CIMA Exam Practice Kit

Management Accounting Decision Management

AF717665

CIMA Exam Practice Kit

CIMA PUBLISHING

Management Accounting Decision Management

Simon Dawkins
Ian Barnett

ELSEVIER

AMSTERDAM • BOSTON • HEIDELBERG • LONDON • NEW YORK • OXFORD
PARIS • SAN DIEGO • SAN FRANCISCO • SINGAPORE • SYDNEY • TOKYO

CIMA Publishing
An imprint of Elsevier
Linacre House, Jordan Hill, Oxford OX2 8DP
30 Corporate Drive, Burlington, MA 01803

First published 2006

Copyright © 2006, Elsevier Ltd. All rights reserved

No part of this publication may be reproduced in any material form (including photocopying or storing in any medium by electronic means and whether or not transiently or incidentally to some other use of this publication) without the written permission of the copyright holder except in accordance with the provisions of the Copyright, Designs and Patents Act 1988 or under the terms of a licence issued by the Copyright Licensing Agency Ltd, 90 Tottenham Court Road, London, England W1T 4LP. Applications for the copyright holder's written permission to reproduce any part of this publication should be addressed to the publisher

Permissions may be sought directly from Elsevier's Science and Technology Rights Department in Oxford, UK: phone: (+44) (0) 1865 843830; fax: (+44) (0) 1865 853333; e-mail: permissions@elsevier.com. You may also complete your request on-line via the Elsevier homepage (http://www.elsevier.com), by selecting 'Customer Support' and then 'Obtaining Permissions'

British Library Cataloguing in Publication Data
A catalogue record for this book is available from the British Library

Library of Congress Cataloguing in Publication Data
A catalogue record for this book is available from the Library of Congress

ISBN 0 7506 6929 2

For information on all CIMA Publishing Publications
visit our website at www.cimapublishing.com

Typeset by Integra Software Services Pvt. Ltd, Pondicherry, India
www.integra-india.com
Printed and bound in The Netherlands

Working together to grow
libraries in developing countries

www.elsevier.com | www.bookaid.org | www.sabre.org

ELSEVIER BOOK AID International Sabre Foundation

Contents

About the Authors

Simon Dawkins qualified as an accountant with KPMG in 1989. After qualifying he moved rapidly into training working at first for The Financial Training Company before moving to BPP and quickly becoming a director. Simon was a co-founder of Revelation Training and has constantly been in high demand with both corporate clients and training organisations for his exceptional communication skills. Simon specialises in financial management, corporate decision-making and management accounting.

Ian Barnett qualified as an accountant with KPMG in 1988. After qualifying he moved rapidly into training working regularly with The Financial Training Company, BPP and a large number of independent providers. He has had his own training company for 13 years providing corporate training as well as lectures for students studying for professional exams. His most recent innovation is with a business game which allows delegates to understand the importance of financial control whilst highlighting the interaction of business functions. Ian specialises in performance management, management accounting and financial management.

Introduction

Welcome to the CIMA Exam Practice Kit which has been launched to coincide with a major change in the syllabus in May 2005.

This Kit has been designed with the needs of home study and distance candidates in mind. It is also ideal for fully taught courses or for students resitting papers from the old syllabus.

These hints, question and answers have been produced by some of the best known free-lance tutors in the United Kingdom who have specialized in their respective papers. The questions and topics selected are relevant for the May 2006 and November 2006 examinations.

The exam practice kits complement CIMA's existing study manuals with the Q&As from May 2005 published in the 2006 edition of the CIMA study manual and the Q&As from November 2005 examination published in this edition of the Exam Practice Kit.

Good luck with your studies.

Syllabus Guidance, Learning Objectives and Verbs

A The syllabus

The syllabus for the CIMA Professional Chartered Management Accounting qualification 2005 comprises three learning pillars:

- Management Accounting pillar
- Business Management pillar
- Financial Management pillar.

Within each learning pillar there are three syllabus subjects. Two of these subjects are set at the lower "Managerial" level, with the third subject positioned at the higher "Strategic" level. All subject examinations have a duration of three hours and the pass mark is 50%.

Note: In addition to these nine examinations, students are required to gain three years relevant practical experience and successfully sit the Test of Professional Competence in Management Accounting (TOPCIMA).

B Aims of the syllabus

The aims of the syllabus are:

- To provide for the Institute, together with the practical experience requirements, an adequate basis for assuring society that those admitted to membership are competent to act as management accountants for entities, whether in manufacturing, commercial or service organisations, in the public or private sectors of the economy.
- To enable the Institute to examine whether prospective members have an adequate knowledge, understanding and mastery of the stated body of knowledge and skills.
- To complement the Institute's practical experience and skills development requirements.

C Study weightings

A percentage weighting is shown against each topic in the syllabus. This is intended as a guide to the proportion of study time each topic requires.

All topics in the syllabus must be studied, since any single examination question may examine more than one topic, or carry a higher proportion of marks than the percentage study time suggested.

The weightings *do not* specify the number of marks that will be allocated to topics in the examination.

D Learning outcomes

Each topic within the syllabus contains a list of learning outcomes, which should be read in conjunction with the knowledge content for the syllabus. A learning outcome has two main purposes:

1 to define the skill or ability that a well-prepared candidate should be able to exhibit in the examination;
2 to demonstrate the approach likely to be taken by examiners in examination questions.

The learning outcomes are part of a hierarchy of learning objectives. The verbs used at the beginning of each learning outcome relate to a specific learning objective, for example, evaluate alternative approaches to budgeting.

The verb "evaluate" indicates a high-level learning objective. As learning objectives are hierarchical, it is expected that at this level, students will have knowledge of different budgeting systems and methodologies and be able to apply them.

A list of the learning objectives and the verbs that appear in the syllabus learning outcomes and examinations, follows:

Learning objective	*Verbs used*	*Definition*
1 **Knowledge**		
What you are expected to know	List	Make a list of
	State	Express, fully or clearly, the details of/ facts of
	Define	Give the exact meaning of
2 **Comprehension**		
What you are expected to understand	Describe	Communicate the key features of
	Distinguish	Highlight the differences between
	Explain	Make clear or intelligible/State the meaning of
	Identify	Recognise, establish or select after consideration
	Illustrate	Use an example to describe or explain something

Level	Verb	Definition
3 Application *How you are expected to apply your knowledge*	Apply	To put to practical use
	Calculate/compute	To ascertain or reckon mathematically
	Demonstrate	To prove with certainty or to exhibit by practical means
	Prepare	To make or get ready for use
	Reconcile	To make or prove consistent/compatible
	Solve	Find an answer to
	Tabulate	Arrange in a table
4 Analysis *How you are expected to analyse the detail of what you have learned*	Analyse	Examine in detail the structure of
	Categorise	Place into a defined class or division
	Compare and contrast	Show the similarities and/or differences between
	Construct	To build up or compile
	Discuss	To examine in detail by argument
	Interpret	To translate into intelligible or familiar terms
	Produce	To create or bring into existence
5 Evaluation *How you are expected to use your learning to evaluate, make decisions or recommendations*	Advise	To counsel, inform or notify
	Evaluate	To appraise or assess the value of
	Recommend	To advise on a course of action

Learning Outcomes, Syllabus Content and Examination Format

Paper P2 – Management Accounting Decision Management

Syllabus outline

The syllabus comprises:

Topic and study weighting

• A	Financial Information for Short-term decision-making	30%
• B	Financial Information for Long-term decision-making	25%
• C	The Treatment of Uncertainty in decision-making	15%
• D	Cost Planning and Analysis for Competitive Advantage	30%

Learning aims

Students should be able to:

- separate costs into their fixed and variable components and use these in breakeven analysis and in decision-making under multiple constraints;
- establish relevant cash flows for decision-making and apply these principles in a variety of contexts including process/product viability and pricing including evaluation of the tension between short-term, "contribution based" pricing and long-term, "return on investment" pricing;
- develop relevant cash flows for long-term projects taking account of inflation and taxation where appropriate, evaluate projects using discounting and traditional methods, critically assess alternative methods of evaluation and place evaluation techniques in the context of the whole process of investment decision-making;
- apply learning curves in forecasting future costs and the techniques of activity-based management, target costing and value analysis in managing future costs and evaluate

the actual and potential impacts of contemporary techniques such as JIT, TOC and TQM on efficiency, inventory and cost;
- undertake sensitivity analysis and assess the impact of risk in decision models using probability analysis, expected value tables and decision trees as appropriate;
- discuss externally oriented management accounting techniques and apply these techniques to the value chain, "gain sharing" arrangements and customer/channel profitability analysis.

Assessment strategy

There will be a written examination paper of three hours, with the following sections.

Section A – 20 marks
A variety of compulsory objective test questions, each worth between 2 and 4 marks. Mini-scenarios may be given, to which a group of questions relate.

Section B – 30 marks
Three compulsory medium answer questions, each worth 10 marks. Short scenarios may be given, to which some or all questions relate.

Section C – 50 marks
Two questions, from a choice of three, each worth 25 marks. Short scenarios may be given, to which questions relate.

A – Financial information for short-term decision-making – 30%

Learning outcomes

On completion of their studies students should be able to:

1. discuss the principles of decision-making including the identification of relevant cash flows and their use alongside non-quantifiable factors in making rounded judgements;
2. explain the particular issues that arise in pricing decisions and the conflict between "marginal cost" principles and the need for full recovery of all costs incurred;
3. apply an approach to pricing based on profit maximisation in imperfect markets and evaluate the financial consequences of alternative pricing strategies;
4. explain the possible conflicts between cost accounting for profit reporting and stock valuation and the convenient availability of information for decision-making;
5. explain why joint costs must be allocated to final products for financial reporting purposes, but why this is unhelpful when decisions concerning process and product viability have to be taken;
6. discuss the usefulness of dividing costs into variable and fixed components in the context of short-term decision-making;
7. apply variable/fixed cost analysis in multiple product contexts to breakeven analysis and product mix decision-making, including circumstances where there are multiple constraints and linear programming methods are needed to reach "optimal" solutions;
8. discuss the meaning of "optimal" solutions and show how linear programming methods can be employed for profit maximising, revenue maximising and satisfying objectives.

Syllabus content

- Relevant cash flows and their use in short-term decisions, typically concerning acceptance/rejection of contracts, pricing and cost/benefit comparisons.
- The importance of strategic, intangible and non-financial judgements in decision-making.
- Pricing decisions for profit maximising in imperfect markets. (Note: tabular methods of solution are acceptable).
- Pricing strategies and the financial consequences of market skimming, premium pricing, penetration pricing, loss leaders, product bundling/optional extras and product differentiation to appeal to different market segments.
- The allocation of joint costs and decisions concerning process and product viability based on relevant costs and revenues. Multi-product breakeven analysis, including breakeven and profit/volume charts, contribution/sales ratio, margin of safety etc.
- Simple product mix analysis in situations where there are limitations on product/service demand and one other production constraint.
- Linear programming for more complex situations involving multiple constraints. Solution by graphical methods of two variable problems, together with understanding of the mechanics of simplex solution, shadow prices etc. (Note: questions requiring the full application of the simplex algorithm will not be set although candidates should be able to formulate an initial tableau, interpret a final simplex tableau and apply the information it contained in a final tableau.)

B – Financial information for long-term decision making – 25%

Learning outcomes

On completion of their studies students should be able to:

1 explain the processes involved in making long-term decisions;
2 apply the principles of relevant cash-flow analysis to long-run projects that continue for several years;
3 calculate project cash flows, accounting for tax and inflation, and apply perpetuities to derive "end of project" value where appropriate;
4 apply activity-based costing techniques to derive approximate "long-run" product or service costs appropriate for use in strategic decision-making;
5 explain the financial consequences of dealing with long-run projects, in particular the importance of accounting for the "time value of money";
6 evaluate project proposals using the techniques of investment appraisal;
7 compare, contrast and evaluate the alternative techniques of investment appraisal;
8 evaluate and rank projects that might be mutually exclusive, involve unequal lives and/or be subject to capital rationing;
9 apply sensitivity analysis to cash-flow parameters to identify those to which net present value is particularly sensitive;
10 produce decision support information for management, integrating financial and non-financial considerations.

Syllabus content

- The process of investment decision-making, including origination of proposals, creation of capital budgets, go/no go decisions on individual projects (where judgements on qualitative issues interact with financial analysis), and post audit of completed projects.

- Generation of relevant project cash flows taking account of inflation, tax and "final" project value where appropriate.
- Activity-based costing to derive approximate "long-run" costs appropriate for use in strategic decision-making.
- The techniques of investment appraisal: payback, discounted payback, accounting rate of return, net present value and internal rate of return.
- Application of the techniques of investment appraisal to project cash flows and evaluation of the strengths and weaknesses of the techniques.
- Sensitivity analysis to identify the input variables that most effect the chosen measure of project worth (payback, ARR, NPV or IRR).
- Methods of dealing with particular problems: the use of annuities in comparing projects with unequal lives and the profitability index in capital rationing situations.

C – The treatment of uncertainty in decision-making – 15%

Learning outcomes

On completion of their studies students should be able to:

1 evaluate the impact of uncertainty and risk on decision models that may be based on CVP analysis, relevant cash flows, learning curves, discounting techniques etc.;
2 apply sensitivity analysis on both short- and long-run decision models to identify variables that might have significant impacts on project outcomes;
3 analyse risk and uncertainty by calculating expected values and standard deviations together with probability tables and histograms;
4 prepare expected value tables and ascertain the value of information;
5 prepare and apply decision trees.

Syllabus content

- The nature of risk and uncertainty.
- Sensitivity analysis in decision modelling and the use of computer software for "what-if" analysis.
- Assignment of probabilities to key variables in decision models. Analysis of probabilistic models and interpretation of distributions of project outcomes.
- Expected value tables and the value of information. Decision trees for multi-stage decision problems.

D – Cost planning and analysis for competitive advantage – 30%

Learning outcomes

On completion of their studies students should be able to:

1 compare and contrast value analysis and functional cost analysis;
2 evaluate the impacts of just-in-time production, the theory of constraints and total quality management on efficiency, inventory and cost;
3 explain the concepts of continuous improvement and Kaizen costing that are central to total quality management and prepare cost of quality reports;

4 explain and apply learning and experience curves to estimate time and cost for new products and services;
5 apply the techniques of activity-based management in identifying cost drivers/activities and explain how process re-engineering can be used to eliminate non-value adding activities and reduce activity costs;
6 explain how target costs can be derived from target prices and describe the relationship between target costs and standard costs;
7 explain the concept of life cycle costing and how life cycle costs interact with marketing strategies at each stage of the life cycle;
8 explain the concept of the value chain and discuss the management of contribution/profit generated throughout the chain;
9 discuss gain sharing arrangements whereby contractors and customers benefit if contract targets for cost, delivery and so on are beaten;
10 apply activity-based costing ideas to analyse "direct customer profitability" and extend this analysis to distribution channel profitability;
11 apply Pareto analysis as a convenient technique for identifying key elements of data and in presenting the results of other analyses, such as activity-based profitability calculations.

Syllabus content

- Value analysis and quality function deployment.
- The benefits of just-in-time production, total quality management and theory of constraints and the implications of these methods for decision-making in the "new manufacturing environment".
- Kaizen costing, continuous improvement and cost of quality reporting.
- Learning curves and their use in predicting product/service costs, including derivation of the learning rate and the learning index.
- Activity-based management in the analysis of overhead and its use in improving the efficiency of repetitive overhead activities. Target costing.
- Life cycle costing and implications for marketing strategies. The value chain and supply chain management, including the trend to outsource manufacturing operations to eastern Europe and the far East.
- Gain sharing arrangements in situations where, because of the size of the project, a limited number of contractors or security issues (e.g. in defence work), normal competitive pressures do not apply.
- The use of direct and activity-based cost methods in tracing costs to "cost objects", such as customers or distribution channels, and the comparison of such costs with appropriate revenues to establish "tiered" contribution levels, as in the activity-based cost hierarchy.
- Pareto analysis.

Examination Techniques

Essay questions

Your essay should have a clear structure, that is, an introduction, a middle and an end. Think in terms of 1 mark for each relevant point made.

Numerical questions

It is essential to show workings in your answer. If you come up with the wrong answer and no workings, the examiner cannot award any marks. However, if you get the wrong answer but apply the correct technique then you will be given some marks.

Reports and memorandum

Where you are asked to produce an answer in a report type format you will be given easy marks for style and presentation.

- A *report* is a document from an individual or group in one organisation sent to an individual or group in another.
- A *memorandum* is an informal report going from one individual or group to another individual or group in the same organisation.

You should start a report as follows:

To: J. SMITH, CEO, ABC plc

From: M ACCOUNTANT

Date: 31 December 2000

Terms of Reference: Financial Strategy of ABC plc

Multiple choice questions managerial level

From May 2005 some multiple choice questions will be worth more than two marks. Even if you get answer wrong, you may still get some marks for technique. Therefore show all workings on such questions.

INDICATIVE MATHS TABLES AND FORMULAE

Present Value Table

Present value of £1 i.c. $(1 + r)^{-n}$ where r = interest rate; n = number of periods until payment or receipt.

Periods (n)	Interest rates (r)																			
	1%	2%	3%	4%	5%	6%	7%	8%	9%	10%	11%	12%	13%	14%	15%	16%	17%	18%	19%	20%
1	0.990	0.980	0.971	0.962	0.952	0.943	0.935	0.926	0.917	0.909	0.901	0.893	0.885	0.877	0.870	0.862	0.855	0.847	0.840	0.833
2	0.980	0.961	0.943	0.925	0.907	0.890	0.873	0.857	0.842	0.826	0.812	0.797	0.783	0.769	0.756	0.743	0.731	0.718	0.706	0.694
3	0.971	0.942	0.915	0.889	0.864	0.840	0.816	0.794	0.772	0.751	0.731	0.712	0.693	0.675	0.658	0.641	0.624	0.609	0.593	0.579
4	0.961	0.924	0.888	0.855	0.823	0.792	0.763	0.735	0.708	0.683	0.659	0.636	0.613	0.592	0.572	0.552	0.534	0.516	0.499	0.482
5	0.951	0.906	0.863	0.822	0.784	0.747	0.713	0.681	0.650	0.621	0.593	0.567	0.543	0.519	0.497	0.476	0.456	0.437	0.419	0.402
6	0.942	0.888	0.837	0.790	0.746	0.705	0.666	0.630	0.596	0.564	0.535	0.507	0.480	0.456	0.432	0.410	0.390	0.370	0.352	0.335
7	0.933	0.871	0.813	0.760	0.711	0.665	0.623	0.583	0.547	0.513	0.482	0.452	0.425	0.400	0.376	0.354	0.333	0.314	0.296	0.279
8	0.923	0.853	0.789	0.731	0.677	0.627	0.582	0.540	0.502	0.467	0.434	0.404	0.376	0.351	0.327	0.305	0.285	0.266	0.249	0.233
9	0.914	0.837	0.766	0.703	0.645	0.592	0.544	0.500	0.460	0.424	0.391	0.361	0.333	0.308	0.284	0.263	0.243	0.225	0.209	0.194
10	0.905	0.820	0.744	0.676	0.614	0.558	0.508	0.463	0.422	0.386	0.352	0.322	0.295	0.270	0.247	0.227	0.208	0.191	0.176	0.162
11	0.896	0.804	0.722	0.650	0.585	0.527	0.475	0.429	0.388	0.350	0.317	0.287	0.261	0.237	0.215	0.195	0.178	0.162	0.148	0.135
12	0.887	0.788	0.701	0.625	0.557	0.497	0.444	0.397	0.356	0.319	0.286	0.257	0.231	0.208	0.187	0.168	0.152	0.137	0.124	0.112
13	0.879	0.773	0.681	0.601	0.530	0.469	0.415	0.368	0.326	0.290	0.258	0.229	0.204	0.182	0.163	0.145	0.130	0.116	0.104	0.093
14	0.870	0.758	0.661	0.577	0.505	0.442	0.388	0.340	0.299	0.263	0.232	0.205	0.181	0.160	0.141	0.125	0.111	0.099	0.088	0.078
15	0.861	0.743	0.642	0.555	0.481	0.417	0.362	0.315	0.275	0.239	0.209	0.183	0.160	0.140	0.123	0.108	0.095	0.084	0.074	0.065
16	0.853	0.728	0.623	0.534	0.458	0.394	0.339	0.292	0.252	0.218	0.188	0.163	0.141	0.123	0.107	0.093	0.081	0.071	0.062	0.054
17	0.844	0.714	0.605	0.513	0.436	0.371	0.317	0.270	0.231	0.198	0.170	0.146	0.125	0.108	0.093	0.080	0.069	0.060	0.052	0.045
18	0.836	0.700	0.587	0.494	0.416	0.350	0.296	0.250	0.212	0.180	0.153	0.130	0.111	0.095	0.081	0.069	0.059	0.051	0.044	0.038
19	0.828	0.686	0.570	0.475	0.396	0.331	0.277	0.232	0.194	0.164	0.138	0.116	0.098	0.083	0.070	0.060	0.051	0.043	0.037	0.031
20	0.820	0.673	0.554	0.456	0.377	0.312	0.258	0.215	0.178	0.149	0.124	0.104	0.087	0.073	0.061	0.051	0.043	0.037	0.031	0.026

Cumulative Present Value of £1

This table shows the Present Value of £1 per annum. Receivable or Payable at the end of each year for n years $\frac{1-(1+r)^{-n}}{r}$

Periods (n)	Interest rates (r)																			
	1%	2%	3%	4%	5%	6%	7%	8%	9%	10%	11%	12%	13%	14%	15%	16%	17%	18%	19%	20%
1	0.990	0.980	0.971	0.962	0.952	0.943	0.935	0.926	0.917	0.909	0.901	0.893	0.885	0.877	0.870	0.862	0.855	0.847	0.840	0.833
2	1.970	1.942	1.913	1.386	1.859	1.833	1.808	1.783	1.759	1.736	1.713	1.690	1.668	1.647	1.626	1.605	1.585	1.566	1.547	1.528
3	2.941	2.884	2.829	2.775	2.723	2.673	2.624	2.577	2.531	2.487	2.444	2.402	2.361	2.322	2.283	2.246	2.210	2.174	2.140	2.106
4	3.902	3.808	3.717	3.630	3.546	3.463	3.387	3.312	3.240	3.170	3.102	3.037	2.974	2.914	2.855	2.798	2.743	2.690	2.639	2.589
5	4.853	4.713	4.580	4.452	4.329	4.212	4.100	3.993	3.890	3.791	3.696	3.605	3.517	3.433	3.352	3.274	3.199	3.127	3.058	2.991
6	5.795	5.601	5.417	5.242	5.076	4.917	4.767	4.623	4.486	4.355	4.231	4.111	3.998	3.689	3.784	3.685	3.589	3.498	3.410	3.326
7	6.728	6.472	6.230	6.002	5.786	5.582	5.389	5.206	5.033	4.868	4.712	4.564	4.423	4.288	4.160	4.039	3.922	3.812	3.706	3.605
8	7.652	7.325	7.020	6.733	6.463	6.210	5.971	5.747	5.535	5.335	5.146	4.968	4.799	4.639	4.487	4.344	4.207	4.078	3.954	3.837
9	8.565	8.162	7.786	7.435	7.108	6.802	6.515	6.247	5.995	5.759	5.537	5.328	5.132	4.946	4.772	4.607	4.451	4.303	4.163	4.031
10	9.471	8.983	8.530	8.111	7.722	7.360	7.024	6.710	6.418	6.145	5.889	5.650	5.426	5.216	5.019	4.833	4.659	4.494	4.339	4.192
11	10.368	9.787	9.253	8.760	8.306	7.887	7.499	7.139	6.805	6.495	6.207	5.938	5.687	5.453	5.234	5.029	4.836	4.656	4.486	4.327
12	11.255	10.575	9.954	9.385	8.863	8.384	7.943	7.536	7.161	6.814	6.492	6.194	5.918	5.660	5.421	5.197	4.988	4.793	4.611	4.439
13	12.134	11.348	10.635	9.986	9.394	8.853	8.358	7.904	7.487	7.103	6.750	6.424	6.122	5.842	5.583	5.342	5.118	4.910	4.715	4.533
14	13.004	12.106	11.296	10.563	9.899	9.295	8.745	8.244	7.786	7.367	6.982	6.628	6.302	6.002	5.724	5.468	5.229	5.008	4.802	4.611
15	13.865	12.849	11.938	11.118	10.380	9.712	9.108	8.559	8.061	7.606	7.191	6.811	6.462	6.142	5.847	5.575	5.324	5.092	4.876	4.675
16	14.718	13.578	12.561	11.652	10.838	10.106	9.447	8.851	8.313	7.824	7.379	6.974	6.604	6.265	5.954	5.668	5.405	5.162	4.938	4.730
17	15.562	14.292	13.166	12.166	11.274	10.477	9.763	9.122	8.544	8.022	7.549	7.120	8.729	6.373	6.047	5.749	5.475	5.222	4.990	4.775
18	16.398	14.992	13.754	12.659	11.690	10.828	10.059	9.372	8.756	8.201	7.702	7.250	6.840	6.467	6.128	5.818	5.534	5.273	5.033	4.812
19	17.226	15.679	14.324	13.134	12.085	11.158	10.336	9.604	8.950	8.365	7.839	7.366	6.938	6.550	6.198	5.877	5.584	5.316	5.070	4.843
20	18.046	16.351	14.878	13.590	12.462	11.470	10.594	9.818	9.129	8.514	7.963	7.469	7.025	6.623	6.259	5.929	5.628	5.353	5.101	4.870

Formulae

Time series

Additive model:

Series = Trend + Seasonal + Random

Multiplicative model:

Series = Trend * Seasonal * Random

Regression analysis

The linear regression equation of Y on X is given by:

$$Y = a + bX \text{ or } Y - \overline{Y} = b(X - \overline{X}),$$

where:

$$b = \frac{\text{Covariance }(XY)}{\text{Variance }(X)} = \frac{n\Sigma XY - (\Sigma X)(\Sigma Y)}{n\Sigma X^2 - (\Sigma X)^2}$$

and $a = \overline{Y} - b\overline{X}$

or solve

$$\Sigma Y = na + b\Sigma X$$
$$\Sigma XY = a\Sigma X + b\Sigma X^2$$

Exponential $Y = ab^x$

Geometric $Y = aX^b$

Learning curve

$$Y_x = aX^b$$

where

Y_x = the cumulative average time per unit to produce X units;

a = the time required to produce the first unit of output;

X = the cumulative number of units;

b = the index of learning.

The exponent b is defined as the log of the learning curve improvement rate divided by log 2.

Relevant Costing

1

When making decisions, businesses should only take into account those costs and revenues which are relevant to the decision. This principle underpins virtually all of the syllabus.

Typical decisions could relate to

- The minimum price to tender for a new contract or a piece of work.
- Whether to shut down a division or keep it open.
- The minimum price to accept from a customer who requires a product which will require transfer of resources away from more profitable uses.
- Whether a manufacturing company should make for itself or buy in a component used in production of a product in its product range.

A *general rule* can be applied when attempting relevant costing questions.

General rule: "Items of income or expense are only relevant to the decision if they make the business *richer* or *poorer* when the business goes ahead with the decision."

For example, *non-cash items* are non-relevant (such as depreciation of fixed assets), since to become *richer* the business must receive cash as a result of their decision and to become *poorer* the business must spend cash.

This would also help to explain the concept of *opportunity cost* – where *another opportunity* is foregone if the business goes ahead with the decision under consideration. The amount by which they would be *poorer* is relevant and is called the *opportunity cost*.

It is important that you know which revenues and costs are relevant and which are non-relevant:

Relevant	*Non-relevant*
Cash	Sunk costs
Opportunity costs	Committed costs
Incremental cash flows	Non-cash items
	Share of group-wide fixed overheads

Questions

1.1 Which of the following phrases are characteristics of relevant costs used for decision-making?

(i) Unavoidable costs
(ii) Past costs
(iii) Incremental costs
(iv) Future costs

A (i) and (ii) only
B (ii) and (iii) only
C (i), (ii) and (iv) only
D (ii), (iii) and (iv) only
E (iii) and (iv) only

(2 marks)

Use the following information to answer the next two questions.

Shultz Ltd is about to tender for a contract.

The following information has been provided by the company accountant.

	£
Labour required	
Skilled (200 hours at £10/hour)	2,000
Semi-skilled (60 hours at £8.50/hour)	510
Unskilled (400 hours at £6/hour)	2,400
Material required	
R (150 kg at £5/kg)	750
T (250 litres at £8/litre)	2,000
	7,660

Skilled labour is currently idle. However, the unskilled labour will have to be diverted from another project which currently generates contribution of £12 per unit, each unit uses four hours of unskilled labour. Semi-skilled labour will be recruited from outside the company if the contract is awarded to Shultz.

The original purchase price of material R was £5 per kg. If purchased now, it will cost £8 per kg. It could be sold as scrap for £2.50 per kg. Current stock is 80 kg.

Material R has not been used in the company for as long as anyone can remember.

The original purchase price of material T was £8 per litre. If purchased now, it will cost £10 per litre. It could be sold as scrap for £3.50 per litre. Current stock is 50 litres and this material is in constant use.

1.2 What is the relevant cost of labour for the contract?

A £1,710
B £3,600
C £3,710
D £4,110
E £4,910

(4 marks)

1.3 What is the relevant cost of materials for the contract?

A £2,750
B £2,760
C £3,260
D £3,375
E £3,460

(4 marks)

1.4 A company makes three products M, N and P. The following information are available

	M	*N*	*P*
	£	£	£
Sales	20,000	40,000	75,000
Variable costs	12,000	33,000	55,000
Fixed costs	5,000	9,000	16,000
Profit/(Loss)	3,000	(2,000)	4,000

It is believed that a percentage of the fixed costs relating to product N are avoidable.

What is the minimum percentage of fixed costs that must be avoidable if the company is to cease producing product N. Calculate to the nearest whole percentage.

A 0%
B 22%
C 29%
D 78%
E 100%

(3 marks)

1.5 Hulme has three divisions. Budgeted information for the forthcoming period is as follows:

	Division T	*Division H*	*Division E*	*Total*
	£'000	£'000	£'000	£'000
Sales	320	370	160	850
Variable costs	220	350	80	650
Contribution	100	20	80	200
Fixed costs				150
Profit				50

Forty five per cent of the fixed costs are specific to each division being split equally between them.

Which divisions should be kept open by Hulme given that their objective is to maximise profit?

A T, H and E
B T and H only
C H and E only
D T and E only
E T only

(3 marks)

1.6 A company is calculating the relevant cost of the material to be used on a particular contract.

The contract requires 4,200 kg of material H and this can be bought for $6.30 per kg.

The company bought 10,000 kg of material H some time ago when it paid $4.50 per kg. Currently 3,700 kg of this remains in stock. The stock of material H could be sold for $3.20 per kg.

The company has no other use for material H other than on this contract, but it could modify it at a cost of $3.70 per kg and use it as a substitute for material J. Material J is regularly used by the company and can be bought for $7.50 per kg.

The relevant cost of the material for the contract is

A $17,210
B $19,800
C $26,460
D $30,900

(2 marks)

Use the following information to answer the next two questions.

T plc manufactures a component D12, and two main products F45 and P67. The following details relate to each of these items:

	D12	*F45*	*P67*
	$ per unit	*$ per unit*	*$ per unit*
Selling price	–	146.00	159.00
Material cost	10.00	15.00	26.00
Component D12 (bought-in price)	–	25.00	25.00
Direct labour	5.00	10.00	15.00
Variable overheads	6.00	12.00	18.00
Total variable cost per unit	21.00	62.00	84.00
Fixed overhead costs:	*$ per annum*	*$ per annum*	*$ per annum*
Avoidable*	9,000	18,000	40,000
Non-avoidable	36,000	72,000	160,000
Total	45,000	90,000	200,000

* The avoidable fixed costs are product-specific fixed costs that would be avoided if the product or component were to be discontinued.

1.7 Assuming that the annual demand for component D12 is 5,000 units and that T plc has sufficient capacity to make the component itself, the maximum price that should be paid to an external supplier for 5,000 components per year is

A $105,000
B $114,000
C $141,000
D $150,000

(2 marks)

1.8 Assuming that component D12 is bought from an external supplier for $25.00 per unit, the number of units of product F45 that must be sold to cover its own costs without contributing to T plc's non-avoidable fixed costs is closest to

A 188 units
B 214 units
C 228 units
D 261 units

(2 marks)

1.9 You are currently in employment earning £30,000 per annum. However, you have become bored and after having considered various job offers, you have now decided to form a business of your own – selling flowers from a shop that you intend to rent in a nearby town.

How should your current salary be treated when deciding whether or not to start your own business?

A as an irrelevant cost
B as a sunk cost
C as an incremental cost
D as a committed cost
E as an opportunity cost

(2 marks)

1.10 IB Ltd is a construction company and has been asked to tender for a contract to build a one-kilometre stretch of motorway as part of the government's road-building strategy.

IB Ltd believes that the construction will take a period of six months.

Five employees would need to be recruited on an annual salary of £45,000. A works foreman would be required to supervise these employees. An existing works foreman would be used whose annual salary is currently £55,000. He would be expected to devote 30% of his time on the new contract.

The new employees would have to go through a "Road Builders Diploma" training programme in order to get approval to work on government contracts. This would cost £3,000 per employee, but it is anticipated that a grant of 20% towards this cost will be obtainable from the local development agency.

Alternatively, IB Ltd could subcontract the work (with the government's agreement) to another road building firm that it sometimes uses for joint venture projects. It is anticipated that the subcontract firm would demand a fee of £135,000 to undertake the work.

The relevant cost of labour for this contract would be

A £124,500
B £127,500
C £135,000
D £141,000
E £144,000

(3 marks)

1.11 Right-Tyres Ltd has three depots selling car tyres. The depots are based in Nottingham, Luton and Manchester.

The average selling price per tyre is £25.

Budgets have been produced for the forthcoming period as follows:

	Nottingham £	*Luton* £	*Manchester* £
Sales	2,000,000	1,500,000	2,500,000
Costs:			
Purchase price of tyres	1,200,000	900,000	see below
Wages and salaries	250,000	220,000	358,000
Overheads	450,000	430,000	600,000
	1,900,000	1,550,000	see below

The average purchase price per tyre charged by suppliers is the same for both the Nottingham and Luton depots. However, due to a higher volume of tyres being purchased by the Manchester depot, the Manchester depot benefits from a 20% discount compared to the price charged to the Nottingham and Luton depots.

The management of Right-Tyres Ltd believes that some of the overheads included in the above budgets would not be incurred if the decision was taken to close any of the depots.

At a recent board meeting, doubt was cast over the future of the Luton depot given its budgeted loss of £50,000.

The percentage of overheads which are variable costs and would not be incurred if a depot were to be closed differs with each depot and are as follows:

Depot	%
Nottingham	25
Luton	15
Manchester	20

If a depot were to be closed it is not expected that there would be any major consequences upon the sales volumes achieved at the remaining depots due to the geographical distances between the depots.

Requirements

(a) Discuss whether the Luton depot should be closed purely on the basis of financial considerations.

(2 marks)

(b) Assuming that 80% of wages and salaries at each depot are variable costs, calculate the number of tyres that must be sold by the whole company in order to breakeven. (For this requirement, assume that the Luton depot will be kept open and that sales will be made at the depots in the ratio used in the original budget.)

(5 marks)

(c) Discuss the key non-financial factors that should be considered when making a decision to close part of a business such as the Luton depot.

(3 marks)

(Total = 10 marks)

1.12 Relco plc is a construction company which has been asked to submit a tender to build a new hotel for a well-known national hotels group based in the UK. The specification for the hotel is as follows.

Six floors including ground floor reception and meeting rooms.
Seventy bedrooms all of similar layout and size.

A team of 100 construction workers are expected to be required to complete the project in the 18 months allowed by the specification of the project.

These workers would be sourced as follows.

Newly recruited: 50 workers, annual wages: £25,000 per annum.

Currently employed by Relco plc but not being used on any construction projects: 35 workers, annual wages: £28,000 per annum.

Currently employed, by Relco plc on another project building a new shopping centre: 15 workers, annual wages: £30,000 per annum. These 15 workers would be transferred to the hotel project but this will delay the completion of the shopping centre. Relco plc expect that this delay will cause them to have to suffer a penalty of £1.5 million for going beyond the agreed completion date, as well as additional labour costs of £300,000.

Materials are expected to cost £2.1 million and will be purchased from the company's usual suppliers if the tender is awarded to Relco plc. Suppliers typically offer 10% trade discounts to Relco plc.

Specialist equipment such as lifting gear, cement mixers and so on will be required.

Some equipment which is already owned by Relco plc and has a net book value of £500,000 would be used. The company's depreciation policy for equipment is 25% on a reducing balance basis. This equipment is not expected to be required on other projects throughout the next 18 months and beyond. It could be sold now for £600,000. Other equipment will have to be hired at an expected hire cost of £30,000 per month.

The roof of the hotel included in the specification must be strong enough to support the weight of a helicopter as planning permission has already been given for a helipad on top of the building. The materials required for the roof have not been included in the cost set out above. The only viable source of supply of these materials is a company called Helimats GmbH based in Germany who would charge around €600,000.

The exchange rate between the Euro and Sterling is currently £1 = €1.40.

Relco plc typically adds a 35% mark-up on relevant costs to arrive at a tender price.

Requirements

(a) Estimate the tender price for the hotel project with explanatory notes setting out the reasoning behind numbers used. Ignore the time value of money.

(6 marks)

(b) Discuss other factors that should be taken into account when deciding upon the tender price.

(4 marks)
(Total = 10 marks)

1.13 MOV plc (IDEC 5/03)

MOV plc produces custom-built sensors. Each sensor has a standard circuit board (SCB) in it. The current average contribution from a sensor is £400. MOV plc's business is steadily expanding and in the year just ending (2001/02), the company will have produced 55,000 sensors. The demand for MOV plc's sensors is predicted to grow over the next three years:

Year	*Units*
2002/03	58,000
2003/04	62,000
2004/05	65,000

The production of sensors is limited by the number of SCBs the company can produce. The present production level of 55,000 SCBs is the maximum that can be produced without overtime working. Overtime could increase annual output to 60,500, allowing production of sensors to also increase to 60,500. However, the variable cost of SCBs produced in overtime would increase by £75 per unit.

Because of the pressure on capacity, the company is considering having the SCBs manufactured by another company, CIR plc. This company is very reliable and produces products of good quality. CIR plc has quoted a price of £116 per SCB, for orders greater than 50,000 units a year.

MOV plc's own costs per SCB are predicted to be:

	£
Direct material	28
Direct labour	40
Variable overhead	20 (based on labour cost)
Fixed overhead	24 (based on labour cost and output of 55,000 units)
Total cost	112

The fixed overheads directly attributable to SCBs are £250,000 a year; these costs will be avoided if SCBs are not produced. If more than 59,000 units are produced, SCBs' fixed overheads will increase by £130,000.

In addition to the above overheads, MOV plc's fixed overheads are predicted to be:

Sensor production, in units:	54,001 – 59,000	59,001 – 64,000	64,001 – 70,000
Fixed overhead:	£2,600,000	£2,900,000	£3,100,000

MOV plc currently holds a stock of 3,500 SCBs but the production manager feels that a stock of 8,000 should be held if they are bought-in; this would increase stockholding costs by £10,000 a year. A purchasing officer, who is paid £20,000 a year, spends 50% of her time on SCB duties. If the SCBs are bought-in, a liaison officer will have to be employed at a salary of £30,000 in order to liase with CIR plc and monitor the quality and supply of SCBs. At present, 88 staff are involved in the production of SCBs at an average salary of £25,000 a year: if the SCBs were purchased, 72 of these staff would be made redundant at an average cost of £4,000 per employee.

The SCB department, which occupies an area of 240 × 120 square metres at the far end of the factory, could be rented out at a rent of £45 per square metre a year. However, if the SCBs were to be bought-in, for the first year only MOV plc would need the space to store the increased stock caused by outsourcing, until the main stockroom had been reorganised and refurbished. From 2003/04, the space could be rented out; this would limit the annual production of sensors to 60,500 units. Alternatively, the space could be used for the production of sensors, allowing annual output to increase to 70,000 units if required.

Requirements

(a) Critically discuss the validity of the following statement. It was produced by Jim Elliott, the company's accountant, to show the gain for the coming year (2002/03) if the SCBs were to be bought-in.

Saving in:	£
Manufacturing staff – salaries saved: 72 staff × £25,000	1,800,000
Purchasing officer – time saved	10,000
Placing orders for SCB materials: 1,000 orders × £20 per order	20,000
Transport costs for raw materials for SCBs	45,000
Cost saved	1,875,000
Additional cost per SCB: (£116 – £112) × 58,000 units	232,000
Net gain if SCBs purchased	1,643,000

(10 marks)

(b) (i) Produce detailed calculations that show which course of action is the best financial option for the three years under consideration. (Ignore the time value of money.)

(12 marks)

(ii) Advise the company of the long-term advantages and disadvantages of buying-in SCBs.

(3 marks)
(Total = 25 marks)

Answers

1.1 **E**

Any decision to be taken must be based only on an assessment of relevant costs. Relevant items are those items of revenue and cost which will make the business either richer or poorer.

They must relate to the future and be consequences of the business going ahead with the decision. Any unavoidable costs will not make the business any poorer than it would have been, had the decision not been made, and past costs have already affected the wealth of the business.

Relevant costs are those which will have an incremental effect upon the wealth of the business.

1.2 **D**

The relevant cost of labour is

- *Skilled labour*. Skilled labour is currently idle and can therefore be transferred to the new contract at no extra cost to the business.
- *Semi-skilled labour*. This labour will be recruited if the contract goes ahead at a cost of £510.
- *Unskilled labour*. This labour will have to be diverted from another project. The contribution currently being generated will therefore be foregone. The new contract will have to generate the lost contribution to ensure that the company does not suffer.

  So cost for unskilled labour is

	£
Cost 400 hours at £6/hour	2,400
Contribution foregone £12 × 100 units	1,200
(400 hours/4 hour = 100 units of lost contribution)	

Total labour cost = £510 + £2,400 + £1,200 = £4,110.

1.3 **C**

The relevant cost of material R is as follows:

150 kg are needed if we win the contract of which 80 kg is in stock.

Therefore the company will have to buy 70 kg at a current purchase cost of £8/kg = £560.

The 80 kg in stock will be used for the contract. However, the company will no longer be able to sell this 80 kg for scrap proceeds of: 80 kg × £2.50 = £200.

So, relevant cost of material R is: £560 + £200 = £760.

The relevant cost of material T is as follows:

250 litres are needed if we win the contract of which 50 litres is in stock.

Therefore the company will have to buy 200 litres at a current purchase cost of £10/litre = £2,000.

The 50 litres in stock will be used for the contract. However, the company will then have to replace those 50 litres since they are needed in order to be used elsewhere in the business.

To replace these 50 litres will cost £10/litre, that is, 50 × £10 = £500.

So, relevant cost of material T is as follows: £2,000 + £500 = £2,500.

Total relevant cost of materials = £760 + £2,500 = £3,260.

1.4 **D**

It would appear that the company should cease producing product N since it generates a loss. However, for decision-making, contribution should always be used instead of profit.

If the entire £9,000 of fixed cost is avoidable then the company should cease producing N since it will forego contribution of £7,000 but save fixed costs of £9,000 so being £2,000 better off overall.

If, say, only £4,000 of the fixed costs are avoidable, ceasing production of N would result in loss of contribution of £7,000 but save fixed costs of £4,000 so the company would be £3,000 worse off. Here they should continue production of N. Since contribution from N is £7,000 at a minimum the avoidable fixed cost would have to be £7,000.

As a percentage this is £7,000/£9,000 × 100% = 78%.

1.5 **D**

If a division is closed the company will forego any contribution it was expected to generate but it will save any fixed cost that is incurred specifically by that division (no division, no specific fixed cost!).

Therefore, we must look at contribution with less specific fixed costs for each division to see what will be foregone if the division is closed.

	Division T	*Division H*	*Division E*
	£'000	£'000	£'000
Contribution	100	20	80
Specific fixed costs (45% × 150 × 1/3)	22.5	22.5	22.5
	77.5	(2.5)	57.5

So, if Division T were to be closed the company will forego £77,500.

If Division E were closed the company will forego £57,500.

Therefore, both of these divisions should be kept open.

However, if Division H is closed the company will forego £20,000 of contribution but save specific fixed costs of £22,500 – a net saving of £2,500.

So, Division H should be closed.

1.6 **A**

The contract requires 4,200 kg of material H. Currently 500 kg must be purchased at a cost of \$6.30 per kg = \$3,150.

As regards the 3,700 kg in stock, this will be used in the contract, but we must consider the cost to the company of doing so.

There are two possible uses of the 3,700 kg in stock (before the existence of the contract was known).

These are to either

- sell for scrap of \$3.20 per kg

or

- turn it into material J. This would cost \$3.70 per kg to modify but then save the business from having to pay \$7.50 per kg to buy material J. A net saving of \$3.80.

Of these two options, the best use of material H would be to convert it into material J saving the business \$3.80 per kg.

By using this 3,700 kg in stock in the contract, the business is losing the opportunity to save itself \$3.80 per kg. This is therefore the relevant cost of the stock of 3,700 kg.

That is, relevant cost = 3,700 kg × \$3.80 = \$14,060.

Total relevant cost of material H is therefore:

\$3,150 + \$14,060 = \$17,210.

1.7 **B**

This question is testing the "make or buy" decision. The business should choose to do whichever is the cheaper of the two options.

If component D12 is purchased from an external supplier, the maximum it should be prepared to pay is equal to the cost it would incur in making the component itself.

Making component D12 itself cost the business \$21.00 per unit (this being the marginal cost of making each unit) although the avoidable fixed costs of \$9,000. If the component were not manufactured in-house the fixed costs of \$9,000 would not be incurred.

So cost of manufacturing 5,000 units of D12 = \$9,000 + \$21.00 × 5,000 = \$114,000.

This is therefore the maximum amount that the company should be prepared to pay an external supplier.

1.8 **B**

If the component D12 is bought-in at a cost of \$25 per unit, the contribution made by the business from each unit if F45 sold will be:

	\$
Selling price	146
Less:	
Variable costs	(62)
(includes the \$25 for component D12)	
Contribution	84

The avoidable fixed costs associated with making F45 are \$18,000.

(The question asked for the number of units of product F45 that must be sold to cover its own costs without contributing to T plc's non-avoidable fixed costs, that is, to cover the avoidable fixed costs only.)

To cover this cost the business must produce the following number of units of F45:

\$18,000/\$84 = 214.29 units.

So, 214 units to the nearest.

1.9 **E**

By setting up your own business you will be giving up the *opportunity* to earn £30,000 per annum. The salary is therefore an opportunity cost.

Answer A cannot be correct since giving up a salary of £30,000 must be considered and is therefore relevant to your decision.

Answer B cannot be correct since a sunk cost is a past cost. This is future salary you would be forgoing.

Answer C cannot be correct since the salary will be forgone. It will not be an additional (incremental) cost of your new business.

Answer D cannot be correct since a committed cost is a cost which the new business is already obliged to pay (perhaps for contractual reasons).

1.10 **A**

If the contract were to go ahead, five new employees will have to be recruited at an incremental cost of 5 × £45,000 = £225,000 per annum.

This cost would only be for six months.

So cost to the contract would be: £225,000 × 0.5 = £112,500

The cost of the works foreman is irrelevant since he already works for IB Ltd. His salary is therefore a committed cost – even the 30% of time he will spend on the contract!

The "Road Builders Diploma" training programme would cost:

5 employees × £3,000 × 80% = £12,000

So total relevant cost if IB Ltd were to build the stretch of motorway would be:

£112,500 + £12,000 = £124,500

Instead, IB Ltd could subcontract the work at a cost of £135,000.

The cheaper option is to employ and train the five new employees. Hence, relevant cost of labour for the contract is £124,500.

1.11

> **!** *Topic being tested*
>
> *Relevant costing for decision-making*
>
> – Whether to close or keep open an apparently unprofitable part of the business.
>
> *Approach*
>
> Part (a) – Always use *contribution* not profit for decision-making purposes.
>
> Part (b) – For breakeven calculations where a company has multiple products sold in a fixed ratio, use a "package" made up of those products in the fixed ratio.
>
> Part (c) – Use common sense to think of non-financial consequences of shutting down part of a business in a local area.

Solution

(a) When considering shutting down part of a business it is necessary to consider the financial and non-financial effects upon the business of the closure.

The financial consequences would be as follows.

If the Luton depot is closed then sales revenue of £1.5 million will be forgone.

However, tyres cost of £900,000, wages and salaries of £220,000 and 15% of overheads (15% × £430,000 = £64,500) would no longer be incurred.

That is, the business would forgo contribution of:

	£
Sales	1,500,000
Tyres cost	(900,000)
Wages and salaries	(220,000)
Overheads	(64,500)
Contribution forgone	315,500

Eighty five per cent of the overheads, that is, £365,500 would still be incurred.

If kept open, the Luton depot will contribute £315,500 towards these overheads.

If the depot were to be closed the loss would be £365,500 rather than £50,000 if it is kept open.

Therefore, the Luton depot should be kept open.

(b) In the original budget the number of tyres to be sold at each depot is as follows:

	Nottingham	*Luton*	*Manchester*
Sales	£2,000,000	£1,500,000	£2,500,000
Selling price	£25	£25	£25
Sale of tyres	80,000 units	60,000 units	100,000 units

This is in the ratio 8:6:10

Contribution per tyre sold at each depot will be:

	Nottingham £	*Luton* £	*Manchester* £
Selling price	25	25	25
Tyres cost:			
$\frac{£1,200,000}{80,000 \text{ units}}$	(15)	(15) (as Nottingham)	(12) (£15 × 80%)
Wages and salaries:			
$\frac{£250,000 \times 80\%}{80,000 \text{ units}}$	(2.50)		
$\frac{£220,000 \times 80\%}{60,000 \text{ units}}$		(2.93)	
$\frac{£358,000 \times 80\%}{100,000 \text{ units}}$			(2.86)
Variable overheads:			
$\frac{£450,000 \times 25\%}{80,000 \text{ units}}$	(1.41)		
$\frac{£430,000 \times 15\%}{60,000 \text{ units}}$		(1.07)	
$\frac{£600,000 \times 20\%}{100,000 \text{ units}}$			(1.20)
Contribution	6.09	6.00	8.94

Consider a "package" made up of eight tyres sold by Nottingham, six tyres sold by Luton depot and 10 tyres sold by Manchester depot (24 tyres in total).

Contribution per package would be:

		£
Nottingham	8 tyres × £6.09	48.72
Luton	6 tyres × £6.00	36.00
Manchester	10 tyres × £8.94	89.40
	24 tyres	174.12

Budgeted fixed overheads are:

		£
Nottingham	75% × £450,000	337,500
Luton	85% × £430,000	365,500
Manchester	80% × £600,000	480,000
		1,183,000

To breakeven, the number of packages comes from:

Number of packages × contribution per package = fixed costs

That is, number of packages × £174.12 = £1,183,000

$$\text{So, number of packages} = \frac{£1{,}183{,}000}{£174.12}$$

$$= 6{,}794.2$$

Say, 6,795 packages.

So total number of tyres that must be sold by the whole company in order to breakeven is

6,795 packages × 24 tyres = 163,080 tyres

(c) Key *non-financial* factors that should be considered when making a decision to close part of a business would include:

- The possible need for redundancies – the effect upon the morale of employees at the depots not being closed and their fear that their depot may be closed at a later date.
- Possible impact upon the brand name of the business and how the business is perceived by customers, suppliers and people in the local community.
- Possible erosion of market share if the closure were to allow a competitor to increase sales, say in Luton, and so gain a larger presence in the UK market.
- Possible bad press for the business.

1.12

> **!** *Topic being tested*
>
> The relevant costs to be considered when making a decision regarding a tender price and other non-financial factors that should be considered.
>
> *Approach*
>
> Part (a) – Read the information carefully and produce a table setting out the relevant costs together with supporting notes explaining which amounts are relevant to the decision and which are not relevant.
>
> Part (b) – Discuss the other non-financial factors that should also be considered. Use common sense here.
>
> Time pressure in such questions typically affects the numerical parts of the question rather than the written part which can usually be answered quickly once you have read the scenario and quickly jotted down some ideas on a plan.
>
> Why not answer part (b) first!

Solution

(a) Statement of relevant costs for hotel project so as to derive a tender price:

	Note	£m	£m
Construction workers			
• new recruits	1	1.875	
• employees not being used	2	–	
• employees from shopping centre project	3	1.800	
			3.675
Materials	4		1.890
Equipment already owned	5	0.600	
Equipment to be hired	6	0.540	
			1.140
Materials for roof	7		0.429
			7.134
35% mark-up			2.497
Tender price			9.631

So the tender price for the hotel project should be £9.631 million.

Supporting notes

Note 1: New recruits

Fifty workers will have to be employed at an incremental cost of:

$$50 \text{ workers} \times £25{,}000 \text{ per annum} \times \frac{18 \text{ months}}{12 \text{ months}} = £1.875\text{m}$$

Note 2: Employees not being used

Thirty-five workers are already employed by Relco plc but are not being used on any existing construction projects.

The salaries of these workers does not represent a relevant cost for the hotel project since the cost is a committed cost for Relco plc (assuming that these 35 workers were not about to be made redundant).

Relco plc will have to pay this cost whether they tender for the hotel project or not.

Note 3: Employees to be transferred from shopping centre project

The salaries of the 15 workers will have to be paid by Relco plc whether it tenders for the hotel project or not. So the salaries cost is not relevant to the decision. However, the penalty cost of £1.5 million is relevant. It would only be suffered if the hotel project were to go ahead and so must be covered by the tender price. Also, the additional labour costs of £300,000 associated with the shopping centre project are relevant for the same reason.

So relevant cost = £1.5m + £0.3m = £1.8m

Note 4: Materials

Materials for the hotel will cost £2.1 million less the 10% discount expected to be offered by suppliers.

Therefore, relevant cost is 90% × £2.1m = £1.89m

Note 5: Equipment already owned

The net book value of £500,000 is irrelevant, being made up of the original cost of the equipment (sunk) and less accumulated depreciation (non-cash).

The equipment has no other use at present but could be sold for £600,000. This amount would be foregone if the hotel project were to go ahead and is hence a relevant cost.

So relevant cost is £600,000.

Note 6: Equipment to be hired

This is an incremental (hence relevant) cost of:

18 months × £30,000 per month = £540,000

Note 7: Materials for roof

This is an incremental (hence relevant) cost, and at today's exchange rate the cost is:

$$\frac{€600{,}000}{€1.40} = £428{,}571$$

(b) Other factors that should be taken into account would include:

Exchange rate £:€

If it is expected that the £:€ exchange rate may move against the company, an estimate should be made of the roof materials cost using a forecast exchange rate.

It would be useful for a contract to be drawn up containing a clause specifying that the tender price is subject to alteration if the exchange rate changes beyond a certain amount of € per £1.

Competitor's tender prices

If possible, the likely tender price that competitors may submit for the contract should be considered. However, this information may be difficult to ascertain. Also it should be remembered that the lowest price tendered for a contract does not always result in the contract being awarded to the lowest cost bidder. Other factors such as reputation, quality, reliability and financial stability of the bidding companies are likely to be taken into consideration by the company awarding the contract.

Other opportunities

Other construction projects may exist that Relco plc could tender for, which might yield a larger potential mark-up than 35% and might possibly lead to further work as well.

Feasibility of 18-month timeframe

Before tendering, Relco plc must assess whether they feel that 18 months is a sufficiently long timeframe in order to complete the hotel construction work to the required specification. There might be hidden penalty clauses for over-running the 18-month time period which have not been brought to Relco plc's attention.

1.13

(a) There are a number of things wrong with Jim Elliott's statement. They are

1 The statement contains mixed-up thinking, which does not compare like with like. It consists of a mix of "relevant costs saved", but not all these costs are saved, and compares this with the additional total cost.
2 If the statement is an attempt to assess the proposal, it should include more than the next year's figures. This is because next year's figures would not be typical because of the inclusion of redundancy costs, for example. Also, demand increases year by year and this should be taken into account by calculating increased revenue and opportunity costs on cost of sales and so on.
3 There is no attempt to include the gain from selling more sensors. The additional cost per SCB is calculated incorrectly: it should be based on bought-in price less marginal cost (£116 − £88). This should then be multiplied by 58,000 units and the directly attributable fixed costs of £250,000 deducted from the total.
4 Assuming the costs under "saving in" are intended to be relevant.
5 The purchasing officer's salary should not be included as it must be assumed that she will still be employed to do the other half of her work and will receive a full salary.
6 Cost of placing an order would normally include the salary cost of the purchasing officer and so Jim's figure seems to be incorrect as the purchasing officer's salary has been dealt with separately.
7 The new liaison officer's salary is omitted.
8 Sixteen members of the production team still appear to be employed – we are not told whether they are transferred to other departments and so cannot judge what should be done with this cost. However, it should probably be included as a saving with the other 72, on the basis that they must be going to do a useful job elsewhere in the factory.
9 No redundancy costs are included: these are 72 staff × £4,000 = £288,000.

10 Costs for transportation of materials are included. These would normally be included in the direct material cost, which has been brought into the "additional cost calculation per SCB" and so should not be included here as a separate item.

(b) *Note*: There are a number of different ways of answering this question.

	Year 2002/03	Year 2003/04	Year 2004/05	Total
CURRENT POSITION – Units	58,000	60,500	60,500	
	£'000	£'000	£'000	£'000
Additional business £400 × 3,000 units, etc.	1,200	2,200	2,200	
Variable cost £75 × 3,000 units, etc.	(225)	(412.5)	(412.5)	
Fixed costs – SCBs		(130)	(130)	
– sensors		(300)	(300)	
	975	1,357.5	1,357.5	3,690
EXPAND PRODUCTION – Units	58,000	62,000	65,000	
	£'000	£'000	£'000	£'000
Additional business:				
2002/03 1,200				
2003/04 – 7,000 units × £400		2,800		
2004/05 – 10,000 units × £400			4,000	
CIF differential £116 − £88 = £28 × 58,000 units, etc.	(1,624)	(1,736)	(1,820)	
Additional costs:				
Stock	(10)	(10)	(10)	
Redundancy	(288)			
Liaison officer	(30)	(30)	(30)	
Fixed costs – SCBs – cost saved	250	250	250	
– sensors		(300)	(500)	
	(502)	974	1,890	2,362
RENTAL OPTION – Units	58,000	60,500	60,500	
	£'000	£'000	£'000	£'000
Rent received 240 × 120 = 28,800 sq.m × £45	–	1,296	1,296	
Additional business	1,200	2,200	2,200	
CIF differential £116 − £88 = £28 × 58,000 units, etc.	(1,624)	(1,694)	(1,694)	
Additional costs:				
Stock	(10)	(10)	(10)	
Redundancy	(288)			
Liaison officer	(30)	(30)	(30)	
Fixed costs – SCBs – cost saved	250	250	250	
– sensors		(300)	(300)	
	(502)	1,712	1,712	2,922

(i) Using the time horizon in the question, it is better to continue producing SCBs and work overtime. The next best option is to buy in SCBs and rent out the space. Working overtime generates (£3,690 – £2,922 = £768,000) more profit over the three years than renting.

(ii) In the long term, there are a number of advantages in buying-in SCBs. These include:

Long-term overtime working is not good for quality production and this could affect sales in the long term.

The company may not be keen on turning down work due to lack of capacity as this may hinder the long-term development of the company.

If demand is sustained at 65,000 sensors or above in the long term, it is financially better to buy in SCBs and expand production. In 2004/05, sales of 65,000 units give a greater return over the overtime option of £532,500, but it would take another three years of production at this level to make it the best option in the long term. However, if production expanded to 68,000 units in year 2005/06 (a similar increase to that of previous years), the annual net gain over the overtime option would be £1,648,500 (see below). This is more than enough to make expansion the best option over a four-year assessment period.

	£
Additional business 13,000 units × £400	5,200
Less: CIF differential 68,000 units × £28	1,904
	3,296
Less: Other costs	290
	3,006

Against this, the main disadvantage is:

SCBs were developed and designed by the company; if they were bought-in, would this lead to a loss of skills? On the other hand, it does not appear that MOV plc can produce them profitably.

Overall, a decision on future capacity of the final product ought to be made separately from a decision on whether to buy-in a component. The company would be advised to try to solve its space problem by finding additional or alternative accommodation.

Linear Programming

2

Linear programming is a graphical decision-making tool to assist businesses in allocating several limited or scarce resources so as to achieve an objective: all of which sounds a bit grandiose!

If a business makes *two* products (this has to be the case for linear programming since we end up drawing a graph and a graph only has two axes – x-axis for one product and y-axis for the other product), and *finite* amounts of available *resources* and possibly other constraints on production as well, then linear programming can be used to determine how many units should be produced of each product.

We need to know what *objective* the business is striving to achieve, typically this will be to maximise profit or maximise revenue or possibly even minimise cost.

(The *simplex* technique can be used where a business makes more than two products.)

The linear programming technique involves six steps which are:

1 Define the variables.
2 Set up the objective function.
3 Set up the constraints.
4 Draw graph for the products, constraint lines and mark the feasible region.
5 Draw an example objective equation on the graph and move it outwards through the feasible region to determine the optimal product mix (move *outwards* if the business wants to *maximise* revenue or profit).
6 Conclude, that is, tell the business how many units of each product that it should produce in order to achieve its objective.

Questions

2.1 A company employs skilled technicians and unskilled labourers. Skilled technicians must not be more than 40% of the total number of persons employed. If skilled technicians are denoted by x and unskilled labourers by y, which of the following inequalities expresses this constraint?

A $\frac{2x}{5} \leq x + y$

B $x \leq \frac{2(x + y)}{5}$

C $\frac{2x}{5} \leq y$

D $x \leq \frac{2y}{5}$

E $4x \leq x + y$

(3 marks)

2.2 There are several limitations associated with the simplex technique. Which of the following is not a limitation of the technique?

A All values used in the technique need to be estimated.
B The technique can only work for two products.
C The technique assumes linear relationships.
D Constraint equations can be difficult to formulate.

(2 marks)

2.3 A company makes four products and is subject to seven constraints (including the non-negativity constraints). It has one objective function. How many slack variables will there be in a simplex model solution?

A 2
B 4
C 5
D 7
E 11

(2 marks)

2.4

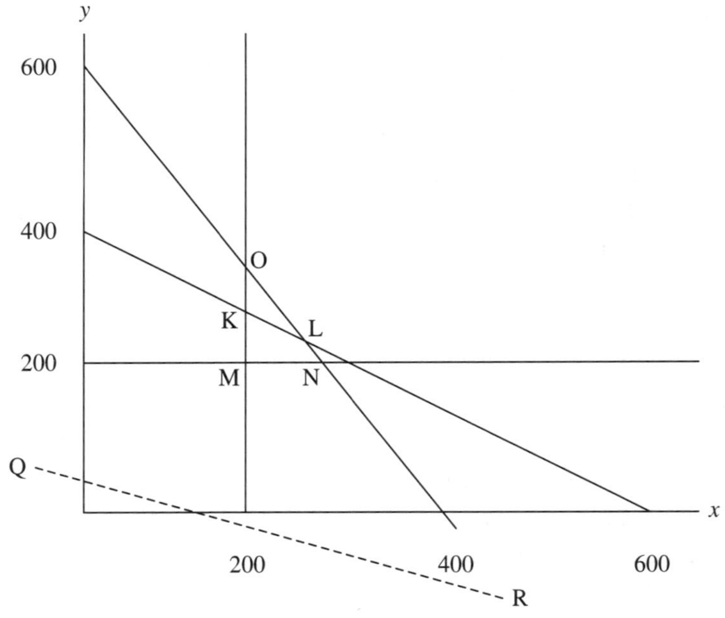

Line QR represents the objective function and the feasible region lies inside KLNM.

The objective of the business is to maximise profit.

At which point on the graph will the business have to produce in order to achieve its objective?

A Point K
B Point L
C Point M
D Point N
E Point O

(3 marks)

2.5 A company using linear programming wishes to determine how many units of its two products, J and N to produce. Annual production of product J will be j units and for product N it will be n units. A binding contract to supply 600 units of J to an existing customer has been signed and will apply for the forthcoming year. However, production of product N is subject to control by an industry regulator such that no more than 1,000 units can be produced in any one year.

Product J requires 90 minutes of labour time per unit. Product N requires 240 minutes of labour time per unit. The company believes that 250,000 hours of labour time will be available during the forthcoming year.

Which of the following is the correct set of constraints?

A $90j + 240n \leq 250{,}000$
$j \geq 600$
$n \leq 1{,}000$

B $1.5j + 4n \leq 250{,}000$
$j \leq 600$
$n \geq 1{,}000$

C $1.5j + 4n \leq 250{,}000$
$j \geq 600$
$n \leq 1{,}000$

D $1.5j + 4n \geq 250{,}000$
$j \geq 600$
$n \leq 1{,}000$

E $1.5j + 4n \geq 250{,}000$
$j + n \leq 1{,}600$

(3 marks)

2.6 A UK-based cake maker has decided to penetrate the Euro-zone by selling in France two cakes from its existing range. The two most popular cakes in terms of sales to the UK market are the "Treatyourself" and the "Chocolatey".

A new factory is to be built in France to manufacture these two products for the French market (at a later date they may even be sold to other countries in the Euro-zone). Three processes are involved in making cakes and the amount of time available for each, given the expected number of machines to be purchased for each process, are as follows:

Process 1: Preparation of ingredients
Process 2: Cooking
Process 3: Quality control and packaging.

Maximum machine time available during first year of operation:

Process 1: 36,000 hours
Process 2: 90,000 hours
Process 3: 22,500 hours

Cakes are made in batches, and spend the following amounts of time in the three separate processes:

	Treatyourself (hours)	*Chocolatey (hours)*
Process 1	3	6
Process 2	15	12
Process 3	4.5	1.5

The expected selling prices and production costs of the two products are:

	Treatyourself (per batch)	*Chocolatey (per batch)*
	€	€
Selling price	30.00	35.00
Variable production costs	20.00	23.00
Fixed production costs	4.00	8.00
Profit	6.00	4.00

The objective of the company is to maximise profit.

Requirement

Using the Linear Programming graphical technique, determine the optimal number of batches of each type of cake that should be made and sold to the French market.

(10 marks)

2.7 MF plc (IMPM 5/02 (Amended))

MF plc manufactures and sells two types of product to a number of customers. The company is currently preparing its budget for the year ending 31 December 2003 which it divides into 12 equal periods.

The cost and resource details for each of the company's product types are as follows:

	Product type M	*Product type F*
	£	£
Selling price per unit	200	210
Variable costs per unit:		
Direct material P (£2.50 per litre)	20	25
Direct material Q (£4.00 per litre)	40	20
Direct labour (£7.00 per hour)	28	35
Overhead (£4.00 per hour)	16	20
Fixed production cost per unit	40	50
	Units	*Units*
Maximum sales demand in Period 1	1,000	3,000

The fixed production cost per unit is based upon an absorption rate of £10 per direct labour hour and a total annual production activity of 180,000 direct labour hours. One-twelfth of the annual fixed production cost will be incurred in Period 1.

In addition to the above costs, non-production overhead costs are expected to be £57,750 in Period 1.

During Period 1, the availability of material P is expected to be limited to 31,250 litres. Other materials and sufficient direct labour are expected to be available to meet demand.

It is MF plc's policy not to hold stocks of finished goods.

Requirements

(a) Calculate the number of units of product types M and F that should be produced and sold in Period 1 in order to maximise profit.

(4 marks)

(b) Using your answer to (a) above, prepare a columnar budgeted profit statement for Period 1 in a marginal cost format.

(4 marks)

After presenting your statement to the budget management meeting, the production manager has advised you that in Period 1 the other resources will also be limited. The maximum resources available will be:

Material P	31,250 litres
Material Q	20,000 litres
Direct labour	17,500 hours

It has been agreed that these factors should be incorporated into a revised plan and that the objective should be to make as much profit as possible from the available resources.

(c) Use graphical linear programming to determine the revised production plan for Period 1. State clearly the number of units of product types M and F that are to be produced.

(10 marks)

(d) Using your answer to part (c) above, calculate the profit that will be earned from the revised plan.

(3 marks)

(e) Calculate and briefly explain the meaning of the shadow price for material Q.

(4 marks)
(Total = 25 marks)

2.8 W plc (IMPM 11/03)

W plc provides two cleaning services for staff uniforms to hotels and similar businesses. One of the services is a laundry service and the other is a dry-cleaning service. Both of the services use the same resources, but in different quantities.

Details of the expected resource requirements, revenues and costs of each service are shown below:

	Laundry *$ per service*	*Dry-cleaning* *$ per service*
Selling price	7.00	12.00
Cleaning materials ($10.00 per litre)	2.00	3.00
Direct labour ($6.00 per hour)	1.20	2.00
Variable machine cost ($3.00 per hour)	0.50	1.50
Fixed costs*	1.15	2.25
Profit	2.15	3.25

* The fixed costs per service were based on meeting the budget demand for December 2003.

W plc has already prepared its budget for December based on sales and operational activities of 8,000 laundry services and 10,500 dry-cleaning services, but it is now revising its plans because of forecast resource problems.

The maximum resources expected to be available in December 2003 are

Cleaning materials	5,000 litres
Direct labour hours	6,000 hours
Machine hours	5,000 hours

W plc has one particular contract which it entered into six months ago with a local hotel to guarantee 1,200 laundry services and 2,000 dry-cleaning services every month. If W plc does not honour this contract it has to pay substantial financial penalties to the local hotel.

Requirements

(a) Calculate the mix of services that should be provided by W plc so as to maximise its profit for December 2003.

(9 marks)

The Sales Director has reviewed the selling prices being used by W plc and has provided the following further information:

- if the price for laundry were to be reduced to $5.60 per service, this would increase the demand to 14,000 services
- if the price for dry-cleaning were to be increased to $13.20 per service, this would reduce the demand to 9,975 services.

(b) Assuming that such selling price changes would apply to all sales and that the resource limitations continue to apply, and that a graphical linear programming solution is to be used to maximise profit,

(i) State the constraints and objective function.

(6 marks)

(ii) Use a graphical linear programming solution to advise W plc whether it should revise its selling prices.

(10 marks)

(Total = 25 marks)

✓ Answers

2.1 **B**

Total employees will be $x + y$

Number of skilled technicians is x

Number of technicians cannot be more than (and so must be less than or at most equal to) 2/5 (i.e. 40%) of the total number of employees.

Therefore, the inequality must be

$$x \leq \frac{2(x + y)}{5}$$

2.2 **B**

A A practical limitation is that selling price, costs and resource requirements have to be estimated for the products involved.

B This is *not* a limitation of the technique. It is a *characteristic* of linear programming that the technique can only be used for a two product company. Remember that simplex technique can be used in the situation of multi-product companies.

C This is a limitation. For example, if a company increases the volume of sales, it may have to offer discounts to selected customers which will have a downward effect upon contribution per unit and hence on the optimal solution. Similarly, as greater volumes are produced it may be possible for the company to achieve quantity discounts on the cost of materials purchased which would also have an effect upon contribution per unit.

D Given that students and others attempting to set up a linear programming problem find the constraints challenging, this limitation should be self-evident.

2.3 **C**

In the simplex model technique, each constraint (other than the non-negativity constraints) requires a slack variable in the initial tableau.

Since there are five such constraints the answer is C.

2.4 **A**

The objective line QR must be pushed outwards as far possible – the more units that can be manufactured of each product on the x-axis and the y-axis, the more profit will be made.

Pushing the line QR outwards into the feasible region, it can be pushed through Points M, N and L and as far as Point K until it can be pushed no further. Point K is therefore the optimal point.

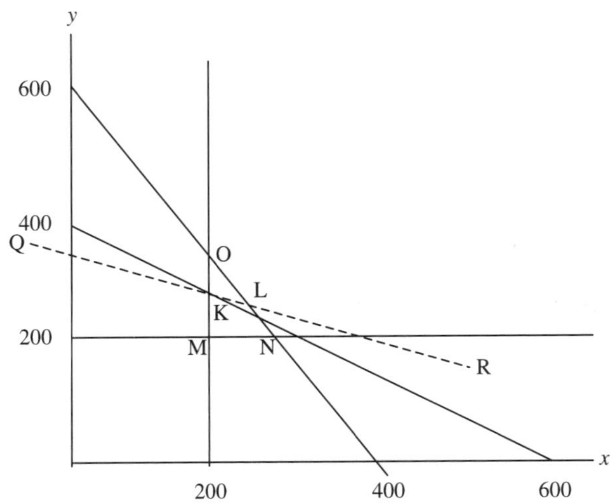

2.5 **C**

At least 600 units of product J must be produced to meet the terms of the recently signed contract. Of course the company may produce more than 600 units in order to supply other customers as well.

So, $j \geq 600$

At most 1,000 units of product N can be produced as a result of control by the industry regulator.

So, $n \leq 1{,}000$

As regards labour hours, at most 250,000 hours are expected to be available. Although product J requires 90 minutes of labour time per unit and product N requires 240 minutes of labour time per unit, these requirements must be converted into hours. So 1.5 hours is required per unit of product J and 4 hours is required per unit of product N.

So the labour hours constraint will be

$1.5j + 4n \leq 250{,}000$.

2.6

> **!** *Topic being tested*
>
> Linear programming as a technique to determine how many batches of two products (cakes in this case) should be produced in order to maximise profits for a bakery business.
>
> *Approach*
>
> Use the following linear programming steps:
>
> 1 Define the variables.
> 2 Set up the objective function.
> 3 Set up the constraints.
> 4 Draw graph for the products, constraint lines and mark the feasible region.
> 5 Draw example objective equation on graph and move outwards through the feasible region to determine the optimal product mix.
> 6 Conclude, that is, tell the bakery how many batches of each type of cake it should produce in order to maximise profit.

Solution

The solution will be found using the linear programming steps as follows:

Step 1 Define the variables

Let x = number of batches of "Treatyourself" to be made.
Let y = number of batches of "Chocolatey" to be made.

Step 2 Set up the objective function

The objective is to maximise profit.

For decision-making purposes we should consider *contribution* since fixed costs will be fixed irrespective of production volumes and the fixed cost per batch of each type of cake is subject to the apportionment technique used.

To maximise profit we must maximise contribution:

Contribution = $10x + 12y$

(Contribution per batch of "Treatyourself" = €30 − €20 = €10)
(Contribution per batch of "Chocolatey" = €35 − €23 = €12)

Step 3 Set up constraints

There is a constraint equation for each process as well as the non-negativity constraint.

$3x + 6y \leq 36{,}000$	Process 1 constraint
$15x + 12y \leq 90{,}000$	Process 2 constraint
$4.5x + 1.5y \leq 22{,}500$	Process 3 constraint
$x \geq 0, y \geq 0$	Non-negativity constraints

To draw these on the graph we first plot the lines:

$3x + 6y = 36{,}000$	Process 1
$15x + 12y = 90{,}000$	Process 2
$4.5x + 1.5y = 22{,}500$	Process 3

$x = 0$
$y = 0$

To plot the line $3x + 6y = 36{,}000$
When $x = 0, y = 6{,}000$
When $y = 0, x = 12{,}000$

To plot the line $15x + 12y = 90{,}000$
When $x = 0, y = 7{,}500$
When $y = 0, x = 6{,}000$

To plot the line $4.5x + 1.5y = 22{,}500$
When $x = 0, y = 15{,}000$
When $y = 0, x = 5{,}000$

For an example objective line we could plot the line:

$10x + 12y = 60{,}000$

For this line
When $x = 0$, $y = 5{,}000$
When $y = 0$, $x = 6{,}000$

Note to student!!

Where did I get the 60,000 from?

Multiplying the numbers in front of x and y together gives $10 \times 12 = 120$

Multiplying by 1,000 since the other lines have values in the '000 gives $120 \times 1{,}000 = 120{,}000$.

I then looked at where this example objective equation would be if I plotted $10x + 12y = 120{,}000$ and it gave me a line out beyond the feasible region on the graph.

So I halved the value and found that plotting $10x + 12y = 60{,}000$.

This gave me a line in the feasible region which I could then move outwards through the feasible region to get to the optimal point.

Steps 4 and 5 Drawing the graph and example objective line

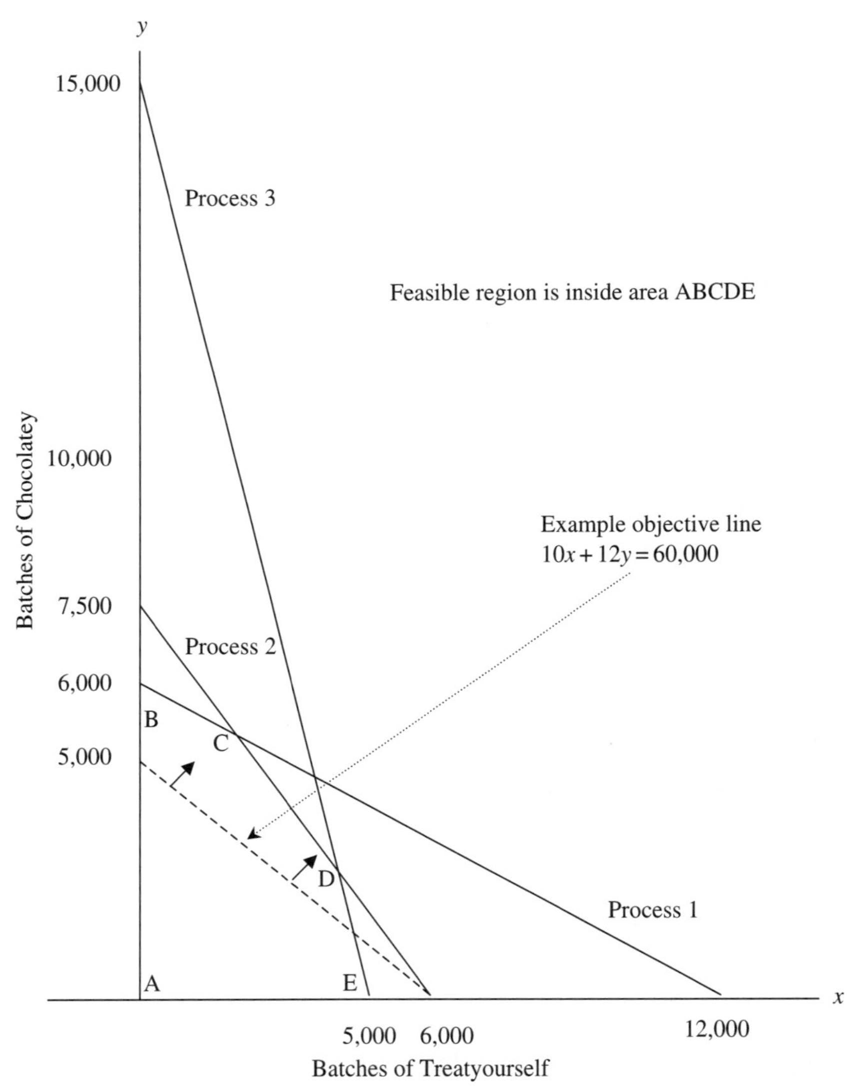

Pushing the example objective line outwards gives Point C as the optimal point. So we now need to find the values of x and y at Point C.

Point C is where the Process 1 and Process 2 lines cross.

That is, where

$3x + 6y = 36{,}000$

and

$15x + 12y = 90{,}000$

we can solve these using simultaneous equations.

Note to student!!

If you can not solve simultaneous equations or are running out of time in the exam, estimate the values of x and y at Point C by reading them off the graph.

$3x + 6y = 36{,}000$ Equation 1
$15x + 12y = 90{,}000$ Equation 2

To remove y:

$2 \times$ Equation 1 $-$ Equation 2

Gives

$$\begin{array}{r} 6x + 12y = 72{,}000 \\ 15x + 12y = 90{,}000 \\ \hline -9x \qquad = -18{,}000 \end{array}$$

So,
$x = 2{,}000$ batches of Treatyourself

Using Equation 1

Note to student!!

We could use Equation 1 or Equation 2 now to get the value of y knowing that the value of x is 2,000. It does not matter which equation we use since using either will give the same answer!

$3x + 6y = 36{,}000$ Equation 1
$3 \times 2{,}000 + 6y = 36{,}000$
$6{,}000 + 6y = 36{,}000$
$6y = 30{,}000$

So,
$y = 5{,}000$ batches of Chocolatey.

Step 6 Conclusion

To maximise contribution and so maximise profit, the company should produce 2,000 batches of Treatyourself (Product X) and 5,000 batches of Chocolatey (Product Y) in the French market.

(At least it will make a change from croissants!)

2.7

(a)

Product type	*M*	*F*
Contribution per product unit (£)	96	110
Material P per unit (litre)	8	10
Contribution per litre of material P (£)	12	11
Ranking	1st	2nd
Production/sales units	**1,000**	**2,325**
Material P used (litre)	8,000	23,250

(b) Budgeted profit statement for Period 1

	Product M £'000	*Product F* £'000	*Total* £'000
Sales	200	488.250	688.250
Variable costs:			
Direct material P	20	58.125	78.125
Direct material Q	40	46.500	86.500
Direct labour	28	81.375	109.375
Overhead	16	46.500	62.500
	104	232.500	336.500
Contribution	**96**	**255.750**	**351.750**
Fixed costs:			
Production			150.000
Non-production			57.750
			207.750
Profit			144.000

Let M be the number of product type M produced and sold.

The iso-contribution line is 96M + 110F (objective function).

The following lines are required for the graph:

$M \leq 1{,}000$ (maximum demand for M)
$F \leq 3{,}000$ (maximum demand for F)
$8M + 10F \leq 31{,}250$ (material P)
$10M + 5F \leq 20{,}000$ (material Q)
$4M + 5F \leq 17{,}500$ (direct labour)

Graph to show profit-maximising production plan.

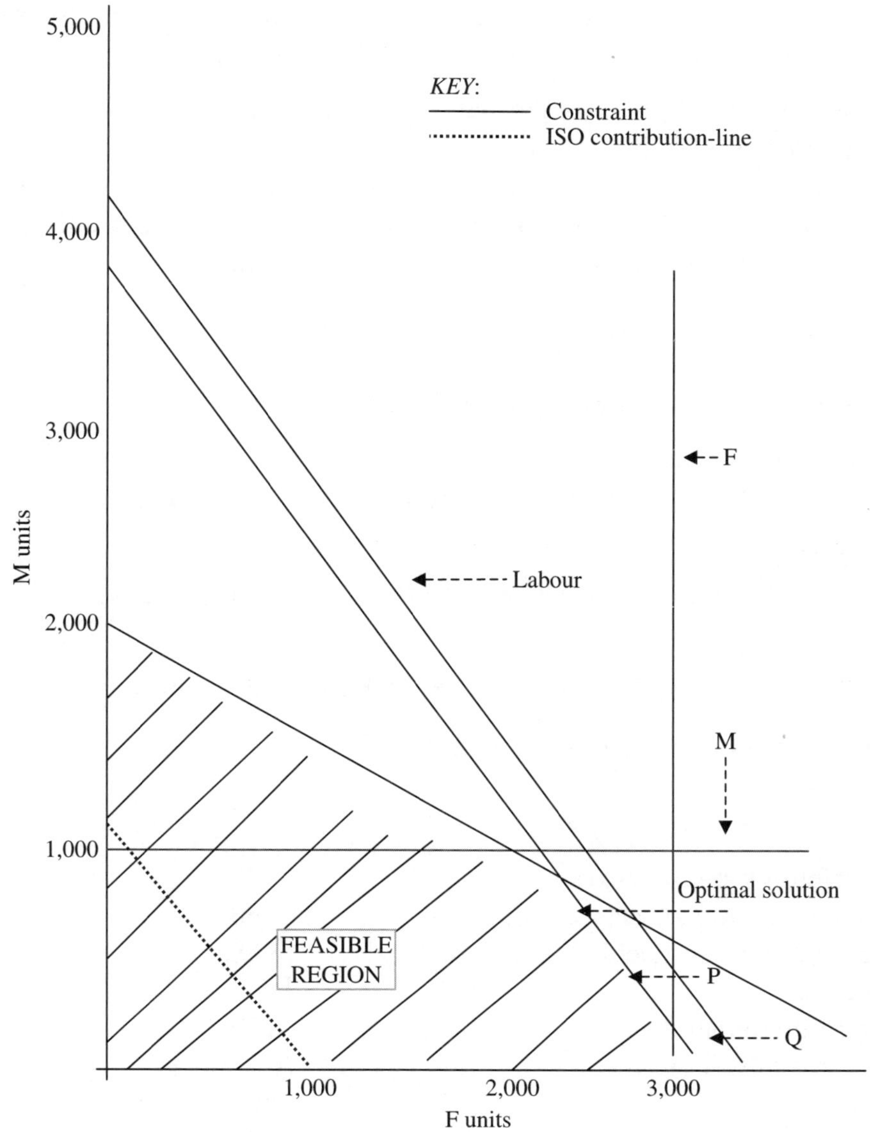

The solution is that production/sales should be:

M	729 units
F	2,542 units

(d) The profit from the revised plan is as follows:

	£
Contribution:	
729M × £96	69,984
2,542F × £110	279,620
	349,604
Less Fixed costs:	
Production	150,000
Non-production	57,750
	207,750
Profit	141,854

(e) There are two constraints that are binding in respect of this revised solution. These are the availability of material P and material Q.

Material P availability was the limiting factor in requirement (a), so the effect of the limited availability of material Q can be measured by comparing the two profit values. There is a reduction in profit of £2,146 as a result of the scarcity of material Q, so this is the shadow price of the extra material Q required (1,625 litres) to return to the original solution from requirement (a).

2.8

(a) Resources required for budgeted activities:

Cleaning materials (8,000L × 0.2 litre) + (10,500DC × 0.3 litre)	4,750 litres
Direct labour (8,000L × 0.2 hour) + (10,500DC × 0.33 hour)	5,065 hours
Machine hours (8,000L × 0.166 hour) + (10,500DC × 0.5 hour)	6,578 hours

Machine hours are the limiting factor

	Laundry	*Dry-cleaning*
Contribution per service unit	£3.30	£5.50
Machine hours per service unit	0.166	0.5
Contribution per machine hour	£19.80	£11.00
Ranking	1st	2nd
Minimum demand	1,200	2,000
Uses (machine hours)	200	1,000
Balance	6,800	5,334
Uses (machine hours)	1,133	2,667
Product mix (units)	8,000	7,334

(b)

Examiner's note: The following proof of the need to use a linear programming solution is included to assist students.

Revised maximum demand levels:

Laundry	14,000
Dry-cleaning	9,975

Revised resource requirements:

Cleaning materials (14,000L × 0.2 litre) + (9,975DC × 0.3 litre)	5,792.5 litres
Direct labour (14,000L × 0.2 hour) + (9,975DC × 0.33 hour)	6,091.75 hours
Machine hours (14,000L × 0.166 hour) + (9,975DC × 0.5 hour)	7,311.5 hours

All resources are now binding – use linear programming to solve

(i) Constraints (L = Laundry, DC = Dry-cleaning):

$$0.2L + 0.3DC \leq 5{,}000$$
$$0.2L + 0.33DC \leq 6{,}000$$
$$0.166L + 0.5DC \leq 5{,}000$$
$$14{,}000 > L \geq 1{,}200$$
$$9{,}975 > DC \geq 2{,}000$$

Objective function: Maximise 1.9L + 6.7DC = C

(ii) The graphical linear programming solution (see graph below) yields:

	£
9,600DC units × £6.70 contribution per unit	64,320
1,200L units × £1.90 contribution per unit	2,280
Total contribution	66,600
Compared to:	
7,334DC units × £5.50 contribution per unit	40,337
8,000L units × £3.30 contribution per unit	26,400
Total contribution	66,737

Thus it appears that the new strategy should not be adopted, as it reduces contribution. However, as the difference is so small, further market research should be carried out.

Graphical linear programming solution

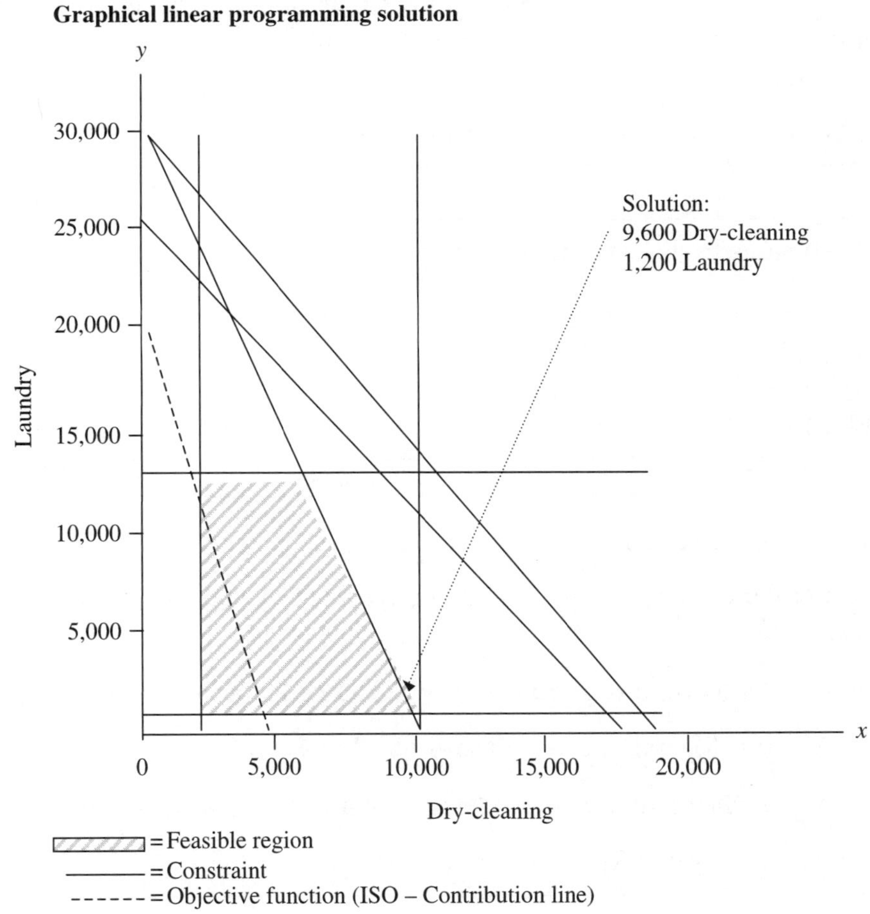

Pricing

3

Businesses must consider many *practical* factors before they can decide upon the eventual selling price of their product or service.

These should include:

- Product cost
- Competitor's prices
- What customers are prepared to pay
- Price of other products in the range, for example, complementary and substitute products
- Elasticity of demand
- Where the product is in the product life cycle
- The company objective, for example, profit maximisation or revenue maximisation
- Whether or not to offer incentives such as discounts
- The degree of product differentiation.

You need to be able to discuss these practical issues.

You must also be able to discuss the following:

- Penetration pricing
- Premium pricing
- Market skimming
- Loss leader pricing
- Product bundling.

π The company may have a *theoretical* objective such as to maximise profit or maximise revenue.

To maximise *profit* the company should produce and sell at a price where,

MC = MR (i.e. Marginal Cost = Marginal Revenue).

To maximise *revenue* the company should produce and sell at a price where,

MR = 0 (i.e. Marginal Revenue equals zero).

? Questions

3.1 The following information relates to a management consultancy:

Wage cost per consultant hour (senior consultant)	£35.00
Wage cost per consultant hour (junior consultant)	£16.00
Overhead absorption rate per consultant hour	£10.50

The firm adds a 30% mark-up on marginal cost to arrive at the price to charge clients.

For client "Octopus" 55 hours of senior consultant time and 40 hours of junior consultant time have been incurred. All staff are paid on an hourly basis.

What price should be charged to Octopus?

A £2,565.00
B £3,334.50
C £3,562.50
D £3,664.29
E £4,631.25

(2 marks)

3.2 When deciding upon the price of a product which of the following items would not be taken into consideration?

A Cost of making the product.
B Price elasticity of demand.
C Cost of making other unrelated products.
D Prices charged by competitors serving the same market segments.
E Level of customer disposable wealth.

(2 marks)

3.3 When is market penetration pricing appropriate?

A If demand is very elastic.
B If the product is new and different.
C If there is little chance of achieving economies of scale.
D If demand is inelastic.
E If there is little competition and high barriers to entry.

(2 marks)

3.4 Which of the following is a recognised method of arriving at the selling price for the products of a business?

(i) Life cycle pricing
(ii) Price skimming
(iii) Penetration pricing
(iv) Target costing

A (i) and (ii) only
B (i), (ii) and (iii) only
C (ii) and (iii) only
D (i), (iii) and (iv) only
E (i), (ii), (iii) and (iv)

(2 marks)

3.5 Dawkins has established the following cost and revenue functions for the single product that it manufactures:

Price = £60 − 0.5 × quantity
Marginal revenue = £60 − 1 × quantity
Total cost = £250,000 + 10 × quantity

What price should Dawkins charge for its product in order to maximise profit?

A £25
B £35
C £100
D £140

(2 marks)

3.6 The variable cost for product Alpha is £40 per unit. Budgeted sales are expected to be 8,000 units during the forthcoming year, and fixed costs are expected to be £30,000. If 8,000 units are sold the profit is expected to be £60,000.

What is the profit margin for product Alpha?

A 14.6%
B 17.1%
C 22.0%
D 25.7%

(2 marks)

3.7 A national opera company is touring a European country and offers discounted tickets to opera-goers who can prove that they are aged over 65 years.

This price discrimination policy is on the basis of

A Place
B Usage
C Market segment
D Time
E Product type

(2 marks)

Use the following information to answer the next two questions.

RJD Ltd makes and sells a single product, Z. The selling price and marginal revenue equations for product Z are as follows:

Selling price = £50 − £0.001x
Marginal revenue = £50 − £0.002x
The variable costs are £20 per unit and the fixed costs are £100,000.

3.8 In order to maximise profit, the selling price per unit should be

A £25
B £30
C £35
D £40
E £50

(3 marks)

3.9 If the selling price was set to maximise *revenue*, the resulting profit would be

A £25,000
B £125,000
C £175,000
D £225,000
E £375,000

(3 marks)

3.10 Market research by Company A has revealed that the maximum demand for product R is 50,000 units each year and that demand will reduce by 50 units for every £1 that the selling price is increased. Based on this information, Company A has calculated that the profit-maximising level of sales for product R for the coming year is 35,000 units.

The selling price of each of the units at the profit-maximising level of sales will be:

A £100
B £300
C £500
D £700
E £900

(2 marks)

3.11 "What Price plc" is about to launch a new product to the UK market, the new product is called the "Wonder Product". Sales demand has been estimated by a firm of marketing consultants who expect demand to be between a low of 50,000 units per month and a high of 400,000 units per month depending upon the price that the company ultimately decides to charge.

The consultants believe that 50,000 units would be sold if the price is set at £400 per unit. They have also advised that for every decrease in price of £12.50 per unit, an additional 25,000 units would be sold.

Fixed costs are expected to be £48 million per annum if the company produces 250,000 units or less. However, if the level of production exceeds 250,000 units, annual fixed costs are expected to increase by £6 million.

If 250,000 units or less are made, the variable production cost per unit is expected to be £240 per unit. If more than 250,000 units are made, the variable production cost per unit is expected to be £210 per unit. Variable selling cost per unit is expected to be £35 per unit if 150,000 units or less are sold, and £40 per unit if more than 150,000 units are sold.

Requirements

(a) Advise the company as to the price that should be set by "What Price plc" given that their primary objective is to maximise profit. Produce a table but consider only production and sales levels of 50,000 units, 100,000 units, 150,000 units, 200,000 units, 250,000 units, 300,000 units, 350,000 units and 400,000 units.

(5 marks)

(b) Briefly explain what is meant by market skimming, penetration pricing and market segmentation in the context of product pricing.

(3 marks)

(c) Briefly discuss the typical issues that a company should consider when setting selling prices for a new product about to be launched.

(2 marks)
(Total = 10 marks)

3.12 Staly plc has two wholly owned UK-based subsidiaries.

One of these subsidiaries, Brompton Ltd, manufactures plastic toys which it sells to toy retailers. Brompton Ltd is about to launch a new product but is unsure what price to charge. A firm of consultants have estimated the level of demand at several different prices. This information is as follows:

Price (£)	5	10	15	20	25	30	35	40
Level of demand in forthcoming year ('000 of units)	200	180	160	135	120	100	75	50

The cost of manufacturing the new toy has been estimated as follows:

	£ per unit
Direct materials	2.00
Direct labour	1.50
Variable overheads	2.50
	6.00

Fixed costs associated with manufacturing the new toy are expected to be £400,000 per annum. However, if production and sales exceed 150,000 units fixed costs are expected to increase by £50,000.

The second subsidiary, Electrics Ltd, assembles desktop computers using components sourced from suppliers of keyboards, microchips, monitors, speakers and so on. It sells these computers under its own brand name through 150 of its own outlets in major shopping centres throughout the UK.

It is to commence selling a new computer aimed at students. The management of Electrics Ltd believe that the price and marginal revenue equations are as follows:

Price equation:
$P = 2{,}000 - 0.01Q$

where P is selling price and Q is sales quantity in units.

Marginal revenue (MR) equation:
$\text{MR} = 2{,}000 - 0.02Q$

The cost of manufacture is expected to be:

	£ per unit
Direct materials (bought-in components)	400
Direct labour (assembly)	150
Variable overheads	50
Fixed overheads (apportioned)	200
	800

Requirements

(a) For Brompton Ltd, determine the price that should be set for the new toy in order to maximise profit for Brompton Ltd.

(4 marks)

(b) For Electrics Ltd, determine the price that should be set for the new computer under two circumstances:

to maximise profit for Electrics Ltd
to maximise revenue for Electrics Ltd.

(6 marks)
(Total = 10 marks)

3.13 R Ltd (IDEC 5/03 (Amended))

Just over two years ago, R Ltd was the first company to produce a specific "off-the-shelf" accounting software packages. The pricing strategy, decided on by the Managing Director, for the packages was to add a 50% mark-up to the budgeted full cost of the packages. The company achieved and maintained a significant market share and high profits for the first two years.

Budgeted information for the current year (Year 3) was as follows:

Production and sales	15,000 packages
Full cost	£400 per package

At a recent board meeting, the Finance Director reported that although costs were in line with the budget for the current year, profits were declining. He explained that the full cost included £80 for fixed overheads. This figure had been calculated by using an overhead absorption rate based on labour hours and the budgeted level of production which, he pointed out, was much lower than the current capacity of 25,000 packages.

The Marketing Director stated that competitors were beginning to increase their market share. He also reported the results of a recent competitor analysis which showed that when R Ltd announced its prices for the current year, the competitors responded by undercutting them by 15%. Consequently, he commissioned an investigation of the market. He informed the Board that the market research showed that at a price of £750 there would be no demand for the packages but for every £10 reduction in price the demand would increase by 1,000 packages.

The Managing Director appeared to be unconcerned about the loss of market share and argued that profits could be restored to their former level by increasing the mark-up.

Note: If price $= a - bx$ then marginal revenue $= a - 2bx$

Requirements

(a) Discuss the Managing Director's pricing strategy in the circumstances described above. Your appraisal must include a discussion of the alternative strategies that could have been implemented at the launch of the packages.

(10 marks)

(b) (i) Based on the data supplied by the market research, calculate the maximum annual profit that can be earned from the sale of the packages from Year 3 onwards.

(7 marks)

(ii) A German computer software distribution company, L, which is interested in becoming the sole distributor of the accounting software packages has now approached R Ltd. It has offered to purchase 25,000 accounting packages per annum at a fixed price of €930 per package. If R Ltd were to sell the packages to L, then the variable costs would be £300 per package.

The current exchange rate is €1 = £0.60.

Requirement

Draw a diagram to illustrate the sensitivity of the proposal from the German company to changes in the exchange rate and then state and comment on the minimum exchange rate needed for the proposal to be worthwhile.

(8 marks)

(Total = 25 marks)

Answers

3.1 **B**

	£
Salary costs:	
Senior consultant 55 hours × £35	1,925.00
Junior consultant 40 hours × £16	640.00
Marginal cost	2,565.00
Mark-up (30%)	769.50
Price to charge client	3,334.50

A This is the marginal cost only without 30% added.
B This is the correct answer.
C This is the full cost including absorbed overheads.
D This is the result of using 30% margin rather than 30% mark-up on marginal cost.
E This is full cost plus 30% added including absorbed overhead.

3.2 **C**

All of the above should be taken into account except for the *cost* of making other unrelated products.

3.3 **A**

A If demand is very elastic, high market share and a market presence could be achieved quickly by charging a low price.
B Here market skimming would be more appropriate. A high price could be charged to the "opinion leaders" who want to be seen to have the new product and are prepared to pay a high price.
C It is difficult to charge a low price for a product where there are few opportunities for economies of scale since cost per unit will still be high irrespective of production volume.

D If demand is inelastic, charging a low price will not have a beneficial effect upon sales volume and profit.

E If there is little competition and high barriers to entry, such as in the pharmaceutical industry, there is no incentive for companies to charge a low price.

3.4 **B**

At first inspection all four appear to be methods of arriving at selling price.

However, target costing is a method to arrive at the cost at which a product should be produced for having worked backwards from the price already set for the product.

It is a method to arrive at product cost not product selling price.

3.5 **B**

To maximise profit Dawkins must produce where MC = MR

(MC is Marginal Cost, MR is Marginal Revenue)

MC = £10
MR = £60 − Q

So to maximise profit:
£10 = £60 − Q

Therefore,
Q = £50

To calculate the price that must be sold:
Price = £60 − 0.5 × quantity

So,
Price = £60 − 0.5 × £50 = £60 − £25 = £35

3.6 **A**

Profit margin = Profit/Sales × 100%

So we need to calculate profit per unit and selling price per unit.

Profit per unit = £60,000/8,000 units = £7.50 per unit

Selling price:

Sales revenue = Variable costs + Fixed costs + Profit
= £40 × 8,000 units + £30,000 + £60,000
= £410,000

So, selling price per unit = £410,000/8,000 units = £51.25 per unit

Profit margin = £7.50/£51.25 × 100% = 14.6%

Alternatively,

Profit margin = Profit/Sales × 100%
= £60,000/£410,000 × 100% = 14.6%

Answer B is profit mark-up on cost (£60,000/£350,000 × 100% = 17.1%)

Answer C is contribution margin (£410,000 − £320,000/£410,000 × 100% = 22%)

Answer D is contribution mark-up on cost (£90,000/£350,000 × 100% = 25.7%)

3.7 **C**

The opera company is discriminating on the grounds of market segment (segmenting using age).

3.8 **C**

In order to maximise profit, a business needs to produce the number of units where marginal cost equals marginal revenue.

In this question the marginal cost is £20 since this is the variable cost per unit.

(Remember that the marginal cost means the additional cost incurred when one additional unit is made – here that is £20.)

The marginal revenue has been given as an equation:
Marginal revenue = £50 − £0.002x

Putting marginal cost equal to marginal revenue gives:
$20 = 50 - 0.002x$

So,
$0.002x = 50 - 20 = 30$
$x = 30 \div 0.002 = 15{,}000$

This is telling us that to maximise profit, the company must produce 15,000 units.

To arrive at the selling price we use the selling price equation given in the question.

Selling price = £50 − £0.001x = £50 − £0.001 × 15,000 = £50 − £15 = £35

So, the answer is £35.

3.9 **A**

In order to maximise revenue, the business needs to produce the number on units where marginal revenue equals zero.

The marginal revenue has been given as an equation:
Marginal revenue = £50 − £0.002x

Putting marginal revenue equal to zero gives:
$50 - 0.002x = 0$

So,
$50 = 0.002x$
$x = 50 \div 0.002 = 25{,}000$

This is telling us that to maximise revenue, the company must produce 25,000 units.

To arrive at the selling price we use the selling price equation given in the question.

Selling price = £50 − £0.001x = £50 − £0.001 × 25,000 = £50 − £25 = £25

At this selling price and volume of output profit would be

	£
Sales (25 × 25,000 units)	625,000
Variable costs (20 × 25,000 units)	(500,000)
Fixed costs	(100,000)
Profit	25,000

So profit is £25,000.

3.10 **B**

To solve this we have to derive an equation as follows:
P = price and let X = demand in units

Then

$$50P = 50{,}000 - X$$

$$P = \frac{50{,}000 - X}{50}$$

$$P = 1{,}000 - 0.02X$$

We are told that the profit maximising level of sales is 35,000 units.

So this is X.

Therefore,
$P = 1{,}000 - 0.02 \times 35{,}000 = 1{,}000 - 700 = £300$

3.11

Topic being tested

Pricing policy

Approach

Part (a) – Arrive at a selling price by using a tabular approach for selected sales volumes and associated prices.
Part (b) – Discuss practical pricing methods and market segmentation using your learned knowledge.
Part (c) – Discuss typical factors to be considered when setting selling prices by doing a quick plan using common sense to generate ideas.

It is often advisable to attempt the written parts of questions of this style first if possible. Time pressure usually applies to numerical parts of questions more so than written parts.

Use short punchy paragraphs with spaces between them in all written answers.

Make it easy to mark!

Solution

(a) The price to set which will maximise profit for "What Price plc" can be found by using a table to calculate the profit resulting for the given price and related sales volumes.

Table for sales levels *per month*

Sales quantity ('000 units)	*50*	*100*	*150*	*200*	*250*	*300*	*350*	*400*
Price per unit (£)	400	375	350	325	300	275	250	225
Revenue (£m)	20	37.5	52.5	65	75	82.5	87.5	90
Variable production cost per unit (£)	240	240	240	240	240	210	210	210
Variable production costs (£m)	12	24	36	48	60	63	73.5	84
Fixed production costs (£m)	4	4	4	4	4	4.5	4.5	4.5
Variable selling cost per unit (£)	35	35	35	40	40	40	40	40
Variable selling costs (£m)	1.75	3.5	5.25	8	10	12	14	16
Profit (£m)	2.25	6.0	7.25	5.0	1.0	3.0	(4.5)	(14.5)

The maximum profit is £7.25 million if 150,000 units are sold at a price of £350 per unit.

So the company should set a selling price of £350 per unit.

(b) *Market skimming*

This is where a high price is initially charged for a new product. It will be aimed at the early adopters who are seen as being the "top of the market", hence the name market skimming – skimming off the "top" customers.

This pricing strategy would be appropriate for the launch of a high-technology product such as plasma screen televisions.

Penetration pricing

This is where the initial price of the new product is low in order to penetrate the market so as to achieve a market presence quickly and hopefully also achieve high market share.

It can be justified by economies of scale cutting product costs if the high market share is achieved.

This pricing strategy would be appropriate for the launch of a low-technology product such as a new chocolate bar.

Market segmentation

Market segmentation involves splitting or segmenting the "mass market" into different subgroups of customers.

Different products or services can then be designed and priced according to the different needs of customers in different segments. Similarly, promotional techniques can be used which focus on these customers.

For example, Porsche sell expensive sports cars to wealthy people at high prices whereas Proton sell relatively cheap cars to people with lower incomes or little interest in expensive cars.

(c) There are several typical issues that a company should consider when setting the selling price for a new product about to be launched. These would include:

- The likely price to be charged by competitors launching a similar new product.
- The price that "early adopters" are expected to be prepared to pay.
- The level of sales in unit terms that the company wishes to achieve in the short term.

The objective of the company:

- high market share, so a fairly low initial price to generate demand, that is, penetration pricing
- high profit per unit, so a high price and low market share, that is, market skimming.

3.12

> **!** *Topic being tested*
>
> Part (a) – Price setting using a tabular approach.
> Part (b) – Price setting using an equation approach.
>
> *Approach*
>
> Part (a) – Given that the price and volume of sales has been presented as a table it makes sense to calculate the profit for each piece and quantity combination also using a tabular approach and then select the price at which the level of profit is maximised.
>
> Part (b) – When equations are given, this should prompt you to remember that to maximise profit we must set MC = MR (Marginal Cost equal to Marginal Revenue), and to maximise revenue we must set MR = 0.

Solution

(a) Brompton Ltd wishes to determine the price at which the new toy should be sold in order to maximise profit. A tabular approach can be used as follows:

Price (£)	*5*	*10*	*15*	*20*	*25*	*30*	*35*	*40*
Quantity of units ('000)	200	180	160	135	120	100	75	50
Sales £'000	1,000	1,800	2,400	2,700	3,000	3,000	2,625	2,000
Variable costs (£6 × no. of units) £'000	1,200	1,080	960	810	720	600	450	300
Fixed costs £'000	450	450	450	400	400	400	400	400
Profit/(Loss)	(650)	270	990	1,490	1,880	2,000	1,775	1,300

Profit is maximised when the price is set at £30 per unit. This is therefore the price that should be set by Brompton Ltd.

(b) In order for Electrics Ltd to *maximise profit* it should produce where

$$MC = MR$$

Since Marginal Cost is the addition to cost of making one more unit, this will be the total *variable* cost of £600 per unit.

MR is given as

$MR = 2{,}000 - 0.02Q$

So setting MC = MR gives
$600 = 2{,}000 - 0.02Q$
$2{,}000 - 600 = 0.02Q$
$1{,}400 = 0.02Q$
$1{,}400 \div 0.02 = Q$

Therefore,
$Q = 70{,}000$ units

So in order to maximise profit, Electrics Ltd should produce and sell 70,000 units per annum.

The selling price should be:
$P = 2{,}000 - 0.01Q$
$P = 2{,}000 - 0.01 \times 70{,}000 = 2{,}000 - 700 = £1{,}300$

So the selling price in order to maximise profit should be £1,300 per computer.

In order for Electrics Ltd to *maximise revenue* it should produce where

$MR = 0$

That is,
$2{,}000 - 0.02Q = 0$

So
$2{,}000 = 0.02Q$
$2{,}000/0.02 = Q$
$Q = 100{,}000$ units

At a price of:
$P = 2{,}000 - 0.01Q$
$P = 2{,}000 - 0.01 \times 100{,}000$
$P = 2{,}000 - 1{,}000 = £1{,}000$

In order to maximise revenue, Electrics Ltd should produce and sell 100,000 computers at a price of £1,000 per computer.

3.13

(a) Appraisal of the current pricing strategy

Managing Director's current pricing method

	£
Cost	400
50% mark-up	200
Selling price	600

Drawbacks

As can be seen, the cost-plus approach adds a mark-up to the cost to arrive at the selling price. There are many drawbacks associated with this pricing method as follows:

- It completely ignores the market, hence the reason why the selling price is out of line with competitors.
- It focuses entirely on internal costs.
- It ignores competitors' reactions which has resulted in the competitors reducing prices as soon as the company released theirs.
- It can result in different selling prices due to the different absorption methods used when determining the total cost.
- It ignores the distinction between incremental and fixed costs.
- It fails to ensure that the quantity produced will be sold since the company does not know if the price is in line with the customer's perceptions of the value of the product.
- It is based on the belief that demand for the software is inelastic, that is, an increase in price will not lead to any significant reduction in demand. If this were true then increasing prices would clearly lead to increased demand. However, this view is not supported by the market research information. Therefore, increasing prices are likely to lead to a fall in demand and hence fall in profitability.

Benefits

There are however, benefits to this method of pricing which include the following:

- It ensures that all costs are covered and a desired profit is achieved. So far this has been achieved with the pricing of the software packages, as they have been profitable to date.
- It is easy to calculate, as once cost is determined a simple mark-up on these costs identifies the selling price.
- It allows the delegation of the price setting to more junior finance staff.
- It allows the company to avoid the costs involved in seeking information about the level of demand in the market.
- It allows the maintenance of relatively stable prices and any price increases are easier to justify to clients.

Alternative pricing strategies

Price skimming

This method of pricing sets high initial prices in an attempt to exploit those sections of the market which are relatively insensitive to price changes. As R Ltd's product was the first of its type it could have initially set high prices to take advantage of the novelty appeal of a new product as demand would have been inelastic. If this approach had been used, R Ltd could have subsequently reduced the price to remain competitive in the market.

Penetration pricing

This method sets very low prices in the initial stages of a product's life cycle to gain rapid acceptance of the product and therefore a significant market share. If R Ltd had used this approach it could have discouraged entrants into the market.

Demand-based approach

With this method R Ltd could have utilised some market research information to determine the selling price and level of demand to maximise company profits. This method, however, does pose the following drawbacks:

- It is dependent on the quality of the market research information.
- It also assumes a competitive market; that is, the actions of competitors will not impact on actual demand for the software package.
- It is difficult to estimate the demand curve.
- It is difficult to incorporate the effect of competition.
- This method assumes that price is the only factor that influences the quantity demanded – other factors like quality, packaging, advertising, promotion, credit terms, after sales service are ignored.
- The marginal cost curve for our packages can only be determined after considerable analysis and the final results (£320) are only an approximation of the true marginal cost function.

However, this method does benefit from

- A useful insight that stresses the need for managers to think about price-demand relationships even if the relationship cannot be measured precisely.
- A consideration of the marketplace.
- Considering only incremental costs.

(b) (i) Optimum selling price and maximum annual profit

Optimum selling price and level of demand can be found when marginal cost equates to marginal revenue:

Demand	£750 − £0.01X
Marginal revenue	£750 − £0.02X
Marginal cost	£320
Marginal cost = marginal revenue	£320 = £750 − £0.02X
	X = 21,500
	Price = £750 − £10/1,000 (21,500) = £535

Revised profit		£
Selling price		535
Variable cost		320
Contribution per unit		215
Total contribution	£215 × 21,500	4,622,500
Less: Fixed costs		1,200,000
Profit		3,422,500

(ii) See diagram on next page.

Workings

Current contribution (b) (i)	£4,622,500
Contribution from exporting to L	
((€930 × 0.60) − £300) × 25,000	£6,450,000

Sensitivity graph

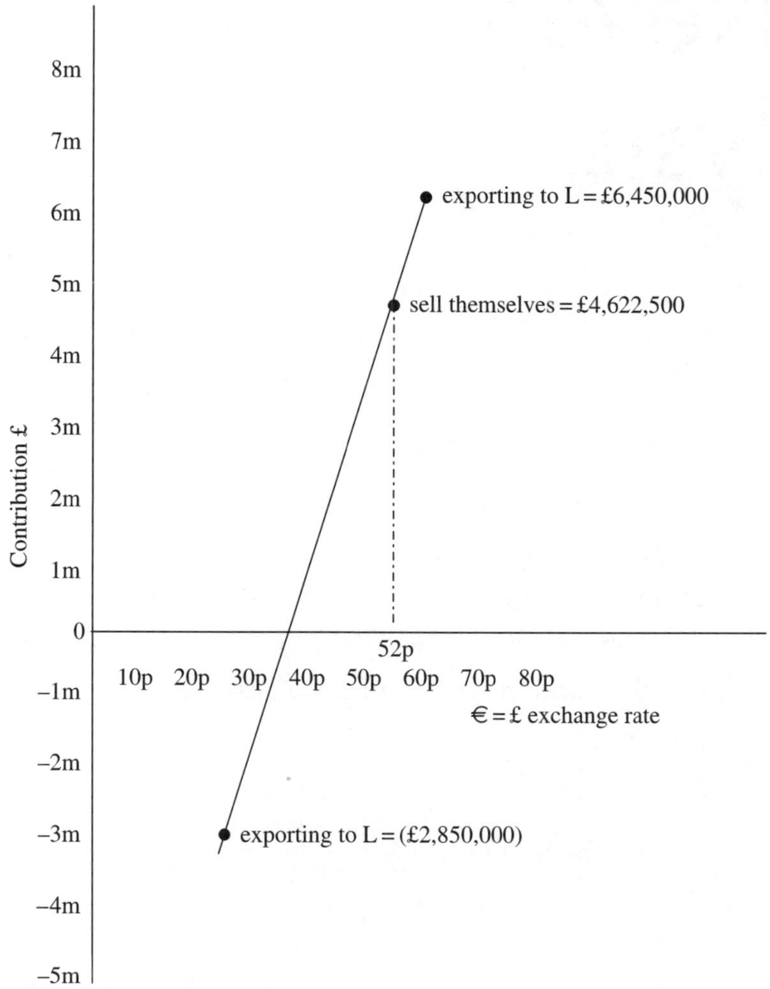

R Ltd should sell all of their output to L as it will increase contribution by £1,827,500.

However, if the exchange rate falls to €1 = £0.20 then negative contribution will be generated:

((€930 × 0.20) – £300) × 25,000 (£2,850,000)

Comment

As can been seen from the graph if the exchange rate falls to €1 = £0.52 (i.e. a 13.33% drop) then R Ltd will be indifferent as to whether they sell the accounting packages themselves or export them to L. If the exchange rate falls below €1 = £0.52, then R Ltd should sell the accounting packages themselves. R Ltd needs to assess the likelihood of the Euro falling in value.

Exporting to L = £6,450,000 in contribution at an exchange rate of 60p

Selling themselves = £4,622,500 in contribution at an exchange rate of 52p

Negative point = £2,850,000 in contribution at an exchange rate of 20p.

Breakeven Analysis

4

Breakeven analysis considers the level of activity in terms of sales units and sales revenue that a business requires to meet in order to breakeven.

It requires mathematical skills and the ability to draw graphs.

π Useful equations:

1 $$\text{Breakeven point (in units)} = \frac{\text{Fixed costs}}{\text{Contribution per unit}}$$

2 $$\text{C/S ratio (Contribution/Sales ratio)} = \frac{\text{Contribution per unit}}{\text{Selling price per unit}}$$

The C/S ratio is also known as P/V ratio (Profit/Volume ratio).

3 $$\text{Breakeven point (in sales revenue terms)} = \frac{\text{Fixed costs}}{\text{C/S ratio}}$$

4 $$\text{Margin of safety} = \frac{\text{Budgeted sales} - \text{Breakeven sales}}{\text{Budgeted sales}} \times 100\%$$

5 Sales required (in units) to achieve a particular profit target

$$= \frac{\text{Fixed costs} + \text{Profit target}}{\text{Contribution per unit}}$$

6 Sales required (in revenue terms) to achieve a particular profit target

$$= \frac{\text{Fixed costs} + \text{Profit target}}{\text{C/S ratio}}$$

You also need to be able to draw two graphs – the Breakeven chart and the Profit/Volume chart.

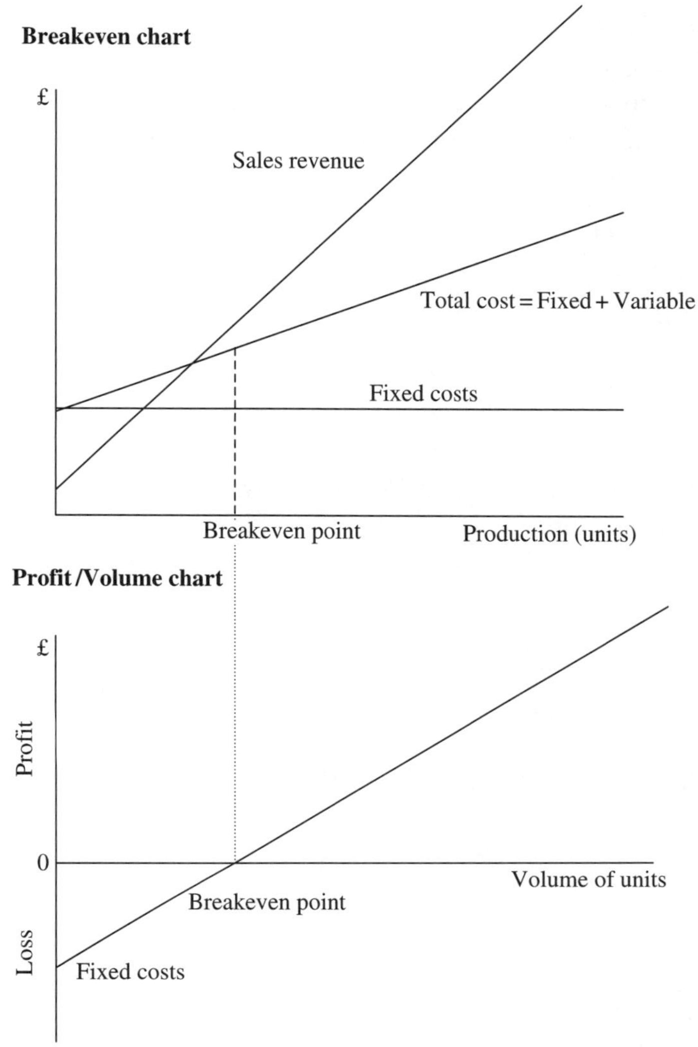

Questions

4.1 PER plc sells three products. The budgeted fixed cost for the period is £648,000. The budgeted contribution to sales ratio (C/S ratio) and sales mix are as follows:

Product	*C/S ratio (%)*	*Mix (%)*
P	27	30
E	56	20
R	38	50

The breakeven sales revenue is nearest to

A £248,000
B £1,606,700
C £1,692,000
D £1,522,700

(2 marks)

4.2 Which of the following may be required to determine the breakeven sales value in a multi-product manufacturing environment?

(i) individual product gross contribution to sales ratio
(ii) the general fixed cost
(iii) the product-specific fixed cost
(iv) the product mix ratio
(v) the method of apportionment of general fixed costs

A (i), (ii), (iii) and (iv) only
B (i), (iii) and (iv) only
C (i), (ii) and (iv) only
D All of them

(2 marks)

4.3 Edward produces a single product. For the forthcoming period, the budget contains the following information:

	£
Revenue	500,000
Fixed overheads	70,000
Contribution	100,000

What is the margin of safety in percentage terms?

A 6%
B 14%
C 20%
D 25%
E 30%

(4 marks)

4.4 Thomas produces three products K, L and M. The products are usually bundled up when sold and have to be sold in the ratio 5:3:2 (K:L:M).

The contribution to sales ratios of the three products are

K 25%
L 30%
M 40%

Budgeted fixed costs are £1,180,000.

What is the budgeted breakeven sales revenue?

A £1,200,000
B £1,242,105
C £3,000,000
D £3,726,317
E £4,000,000

(4 marks)

4.5

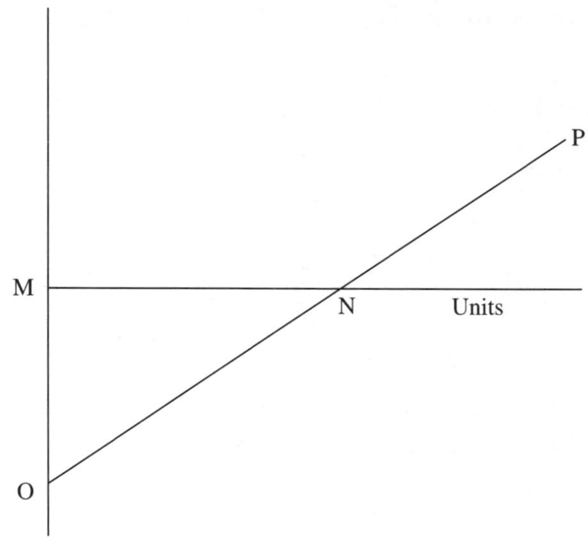

Which of the following statements is true?

	Name of graph	*Breakeven point*	*Fixed costs*
A	Breakeven chart	N	M
B	Breakeven chart	M	O
C	Profit/Volume chart	M	P
D	Profit/Volume chart	P	O
E	Profit/Volume chart	N	O

(2 marks)

4.6 The following information relates to a company making televisions:

	£
Budgeted sales revenue	1,300,000
Budgeted profit	130,000
Budgeted contribution	520,000

What is the budgeted sales revenue to breakeven?

A £325,000
B £500,000
C £910,000
D £975,000
E £1,170,000

(3 marks)

4.7 RT Ltd wants to make a profit of £495,000. It has fixed costs of £247,500 and a C/S ratio of 0.75. The product selling price is £11.

What number of units will RT Ltd have to sell in order to achieve the targeted profit?

A 30,000 units
B 45,000 units
C 67,500 units
D 90,000 units
E 120,000 units

(3 marks)

Use the following information to answer the next two questions.

HG plc manufactures four products. The unit cost and selling price details per unit are as follows:

	Product W	*Product X*	*Product Y*	*Product Z*
	£	£	£	£
Selling price	56	67	89	96
Materials	22	31	38	46
Labour	15	20	18	24
Variable overhead	12	15	18	15
Fixed overhead	4	2	8	7

4.8 Assuming that labour is a unit variable cost, if the products are ranked according to their contribution to sales ratio, the most profitable product is

A W
B X
C Y
D Z

(2 marks)

4.9 Assuming that labour is a unit variable cost, if budgeted unit sales are in the ratio W:2, X:3, Y:3, Z:4 and monthly fixed costs are budgeted to be £15,000, the number of units of W that would be sold at the budgeted breakeven point is nearest to

A 106 units
B 142 units
C 212 units
D 283 units

(2 marks)

4.10 KLQ plc sells three products. The ratio of their total sales values is K2:L3:Q5.

The contribution to sales ratios of the products are

K 30%
L 25%
Q 40%

If fixed costs for the period are expected to be £120,000, the revenue (to the nearest £1,000) needed to earn a marginal costing profit of £34,000 is

A £392,000
B £413,000
C £460,000
D £486,000

(2 marks)

4.11 Footy Shirts Ltd makes replica football shirts which it sells to clothes retailers for £25 per shirt. Retailers typically sell the shirts to consumers for £40 per shirt.

Budgeted production for the forthcoming period is 200,000 shirts. Budgeted fixed overheads are £2.4 million. Variable cost per shirt is expected to be £6.50.

Retailers have started to use their buyer power over Footy Shirts Ltd and have begun to demand a discount off the existing price charged to them. The directors of Footy

Shirts Ltd are concerned that they may lose business if they do not offer some sort of discount to their customers and have asked for advice from the market research consultancy, DropItAndSee.

DropItAndSee have suggested that Footy Shirts Ltd need to decrease the selling price charged to retailers by at least 10% if they are to retain their existing customers. However, they believe that Footy Shirts Ltd can use some buyer power of their own over supplier of materials such that the variable cost per shirt would fall by 5%.

Requirements

(a) Calculate the breakeven point in terms of units and sales revenue, and the margin of safety based upon the existing selling price and variable cost per shirt.

(3 marks)

(b) Draw the Profit/Volume chart based upon the existing selling price and variable cost per shirt.

(3 marks)

(c) Calculate the breakeven point in terms of units and sales revenue, and the margin of safety, assuming the company not only decreases the selling price by 10% but also uses its own buyer power over its suppliers.

(2 marks)

By how many units has the breakeven point changed?

(1 mark)
(Total = 10 marks)

4.12 Laws Stores Ltd owns a large out-of-town store selling sports equipment. For reporting and control purposes it splits the business into four product groups: Ball sports, Racquet sports, Water sports and Outdoor activities.

The board of directors is dominated by the Laws family who have heard a rumour that one of the large quoted sports goods retailers is seeking planning permission to build a new store nearby. The board of Laws Stores Ltd feel that to compete they may have to decrease the prices of their products.

For the forthcoming year, before any price changes are implemented, budgeted information is as follows:

	Ball sports	*Racquet sports*	*Water sports*	*Outdoor activities*
	£	£	£	£
Sales	800,000	400,000	250,000	150,000
Variable costs	500,000	260,000	190,000	126,000

Fixed costs of operating the store are budgeted to be £400,000.

Price decreases are being contemplated as follows:

	Average price decrease (%)
Ball sports	10
Racquet sports	5
Water sports	6
Outdoor activities	4

Although these price decreases are expected to be needed to defend sales volume from the threat posed by new competition, the directors believe that sales volume for Water sports and Outdoor activities might even increase as a result of the lower prices being proposed.

In fact, the *sales volume* changes as a result of the decrease in prices and are expected to be as follows:

Ball sports	Unchanged if prices are decreased by 10%
Racquet sports	Unchanged if prices are decreased by 5%
Water sports	Increase of 15% if prices are decreased by 6%
Outdoor activities	Increase of 10% if prices are decreased by 4%

Requirements

(a) Calculate the C/S ratio and breakeven sales revenue for the store before any changes to product selling prices.

(4 marks)

(b) Calculate the effect upon profit of the proposed price changes and suggest whether they should be implemented. Ignore economies of scale.

(3 marks)

(c) Discuss the other factors that should be considered before implementing the proposed changes to product prices.

(3 marks)
(Total = 10 marks)

Answers

4.1 **C**

$$\text{Budgeted breakeven sales} = \frac{\text{Budgeted fixed costs}}{\text{C/S ratio}}$$

We know the budgeted fixed costs but the C/S ratio is a little more involved since the company produces more than one product.

However, since the three products have to be sold in a given mix we can calculate the average C/S ratio as follows:

Average C/S ratio $= 0.3 \times 27\% + 0.2 \times 56\% + 0.5 \times 38\% = 38.3\%$

So,

$$\text{Budgeted breakeven sales} = \frac{\text{Budgeted fixed costs}}{\text{C/S ratio}} = \frac{£648{,}000}{0.383} = £1{,}691{,}906$$

4.2 **A**

All of the statements are true except statement (v).

Contribution is used when calculating the breakeven point NOT profit.

Apportionment of general fixed costs would only be required if the business wished to calculate the profit generated per product for some reason.

4.3 **E**

The margin of safety is calculated as:

$$\frac{\text{Budgeted sales} - \text{Sales to breakeven}}{\text{Budgeted sales}}$$

So we need to calculate the breakeven sales revenue.

To do this we need the C/S (Contribution/Sales) ratio.

C/S ratio = £100,000/£500,000 = 20%

$$\text{Sales revenue to breakeven} = \frac{\text{Fixed costs}}{\text{C/S ratio}}$$

$$= \frac{£70,000}{0.2} = £350,000$$

$$\text{So margin of safety} = \frac{£500,000 - £350,000}{£500,000} = 30\%$$

4.4 **E**

$$\text{Budgeted breakeven sales} = \frac{\text{Budgeted fixed costs}}{\text{C/S ratio}}$$

We know the budgeted fixed costs but the C/S ratio is a little more involved since the company produces more than one product.

However, since the three products have to be sold in a fixed ratio we can calculate the average C/S ratio as follows:

$$\text{Average C/S ratio} = \frac{5 \times 25\% + 3 \times 30\% + 2 \times 40\%}{10}$$

$$= 29.5\%$$

$$\text{So, budgeted breakeven sales} = \frac{£1,180,000}{0.295}$$

$$= £4,000,000$$

4.5 **E**

The chart is the Profit/Volume chart which passes through the *x*-axis at the breakeven volume of units.

If zero units are made, the business will have no revenue and suffer no variable costs, but will still have to pay its fixed costs.

At zero units the loss would be at point "O" which is equal to the fixed costs of the business.

4.6 **D**

$$\text{Budgeted sales revenue to breakeven} = \frac{\text{Fixed costs}}{\text{C/S ratio}}$$

Fixed cost = Contribution less profit = £520,000 − £130,000 = £390,000

$$\text{C/S ratio} = \frac{£520,000}{£1,300,000} = 0.4$$

$$\text{Budgeted sales revenue to breakeven} = \frac{£390,000}{0.4} = £975,000$$

4.7 **D**

To breakeven

$$\text{Revenue} = \frac{\text{Fixed costs}}{\text{C/S ratio}}$$

To achieve a profit target

$$\text{Revenue} = \frac{\text{Fixed costs} + \text{Profit target}}{\text{C/S ratio}}$$

$$= \frac{£247{,}500 + £495{,}000}{0.75} = £990{,}000$$

Since selling price is £11 per unit, company needs to sell £990,000/£11 = 90,000 units.

4.8 **C**

We need to calculate the C/S ratio for each product and rank them on the grounds of highest to lowest.

	Product W	*Product X*	*Product Y*	*Product Z*
	£	£	£	£
Contribution	7	1	15	11
Sales	56	67	89	96
C/S ratio	7/56	1/67	15/89	11/96
	= 0.125	= 0.015	= 0.169	= 0.115
Ranking	2nd	4th	1st	3rd

Remember that contribution is selling price less all variable costs. Fixed costs are not deducted.

4.9 **D**

Since the four products are to be produced in a set mix, we can consider them being produced as a "package".

That is, every time a package is produced it will consist of 2 units of W, 3 units of X, 3 units of Y and 4 units of Z.

To breakeven, sufficient packages must be produced and sold so that the contribution earned covers the fixed costs of the company.

The fixed costs are expected to be £15,000 (given in question).

So, we need to calculate contribution generated each time that a "package" is produced and sold, as follows:

Package contribution

	£
2 units of W × £7	14
3 units of X × £1	3
3 units of Y × £15	45
4 units of Z × £11	44
Total contribution	106

The number of packages that must be sold therefore is

£106 × number of packages = £15,000

So, number of packages = £15,000/£106 = 141.51 packages.

Remember that the question is asked for the number of units of product W that must be sold.

Given that there are 2 units of W in each package, the answer must be $2 \times 141.51 =$ 283 units.

4.10 **C**

$$\text{Budgeted } \textit{breakeven} \text{ sales} = \frac{\text{Budgeted fixed costs}}{\text{C/S ratio}}$$

However, to achieve a *particular profit target*:

$$\text{Budgeted sales} = \frac{\text{Budgeted fixed costs} + \text{Profit target}}{\text{C/S ratio}}$$

Since the contribution generated by selling the products of the company must be high enough to cover not only the Fixed costs, but also the profit target.

We know the budgeted fixed costs and the profit target but the C/S ratio is a little more involved since the company produces more than one product.

However, since the three products have to be sold in a fixed ratio we can calculate the average C/S ratio as follows:

$$\text{Average C/S ratio} = \frac{2 \times 30\% + 3 \times 25\% + 5 \times 40\%}{10}$$

$$= 33.5\%$$

$$\text{So, budgeted sales} = \frac{£120{,}000 + £34{,}000}{0.335} = £459{,}701$$

4.11

Topic being tested

Breakeven analysis

Approach

Part (a) – Calculate the breakeven volume of units using the breakeven equation.

$$\text{Breakeven volume} = \frac{\text{Fixed costs}}{\text{Contribution per unit}}$$

Breakeven sales revenue is then:
Breakeven sales volume × selling price per unit

The margin of safety is

$$\frac{\text{Budgeted sales} - \text{Breakeven sales}}{\text{Budgeted sales}} \times 100\%$$

Part (b) – Draw the Profit/Volume chart where profit is on the y-axis and volume of units is on the x-axis.

Part (c) – Calculate the breakeven volume of units and breakeven sales revenue using the same approach as in Part (a) but using the revised contribution per unit figure.

Part (d) – Compare breakeven points.

Solution

(a) To calculate the breakeven sales volume:

$$\text{Contribution per unit} \times \text{volume of units} = \text{fixed costs}$$

Therefore,

$$\text{Volume} = \frac{\text{Fixed costs}}{\text{Contribution per unit}}$$
$$= \frac{2{,}400{,}000}{25 - 6.50} = 129{,}730 \text{ football shirts}$$

So, breakeven sales revenue = breakeven sales volume × selling price per shirt
= 129,730 × £25 = £3.24m

The margin of safety is

$$\frac{\text{Budgeted sales} - \text{Breakeven sales}}{\text{Budgeted sales}} \times 100\%$$
$$= \frac{200{,}000 \text{ units} - 129{,}730 \text{ units}}{200{,}000 \text{ units}} \times 100\% = 35.1\%$$

That is, sales could fall below budget by 35% in volume terms before the company needs to worry about making a loss.

(b) Profit/Volume chart (P/V chart)

The Profit/Volume chart relates profit to be achieved with the volume of units to be made and sold. Two points are needed on the line in order to be able to draw the P/V chart.

If no units are made and sold, the loss will be equal to the fixed costs of £2.4 million.

If 129,730 units are made and sold, profit will be zero (129,730 units is the breakeven point from Part (a)).

Profit/Volume chart based on original selling price and variable cost per unit:

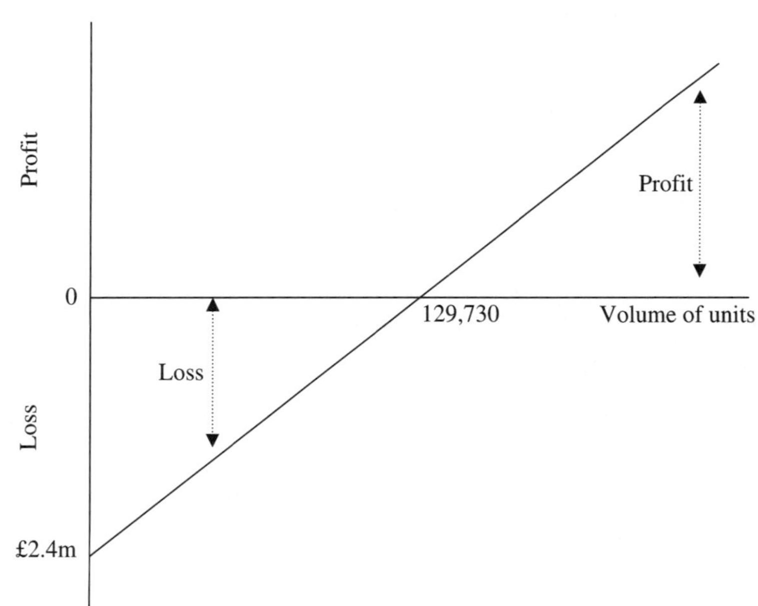

		£
(c)	New selling price per unit (£25 × 90%)	22.50
	New variable cost per unit (£6.50 × 95%)	6.18
	New contribution per unit	16.32

$$\text{New breakeven volume} = \frac{\text{Fixed costs}}{\text{Contribution per unit}}$$
$$= \frac{2{,}400{,}000}{16.32}$$
$$= 147{,}059 \text{ football shirts}$$

New breakeven sales revenue = 147,059 units × £22.50 = £3.31m

That is, the business needs to generate additional sales revenue of £70,000 in order to breakeven.

The new margin of safety is

$$\frac{\text{Budgeted sales} - \text{Breakeven sales}}{\text{Budgeted sales}} \times 100\%$$
$$= \frac{200{,}000 \text{ units} - 147{,}059 \text{ units}}{200{,}000 \text{ units}} \times 100\% = 26.5\%$$

That is, sales could now only fall by 26.5% in volume terms before the company need to worry about making a loss.

(d) The breakeven point has increased by 17,329 units in volume terms and £70,000 in sales revenue terms.

4.12

Topic being tested

Breakeven analysis for a multi-product company (in this question, four product types).

Approach

Part (a) – Calculate the C/S ratio (also known as the P/V ratio).

$$\text{C/S ratio} = \frac{\text{Contribution for the store}}{\text{Sales revenue for the store}}$$

– Calculate breakeven sales revenue using

$$\text{breakeven sales revenue} = \frac{\text{Fixed costs}}{\text{C/S ratio}}$$

Part (b) – Calculate the effect upon profit by calculating the budgeted profit before the price changes are implemented and then recalculate profit once the prices have been changed.

– Conclude whether prices should be changed.

Part (c) – Discuss other factors (other than the effect upon profit) that should be considered before the prices are changed.

Solution

(a)

	Ball sports £	*Racquet sports* £	*Water sports* £	*Outdoor activities* £
Sales	800,000	400,000	250,000	150,000
Variable costs	500,000	260,000	190,000	126,000
Contribution	300,000	140,000	60,000	24,000

Total sales revenue = £1,600,000

Total contribution = £524,000

So, C/S ratio = £524,000/£1,600,000 = 0.3275

That is, for every £1 of sales revenue generated by the store, contribution (on average) is 32.75 pence.

$$\text{Breakeven sales revenue} = \frac{\text{Fixed costs}}{\text{C/S ratio}}$$
$$= \frac{£400{,}000}{0.3275} = £1{,}221{,}374$$

This is 76.3% of the budgeted revenue.

(£1,221,374/£1,600,000 × 100% = 76.3%)

(b) Effect upon profit of proposed changes in selling prices:

Profit before price changes	£
Total contribution (from solution for part (a))	524,000
Less: Budgeted fixed costs	(400,000)
Budgeted profit before price changes	124,000

Profit after price changes

	Ball sports £	*Racquet sports* £	*Water sports* £	*Outdoor activities* £
Sales (W1)	720,000	380,000	270,250	158,400
Variable costs (W2)	500,000	260,000	218,500	138,600
Contribution	220,000	120,000	51,750	19,800

Total contribution	£411,550
Less: Budgeted fixed costs	(£400,000)
Budgeted profit after price changes	£11,550

Conclusion

Budgeted profit is expected to fall by £112,450 if the price changes being proposed are implemented.

On profit grounds, therefore, the price changes should not be implemented.

Workings

	Ball sports £	*Racquet sports* £	*Water sports* £	*Outdoor activities* £
W1: Sales revenue				
Sales (W1)	800,000	400,000	250,000	150,000
	× 90%	× 95%	× 115%	× 110%
			× 94%	× 96%
	= 720,000	= 380,000	= 270,250	= 158,400
W2: Variable costs				
Sales (W1)	unchanged	unchanged	190,000	126,000
			× 115%	× 110%
			= 218,500	= 138,600

(c) Other factors, that should be considered before implementing the proposed changes to product prices, would include:

Rumour relating to new entrant

How likely is it that the rumour is correct relating to the large competitor setting up nearby, is planning permission likely to be granted to them, and how long would it take before their new store would become operational.

Customer loyalty

Is there any customer loyalty amongst local customers such that less dramatic price changes may be possible to stave off the effects of a new local competitor.

Economies of scale

What size of store would the quoted sports goods retailer be likely to open and what cost benefits might they achieve from having a larger store than that of Laws Stores Ltd. (These cost benefits might come in the form of buyer power to demand discounts from their suppliers, perhaps a rent-free period for the early years if the store is to be rented rather than owned, and so on.)

Specialisation

Would it be possible for Laws Stores Ltd to sell a narrower range of sports goods than at present and compete by being seen to be the specialist provider for the local area and beyond.

5 Product Mix Analysis and Joint Costs

Product mix analysis helps businesses to decide which products to produce in the situation where a resource is in limited supply. This resource could be labour time or machine time available.

When the resources required are in unlimited supply then the business should produce those products that generate a positive contribution.

Linear programming (Chapter 2) is one technique for dealing with this situation, however it will only deal with two product situations.

When a company has more than two products it needs to consider the following.

> When resources are in limited supply such that the business cannot possibly make all of the products that it wishes to, then the scarce resource must be rationed amongst the competing products in such a way as to generate the maximum contribution.

The rationing technique is as follows:

> Calculate contribution per unit of the scarce resource for each product, for example, contribution per labour hour, if labour is scarce.
>
> Rank the products from best to worst performer on the grounds of contribution per unit of the scarce resource.
>
> Create a production schedule to illustrate which products should be produced and in which quantities in order to maximise contribution for the business.

Joint costs

The cost of a process that makes several products simultaneously from common resources is called the joint cost.

For accounting purposes this cost is often split between the resulting joint products.

Techniques to split the costs between the joint products include

- physical measure (tonnage, volume, etc.)
- sales value at the split off point (if products can be sold without the need for post-separation further processing)
- final sales value after further processing
- net realisable value (= final sales value less further processing costs post).

A useful technique when answering this type of question is to *draw a diagram* representing the information you are given.

In the exam the option to process products further may need to be considered. The following principle must be adhered to (it is a direct consequence of the relevant costing principles covered earlier).

> A product should only be processed further if the extra revenues generated exceed the extra costs involved.
> Any joint costs are irrelevant in relation to this decision.

? Questions

Use the following information to answer the next two questions.

A company produces three products P, Q and R.

The cost cards are as follows:

	P £	*Q* £	*R* £
Selling price	50	65	80
Materials (at £5/kg)	15	15	25
Labour (at £8/hour)	8	12	16
Fixed overheads	9	19	8
Profit/unit	18	19	31
Maximum demand per annum (units)	2,000	1,500	1,000

Only 12,000 kg of material and 7,500 hours of labour are expected to be available during the next year.

5.1 What is the optimal production mix for the company?

	P units	*Q units*	*R units*
A	2,000	1,500	300
B	2,000	1,500	1,000
C	833	1,500	1,000
D	300	1,500	1,000
E	2,000	1,000	1,000

(3 marks)

5.2 What is the maximum contribution that the company can generate?

A £118,700
B £120,700
C £122,700
D £124,700
E £126,700

(3 marks)

5.3 The following details relate to three services provided by JHN plc.

	Service J £	*Service H* £	*Service N* £
Fee charged to customers	84	122	145
Unit service costs:			
Direct materials	12	23	22
Direct labour	15	20	25
Variable overheads	12	16	20
Fixed overheads	20	42	40

All three services use the same type of direct labour which is paid £30 per hour.

The fixed overheads are general fixed overheads that have been absorbed on the basis of machine hours.

If direct labour is a scarce resource, the most and least profitable uses of it are

	Most profitable	*Least profitable*
A	H	J
B	H	N
C	N	J
D	N	H

(2 marks)

5.4 M Ltd manufactures four products from different quantities of the same material which is in short supply. The following budgeted data relates to the products:

Product name	*M1* *£/unit*	*M2* *£/unit*	*M3* *£/unit*	*M4* *£/unit*
Selling price	70	92	113	83
Material (£4/kg)	16	22	34	20
Conversion costs	39	52	57	43
	55	74	91	63
Profit	15	18	22	20
Machine time per unit (in *minutes*)	40	40	37.5	45

The conversion costs include general fixed costs that have been absorbed using a rate of £24 per machine hour.

The most profitable use of the raw materials is to make

A Product M1
B Product M2
C Product M3
D Product M4

(2 marks)

5.5 A company produces three products M, T and D.

The cost cards are as follows:

	M	*T*	*D*
	£	£	£
Selling price	120.00	156.00	192.00
Materials (£12/kg)	36.00	36.00	60.00
Labour (£19.20/hour)	19.20	28.80	38.40
Fixed overheads	21.60	45.60	19.20
Profit/unit	43.20	45.60	74.40
Maximum demand per annum (units)	4,000	3,000	2,000

Only 24,000 kg of material and 15,000 hours of labour are expected to be available during the next year.

The company wishes to determine the number of units of each product it should produce in order to maximise profits. Which of the following comments is correct?

A The solution can be arrived at by ranking the products on the basis of contribution per kg of materials.
B The solution can be arrived at by ranking the products on the basis of contribution per hour of labour.
C The solution can be arrived at by ranking the products on the basis of profit per unit.
D The solution can only be arrived at by using the linear programming technique.
E The solution can only be arrived at by using the simplex technique.

(4 marks)

5.6 Which of the following best describes a by-product?

A A product produced at the same time as the other products which has no value.
B A product produced at the same time as other products which has a relatively high value compared to those other products.
C A product produced at the same time as other products which has a relatively low value compared to those other products.
D A product produced at the same time as other products which has to be processed further in order to be saleable.
E A product which can be produced on its own.

(2 marks)

5.7 RT Ltd manufactures three joint products R, S and T in a process where the total cost of manufacturing is £200,000.

Output and sales of the products were as follows:

	Production (units)	*Sales (units)*	*Selling price (£ per unit)*
R	30,000	25,000	5
S	20,000	12,000	4
T	40,000	30,000	6

Costs are apportioned between the products on the basis of market value, what cost is associated with product S?

A £27,195
B £34,043
C £35,821
D £44,441
E £48,000

(2 marks)

Use the following information to answer the next two questions.

ST plc manufactures two joint products S and T. The production process from which the products eventually result involves the following costs:

	£
Variable costs	170,000
Fixed costs	50,000

Other information:

	Production and sales (units)	*Selling price (£ per unit)*
S	10,000	20
T	6,000	15

5.8 If costs are apportioned over the joint products using final sales value, what is the total cost of product S (to the nearest £100)?

A £68,276
B £82,500
C £137,500
D £151,724

(2 marks)

5.9 If costs are apportioned over the joint products using physical units, what is the total cost of product T?

A £68,276
B £82,500
C £137,500
D £151,724

(2 marks)

5.10 TEH Ltd produces three joint products incurring common costs of £400,000.

Each product can be sold immediately as the production process ceases, or sold for a higher price after further processing work has been undertaken.

Relevant information is as follows:

Product	*T*	*H*	*E*
Units produced	10,000 units	6,000 units	4,000 units
Selling price at separation point	£8 per unit	£10 per unit	£6 per unit
Further processing costs	£25,000	£35,000	£20,000
Final selling price	£10 per unit	£16 per unit	£12 per unit

For which product(s) is it worth the company undertaking further processing?

A Product T and Product H and Product E
B Product T and Product H only
C Product T and Product E only
D Product H and Product E only
E Product T only

(4 marks)

5.11 Aber Machinery Ltd manufactures four electrical components used in the motor industry. The components are products F, G, H and J.

Due to the nature of the components, they are handcrafted with only a small amount of machine time being used during manufacture. Labour is skilled and a maximum of 1,845 hours of handcrafting time is available during the forthcoming month.

Budgeted information is as follows:

	Product F per unit (£)	*Product G per unit (£)*	*Product H per unit (£)*	*Product J per unit (£)*
Selling price	23.30	25.00	37.50	35.00
Direct materials	2.00	2.50	5.00	8.00
Direct labour	5.00	5.20	7.50	6.50
Variable overheads	3.00	3.20	6.00	4.00
Fixed overheads	4.00	4.00	7.00	6.00
Labour hours required	2 hours	3 hours	2.5 hours	3 hours
Machine hours required	0.25 hour	0.15 hour	0.30 hour	0.5 hour
Maximum demand	300 units	150 units	270 units	120 units

Budgeted fixed costs are £4,410.

Requirements

(a) Determine the production plan which will maximise profit during the forthcoming month.

(5 marks)

(b) A new customer has asked Aber Machinery Ltd to quote a price to supply 100 units of product G. Calculate the minimum price that Aber Machinery Ltd should quote to the new customer.

(5 marks)
(Total = 10 marks)

Answers

5.1 **A**

Maximum amount of material required:

	P	*Q*	*R*	*Total*
Maximum demand per annum (units)	2,000	1,500	1,000	
Materials required per unit	3 kg	3 kg	5 kg	
Material required	6,000 kg	4,500 kg	5,000 kg	15,500 kg
Labour hours required per unit	1 hour	1.5 hours	2 hours	
Labour hours required	2,000 hours	2,250 hours	2,000 hours	6,250 hours

Insufficient material is available although labour is in sufficient supply.

We must ration materials by calculating contribution per kg of material.

Remember that *contribution* is used for decision-making NOT profit!

	P £	*Q* £	*R* £
Contribution	27	38	39
Materials required per unit (kg)	3 kg	3 kg	5 kg
Contribution per kg	£9/kg	£12.67/kg	£7.80/kg
Order of production	2	1	3

Optimal production schedule

Product	*No. of units*	*Materials* (kg)	*Contribution* (£)
Q	1,500	4,500	57,000 (1,500 units × £38)
P	2,000	6,000	54,000 (2,000 units × £27)
		10,500	
Amount left to use for R		1,500	
R	300		11,700
Maximum contribution			122,700

5.2 **C**

(workings above)

5.3 **A**

In order to be able to rank the services, we need to calculate contribution per unit of the scarce resource – in this case, labour – for each service provided by the business.

	Service J	*Service H*	*Service N*
Contribution	£45	£63	£78
Hours of labour required (cost ÷ £30)	0.5 hour	0.67 hour	0.83 hour

So,
Contribution per hour of scarce labour for each service provided and the resulting ranking is as follows:

	Service J	*Service H*	*Service N*
Contribution	£45	£63	£78
Hours of labour required (cost ÷ £30)	0.5 hour	0.67 hour	0.83 hour
Contribution per hour of labour	£45/0.5	£63/0.67	£78/0.83 hour
	= £90/hour	= £94.50/hour	= £93.98/hour
Ranking	3rd	1st	2nd

So most profitable service is H and least profitable is J.

(Remember that contribution is selling price less all *variable* costs. Fixed costs are not deducted.)

5.4 **A**

In order to be able to rank the products, we need to calculate *contribution* per unit of the scarce resource – in this case, materials – for each product produced by the business.

Contribution is selling price less variable costs. Part of the conversion costs are fixed costs.

So we must deduct the fixed costs from the conversion costs in order to arrive at the underlying variable costs.

Product name	*M1* *£/unit*	*M2* *£/unit*	*M3* *£/unit*	*M4* *£/unit*
Conversion costs	39	52	57	43
Less:				
Fixed costs (machine time × £24/hour)	16	16	15	18
Variable conversion costs	23	36	42	25

So contribution is:

Product name	*M1* *£/unit*	*M2* *£/unit*	*M3* *£/unit*	*M4* *£/unit*
Selling price	70	92	113	83
Less:				
Material (£4/kg)	16	22	34	20
Variable conversion costs	23	36	42	25
Contribution	31	34	37	38

So,
Contribution per kg of scarce material and the resulting ranking is as follows:

Product name	*M1*	*M2*	*M3*	*M4*
Contribution	31	34	37	38
Material required	4 kg	5.5 kg	8.5 kg	5 kg
Contribution per kg of materials (cost of material ÷ £4/kg)	£31/4	£34/5.5	£37/8.5	£38/5
	£7.75/kg	£6.18/kg	£4.35/kg	£7.60/kg
Ranking	1st	3rd	4th	2nd

So, most profitable product is M1.

5.5 **A**

To check whether A or B is correct we need to determine whether materials or labour or possibly both of those resources are scarce, that is, in insufficient supply.

Maximum amount of material required:

	M	*T*	*D*	*Total*
Maximum demand (units)	4,000	3,000	2,000	
Materials required per unit	3 kg	3 kg	5 kg	
Material required	12,000	9,000	10,000	
Total material required				31,000 kg
Labour hours required per unit	1 hour	1.5 hours	2 hours	
Labour hours required	4,000 hours	4,500 hours	4,000 hours	
Total labour hours required				12,500 hours

Insufficient material is available although labour is in sufficient supply.

So we must ration materials by calculating contribution per kg of material.

Answer C cannot be correct. Decision should always be made using contribution NOT profit.

Answer D cannot be correct. Linear programming is used when there are several scarce resources (in our example, only the materials are scarce). Also linear programming can only be used for a TWO product firm. Our company manufactures THREE products.

Answer E cannot be correct. It appears to be correct but must be read carefully.

We could use simplex technique to solve this problem, however, it is not the ONLY method of arriving at a solution!

5.6 **C**

By definition a by-product results from a process intended to produce "proper" saleable products, that is, joint products. The by-product cannot be produced on its own but will be of little sales value to the business.

5.7 **B**

Although production in this period is more than sales so that there is closing stock at the period end, all production will eventually be sold and therefore the market value is the units produced multiplied by the selling price. These market values are then used to apportion the joint cost of £200,000.

	Production (units)		*Selling price* (£)	*Market value* (£)	*Joint cost* (£)
R	30,000	×	5	150,000 (150/470)	63,830
S	20,000	×	4	80,000 (80/470)	34,043
T	40,000	×	6	240,000 (240/470)	102,127
				470,000	200,000

A is the apportioned cost using the value of sales units
C is the apportioned cost using sales units
D is the apportioned cost using production units
E is the sales value of the units of product S.

5.8 **D**

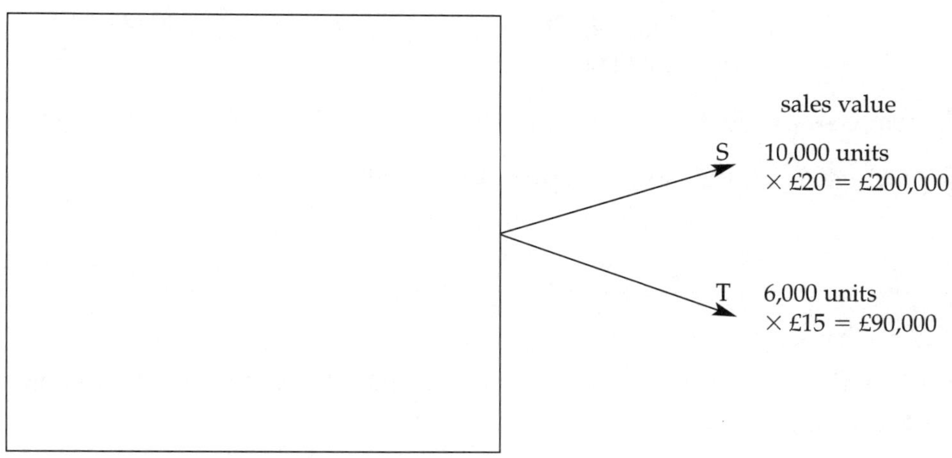

Apportionment of joint cost:

S £220,000 × 200,000/290,000 = £151,724
T £220,000 × 90,000/290,000 = £68,276
£220,000

5.9 **B**

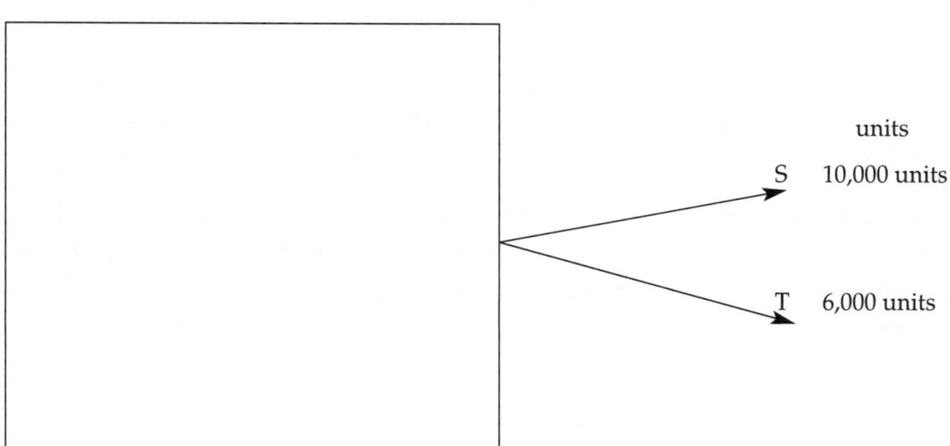

Apportionment of joint cost:

S £220,000 × 10,000/16,000 = £137,500
T £220,000 × 6,000/16,000 = £82,500
£220,000

5.10 **D**

It is only worth undertaking further processing if the additional revenue generated exceeds the additional processing cost incurred. This type of further processing decision does not depend on how the joint or common cost is apportioned over the products.

Product	*Additional revenue if processed further*	*Additional cost if processed further*
T	(£10 – £8) × 10,000 units = £20,000	£25,000

To further process product T would lose £5,000. (Do not process further)

H	(£16 – £10) × 6,000 units = £36,000	£35,000

To further process product H would increase profit by £1,000. (Process further)

E	(£12 – £6) × 4,000 units = £24,000	£20,000

To further process product E would increase profit by £4,000. (Process further)

So, only products H and E should be processed further.

5.11

Topic being tested

Part (a) – Which products to make in order to maximise profits when subject to a single scarce resource.

Part (b) – Minimum price to quote to a new customer where it is only possible to supply the new customer's demands if we use labour time currently intended to be used on another more profitable product.

Remember that although the company wishes to maximise profit, we always use *contribution* for decision-making purposes. Given that fixed costs are fixed, the contribution maximising production mix will also be the profit maximising production mix.

Approach

Part (a) – Rank the products from best to worst by calculating contribution per labour hour to determine how best to use the scarce labour available.

Part (b) – The minimum price to quote to the new customer must include the contribution forgone from any product that was originally planned to be made and sold using the labour time required to meet the new customer's product demands.

Solution

(a) In order to maximise profit we will maximise contribution by calculating contribution per labour hour for each product if labour turns out to be in scarce supply.

Is labour available of 1,845 hours sufficient to meet maximum demand for the company's products or is it a scarce resource?

Product	*Maximum demand (units)*	*Labour hours required per unit*	*Labour hours required*
F	300	2	600
G	150	3	450
H	270	2.5	675
J	120	3	360
Total labour hours required to meet maximum demand			2,085

Since only 1,845 hours of labour time is available, labour is scarce and must be rationed among the products.

Contribution per labour hour:

Product	*Contribution per unit (£)*	*Labour hours per unit (hours)*	*Contribution per labour hour (£)*	*Ranking*
F	13.30	2	6.65	2nd
G	14.10	3	4.70	4th
H	19.00	2.5	7.60	1st
J	16.50	3	5.50	3rd

Note to student!!

Remember that contribution is selling price less *variable* costs not *fixed* costs.

Production plan

Product	*Number of units*	*Labour hours used*	*Contribution (£)*
H	270	675	5,130 (270 units × £19)
F	300	600	3,990 (300 units × £13.30)
J	120	360	1,980 (120 units × £16.50)
		1,635	
G	70	210	987 (70 units × £14.10) (balancing amount)
		1,845	12,087

Maximum contribution that can be earned	£12,087
Less: Fixed costs	(£4,410)
Maximum profit that can be earned	£7,677

(b) A new customer has asked Aber Machinery Ltd to supply 100 units of product G.

At present the company would only wish to make 70 units of product G as per the solution to Part (a). Therefore, to produce 100 units of G it would require an additional 30 units of G to be made. These additional 30 units of G would require 90 hours of labour time which would have to be diverted away from another product.

It makes sense to divert these 90 hours away from production of whichever product would generate the least return. This would mean diverting 90 hours of labour time away from producing product J as per the solution to Part (a).

90 hours of time diverted from production of J would necessitate producing 30 units less of product J (90 hours/3 hours per unit of J).

This would result in lost contribution of:

	£
30 units of J × £16.50 per unit =	495
70 units of G × £14.10 per unit =	987
	1,482

So the minimum price to quote to the new customer for 100 units of product G is:

	£
Cost of making 100 units of G (100 units × £10.90)	1,090
Add: lost contribution (above)	1,482
Minimum price to quote	2,572

Investment Appraisal

6

A key topic that you will see throughout your accountancy studies is *investment appraisal.*

When businesses are considering investing in land and buildings, plant and machinery, marketing campaigns, staff training, computerisation and so on, they must be able to determine whether the proposed investment is likely to be worthwhile – this is where investment appraisal techniques come in.

Investment appraisal techniques fall into those which are *cash flow based* (i.e. based on the relevant cost principles covered elsewhere) and those which are *profit based.*

Cash flow based
Net present value
Internal rate of return
Payback period
Discounted payback period
Profitability index

Profit based
Accounting rate of return
Net profit targets

Note that the *Profitability* Index is based on *cash flows* not profit. It is equal to

$$\frac{\text{Present value of net cash inflows}}{\text{Initial cash outlay}}$$

The accounting rate of return (ARR) is also known as return on capital employed (ROCE).

Net present value (NPV) is the most important of these techniques.

Make sure you can deal with the following.

Corporation tax. Deduct the tax payable from the operational flows and add back the tax saving from the capital allowances. Watch the timing.
Inflation. Inflate up the cash flows to the nominal amounts (money flows) and discount at the nominal (money) cost of capital. Alternatively, use real flows and real rates.
Working capital. Include the change in working capital as a cash flow.

? Questions

6.1 R Ltd is deciding whether to launch a new product. The initial outlay for the new product is £20,000. The forecast possible annual cash inflows and their associated probabilities are shown below.

	Probability	*Year 1 (£)*	*Year 2 (£)*	*Year 3 (£)*
Optimistic	0.20	10,000	12,000	9,000
Most likely	0.50	7,000	8,000	7,600
Pessimistic	0.30	6,400	7,200	6,200

The company's cost of capital is 10% per annum.

Assume the cash inflows are received at the end of the year and that the cash inflows each year are independent.

The expected NPV for the product is

A £(582)
B £(1,170)
C £(10,660)
D £10,430
E £22,286

(3 marks)

6.2 A company is appraising an investment project which has the following expected cash flows:

Time	*Cash flow per annum* £
0	(35,200)
1–4	5,280
5–8	12,320
10	(17,600)

The company's cost of capital is 8%.

What is the NPV for the project?

A £(4,252)
B £4,137
C £12,287
D £12,401

(2 marks)

6.3 The following graph represents the relationship between the net present value and the cost of capital for an investment project.

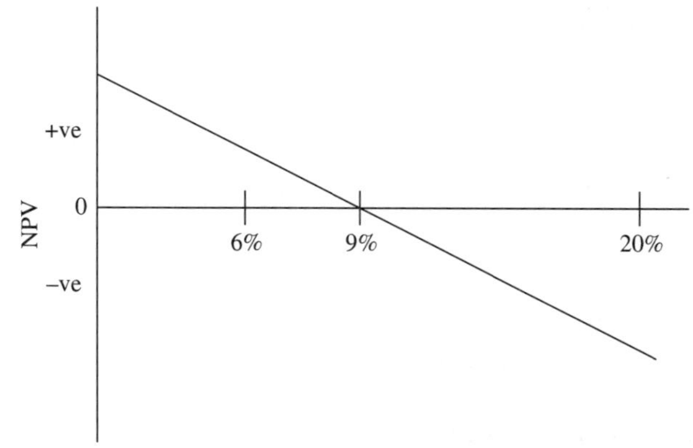

Which of the following statements are correct?

(i) The project cash flows are an outflow followed by a series of inflows where the total inflows exceed the outflow.
(ii) The internal rate of return (IRR) of the project is 6%.
(iii) The project cash flows are an inflow followed by a series of outflows where the total outflows exceed the inflow.
(iv) If the company's cost of capital is 20%, the project should be rejected.

A (i), (ii), (iii) and (iv)
B (i) and (ii) only
C (ii) and (iii) and (iv) only
D (i) and (iii) only
E (i) and (iv)

(3 marks)

6.4 A company is considering investing in a project with a five-year life. It has calculated the present value of the expected future receipts as £37,500. The first receipt is expected in one year's time.

The future receipt is expected to be the same amount each year, that is, an annuity. The cost of capital is 5% per annum.

What is the amount of the annuity that has been used in the present value calculation?

A £5,357
B £6,218
C £7,037
D £7,500
E £8,663

(2 marks)

6.5 A project is being appraised which has the following expected cash flows:

Time	*Cash flow* (£)
0	(30,000)
1	10,000
2	10,000
3	8,750
4	8,750

The NPV at 9% cost of capital has been calculated as £550 and at 10% cost of capital, the NPV is −£100.

What is the IRR of the project?

A 9.25%
B 9.75%
C 9.85%
D 10.35%
E 11.65%

(3 marks)

6.6 Which of the following statements best describes the IRR of an investment project?

A The only financial decision-making tool.
B The discount rate to be used for appraisal purposes.
C The discount rate at which all proposed projects will have the same NPV.
D The discount rate at which the project NPV is zero.
E The discount rate at which all proposed projects will have a NPV of zero.

(2 marks)

6.7 A company has the opportunity to buy a car park for £5 million. The net cash earnings would be £800,000 per annum. The payback period is

A 4 years
B 5 years
C 6.25 years
D 7.5 years

(2 marks)

6.8 Which of the following is not an advantage of the payback method of investment appraisal?

A It is easy to calculate and understand.
B It favours projects with a quick return.
C It ignores the time value of money.
D It deals with liquidity.

(2 marks)

6.9 The NPV technique is a superior investment measure when compared to the IRR because

A The NPV is a relative measure.
B The NPV has more than one outcome.
C The NPV is consistent with a company's objective of maximising shareholders' wealth.
D It estimates the company's cost of capital.

(2 marks)

6.10 Mags plc publis\hes over 60 magazines with titles covering sport, men's interests, women's interests, business, films, and so on.

One of its proposed new titles is Movies4U which will be a monthly magazine with articles relating to new cinema releases of films and reviews of films being released on DVD and video once their cinema run has come to an end.

If Movies4U goes ahead, Mags plc will have to invest £10 million in printing equipment and computers. Annual fixed running costs (journalists salaries, photography costs, promotional costs, distribution costs, etc.) are expected to be £1 million per annum in current prices. Variable cost per copy (cost of paper, printing ink, etc.) is expected to be £0.60 in current prices.

Many magazines are launched but fail to sell sufficient copies to justify their annual running costs. For this reason, Mags plc's management wish to be prudent and assume only a four year shelf life for the new magazine for decision-making purposes. Revenue is generated not only from sales of magazines to newsagents, supermarket chains, wholesalers and so on; but also from sale of advertising space in magazines to companies wishing to place adverts for their products and services.

Movies4U is expected to be produced in a 90 page format 12 times each year. 18 pages out of the 90 pages in each edition will be sold to advertisers for full-page adverts. Advertising is expected to generate income of £20,000 per page in current prices.

Mags plc expects to be able to sell Movies4U to newsagents, supermarkets, and so on for £2 per copy in current prices (although the "cover price" that newsagents, supermarkets and so on will sell Movies4U to readers at is expected to be £3.60 per copy in current prices).

Running costs are expected to inflate at 6% per annum although magazine selling prices, variable cost per copy and advertising rates are expected to inflate at 2% per annum. The general rate of inflation is expected to be 4% per annum. Fixed operating costs are expected to increase by an extra 5.5% in year 3 (this is in addition to the normal, running cost, inflation).

The company's real cost of capital is 7.7% per annum.

The scrap proceeds for the printing equipment and computers is likely to be negligible in four-years time.

Corporation tax at 30% is payable in the same year as the cash flows to which it relates. Capital allowances are expected to be available on 50% of expenditure on printing equipment and computers on a 25% per annum reducing balance basis.

Requirement

Calculate the number of copies of Movies4U that must be sold each year for the magazine to breakeven, taking account of the time value of money. (Assume that the same number of copies of the magazine will be sold each year.)

(10 marks)

6.11 Barney Ltd is considering investing in a new manufacturing plant which will be used to make bathroom fittings to be sold to "do-it-yourself" retailers.

Planning permission has already been sought and won from the local authority. This process has already cost £400,000. The financial effects of the new investment are set out below.

	0	*1*	*2*	*3*	*4*
	£'000	£'000	£'000	£'000	£'000
Investment:					
Machinery	(800)				
Land	(1,500)				
Buildings	(2,000)				
Sales		2,400	2,800	2,600	2,550
Materials		300	350	420	460
Labour		250	330	360	420
Overheads		400	450	480	500
Interest		500	500	500	500
Depreciation		450	450	450	450
Profit pre-tax		500	720	390	220
Tax at 35%		175	252	137	77
Profit post-tax		325	468	253	143

The following information has not been reflected in the above calculations:

Capital allowances are available on the machinery and buildings as follows – buildings 50% straight line allowance, no capital allowances are available in relation to land or machinery.
Tax is payable one year after the company's year end.
40% of the overheads cost is an apportionment of the head office cost.
Sales, labour and overheads are expected to inflate at 5% per annum.
Materials are expected to inflate at 10% per annum.
The company's nominal cost of capital is 12% per annum.

At the end of four years the disposal value of the assets is expected to be £2,850,000 made up as: land £2,000,000; buildings £800,000; machinery £50,000. (Capital gains on land are tax-free.)
Working capital requirements are believed to be negligible.
The investment is expected to occur at the start of an accounting year.

Requirements

(a) Calculate the NPV for the new investment and recommend whether Barney Ltd should go ahead with the new investment.

(8 marks)

(b) Briefly discuss why sensitivity analysis should be undertaken as part of any investment appraisal decision.

(2 marks)
(Total = 10 marks)

6.12 (a) Explain how inflation affects the NPV of an investment project and distinguish between the real and nominal cost of capital.

(4 marks)

(b) Discuss how taxation can impact upon the NPV of an investment project.
(4 marks)

(c) Discuss the key advantages and disadvantages of the payback period method of investment appraisal.

(2 marks)
(Total = 10 Marks)

6.13 Multinational "P" (IDEC 11/02 (Amended))

P, a multinational organisation, is currently appraising a major capital investment project which will revolutionise its business. This investment involves the installation of an Intranet. [*An Intranet is a private Internet reserved for use by employees and/or customers who have been given the authority and passwords necessary to use that network. It is a private network environment built around Internet technologies and standards.*]

You have recently been appointed as the Management Accountant for this project and have been charged with the responsibility of preparing the financial evaluation of the proposed investment. You have carried out some initial investigations and find that management currently uses a target accounting rate of return of 25% and a target payback period of four years as the criteria for the acceptance or rejection of major capital investments.

You propose to use the NPV method of project appraisal and, having carried out some further investigations, you ascertain the following information for the project.

	£'000
Initial outlay	2,000
Cash savings:	
Years 1 to 3	400 per annum
Years 4 to 5	500 per annum
Years 6 to 8	450 per annum
Years 9 to 10	400 per annum

At the end of the project's life, no residual value is expected for the project.

The company's cost of capital is 15% per annum. All cash savings are assumed to occur at the end of each year.

Ignore taxation and inflation.

Requirements

(a) As Management Accountant for this project, write a report to the management of P which incorporates the following:

(i) a full analysis and evaluation of the existing methods of project appraisal and of your proposed method of project appraisal
(ii) a recommendation on a purely financial basis as to whether or not the project should be undertaken
(iii) a discussion of the difficulties associated with the net present value method when appraising this type of investment.

(15 marks)

(b) Describe how you would undertake a post-completion appraisal (PCA) for this project and discuss the benefits and drawbacks which the management of P might expect when undertaking such an exercise.

(10 marks)
(Total = 25 marks)

6.14 JLX plc (IDEC 5/01 (Amended))

JLX plc is a well-established manufacturing organisation that has recently expanded rapidly, by a series of acquisitions, in a period of favourable trading conditions. The need to integrate the management information and control systems of the rapidly expanding group has imposed a very large workload on the managerial and accounting teams. Consequently, some of the normal procedures at JLX plc have been neglected.

JLX plc uses return on investment (ROI) as the chief performance measure for controlling the operating activities of its divisions, and managers' bonuses are based on the achievement of ROI targets. The company also uses NPV to assess and select investment projects. It used to be standard practice to assess and review all projects after implementation by a PCA. However, PCA has been one area that has been neglected because of the increased workloads, and recently PCA has been applied only to those projects which have been considered unsuccessful.

PRO35 is a major project recently implemented by division X. This project was controversial because of its large capital requirement and high risk level. The Group Finance Director has stated that his department is now considerably understaffed and that he requires more resources to operate effectively. In particular, he is using the need to carry out a PCA on PRO35 as a lever to gain more funds. He has told the Group Chief Executive that he thinks that PRO35 should be subjected to a PCA as he considers that it should be generating a greater return given the continuing favourable trading conditions.

The Group Chief Executive has responded to this by saying that he feels that a PCA for PRO35 is unnecessary as it is generating the predicted net cash flow. To back this up, he cites the fact that division X's performance as measured by ROI is in line with its target. The Group Chief Executive has also said on several occasions that he is worried about behavioural issues if divisions are criticised and monitored unnecessarily.

Requirements

Note: Your answer must relate to the scenario above.

(a) Evaluate whether it is advisable for an organisation such as JLX plc to carry out PCAs.

(7 marks)

(b) Discuss whether a PCA should be carried out on PRO35, a project that appears to be performing satisfactorily.

(5 marks)

(c) Critically evaluate the use of ROI as the performance measure within the JLX plc group.

(13 marks)
(Total = 25 marks)

Answers

6.1 **A**

In order to be able to calculate the NPV, we must first calculate the expected cash flow at the end of each of the three years.

Expected value of cash flows:

Year 1:
$0.20 \times 10{,}000 + 0.50 \times 7{,}000 + 0.30 \times 6{,}400 = 7{,}420$

Year 2:
$0.20 \times 12{,}000 + 0.50 \times 8{,}000 + 0.30 \times 7{,}200 = 8{,}560$

Year 3:
$0.20 \times 9{,}000 + 0.50 \times 7{,}600 + 0.30 \times 6{,}200 = 7{,}460$

We can now use these to calculate the NPV using the cost of capital of 10%.

Time	*Cash*	*DF at 10%*		*PV*
0	(20,000)	1		(20,000)
1	7,420	0.909		6,745
2	8,560	0.826		7,071
3	7,460	0.751		5,602
			NPV	(582)

6.2 **B**

Time	*Cash*	*DF at 8%*		*PV*
0	(35,200)	1		(35,200)
1–4	5,280	3.312		17,487
5–8	12,320	2.435		29,999
10	(17,600)	0.463		(8,149)
			NPV	4,137

Calculation of discount factors:

Factor for Time 1–4 at 8% can be taken from discount factor tables and is 3.312.

For the factor for Time 5–8 at 8%, we must get the factor for eight years from factor tables and deduct from it the factor for four years:

Factor for Time 1–8	5.747
Less: Factor for Time 1–4	3.312
Factor for Time 5–8	2.435

Factor for Time 10 can be taken from discount factor tables and is 0.463.

From the above table, answer is B.

6.3 **E**

(i) Is correct.
The diagram is downward sloping for a "standard" project, that is, a project where the cash flows are an outflow followed by a series of inflows and the total inflows exceed the outflow.

(ii) Is incorrect.
The IRR is where the NPV of the project is zero. From the graph we can see that the IRR is 9% NOT 6%.

(iii) Is incorrect.
For a project where the cash flows are an inflow followed by a series of outflows and the total outflows exceed the inflow, the diagram would be upward sloping as follows:

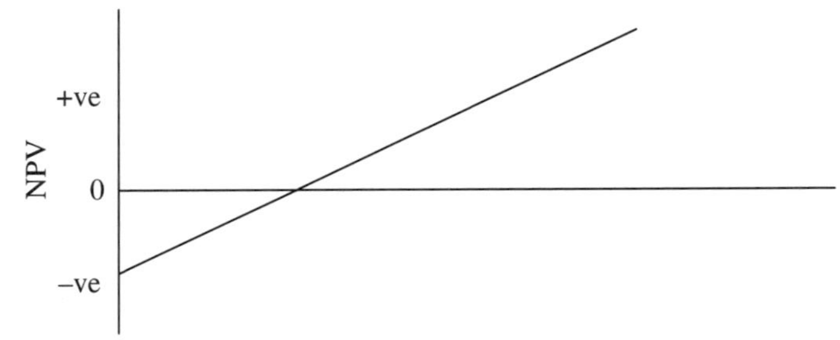

(iv) Is correct.
From the graph we can see that the NPV is negative at a cost of capital of 20%. Therefore, the project should be rejected.

6.4 **E**

We know the present value of the annuity is £37,500. We also know the timing of the receipts (Time 1–5) and the cost of capital of 5%. From discount factor tables, the factor at 5% for five years is 4.329.

So, if we let the amount of the annuity be £A:

Time	*Cash*	*DF at 5%*		*PV*
1–5	*A*	4.329		4.329 × *A*
			NPV	37,500

So,
$4.329 \times A = £37{,}500$

$A = £37{,}500/4.329$

$A = £8{,}663$

6.5 **C**

We have the NPVs at two different costs of capital and can therefore use the IRR equation as follows:

$$\text{IRR} = a + \frac{N_a \times (b - a)}{N_a - N_b}$$

where,
a = lower %
b = higher %
N_a = NPV at a%
N_b = NPV at b%

$$\text{IRR} = a + \frac{N_a \times (b - a)}{N_a - N_b}$$

$$= 9 + \frac{550 \times (10 - 9)}{550 - (-100)}$$

$$= 9 + \frac{550 \times 1}{550 + 100}$$

$$= 9 + \frac{550}{650}$$

$$= 9 + 0.85$$

$$= 9.85\%$$

6.6 **D**

Answer A is incorrect.

There are many investment appraisal tools other than the IRR. These include: NPV, Payback Period, Discounted Payback Period, Accounting Rate of Return.

Answer B is incorrect.

The rate to be used for investment appraisal purposes is the cost of capital not the IRR.

Answer C is incorrect.

Answer D is correct.

This is the definition of the IRR.

Answer E is incorrect. Different projects will have different IRRs due to the differing cash flows involved and the differing project lives.

6.7 **C**

To calculate the payback period we need to know how long it will take for future project cash receipts to pay off the initial cash investment.

The timing of the cash flows is as follows:

Time	*Cash flow*
0	(5,000,000)
1	800,000
2	800,000
3	800,000
4	800,000
5	800,000
6	800,000
7	800,000

and so on.

To calculate the payback period another column, the *cumulative cash flow* column is useful. This shows the cash position to date, so after three years, for example, £5,000,000 has been invested and three lots of £800,000 have been received giving a net outflow of £2,600,000 (£5m − 3 × £0.8m).

Time	*Cash flow*	*Cumulative cash flow*
0	(5,000,000)	(5,000,000)
1	800,000	(4,200,000)
2	800,000	(3,400,000)
3	800,000	(2,600,000)
4	800,000	(1,800,000)
5	800,000	(1,000,000)
6	800,000	(200,000)
7	800,000	600,000

The project pays for itself between the end of Year 6 and the end of Year 7. It is customary to assume that cash flows are received evenly throughout the year.

In the 7th year it was only necessary to receive £200,000 in order to find the payback period.

This is £200,000/£800,000, that is, 0.25 of the way through the year.

So, the payback period is 6.25 years.

6.8 C

The payback method of investment appraisal is easy to understand and calculate (and explain to board of directors). The technique involves management setting a time limit, say five years, by which an investment must pay for itself if it is to be undertaken. It therefore favours projects with a quick return.

The payback period considers how long it will take for future cash receipts to pay off the initial project investment. In so doing it ignores the timing of those cash flows and hence ignores the time value of money. Although this is a characteristic of the payback method, it is one of its key disadvantages and one of the reasons why the NPV technique is superior. Since the payback method deals with cash flows, it deals with liquidity.

6.9 C

A is incorrect.
The NPV is an absolute measure (in £) rather than a relative measure (in %).
B is incorrect.
Any project has only one NPV at the company's cost of capital. (It is possible for a project to have several IRR under certain circumstances but not several NPV.)
C is correct.
The NPV is consistent with a company's objective of maximising shareholders' wealth.
D is incorrect.
The cost of capital is the rate that is used to calculate the NPV. (The IRR is the cost of capital at which the project would have a NPV of zero.)

6.10

> *Topic being tested*
>
> Net present value calculations including tax and inflation in order to find the breakeven volume of sales required to give a NPV of zero.
>
> *Approach*
>
> Set up a NPV proforma.
> Extract relevant cash flows from the question including those relating to taxation and put them onto the proforma.
> Ensure that you treat inflation correctly – since there are *several* inflation rates in this question it is necessary to *inflate up* the cash flows and discount them using the company's *nominal* cost of capital.

Solution

In order to calculate the number of magazines to be sold by Mags plc so as to breakeven, we must set up a NPV calculation using the company's four-year planning horizon.

The breakeven number of copies of the magazine will be that number at which the NPV will be zero.

Since the rate of inflation differs for different cash flows, it is necessary to discount the future cash flows using the company's nominal cost of capital.

This is arrived at using:

$$(1 + r) \times (1 + i) = 1 + n$$

r = real cost of capital
i = general rate of inflation
n = nominal cost of capital

$(1.077) \times (1.04) = 1.12$

So the nominal cost of capital is 12% per annum.

Revenue

From advertising = 12 issues × 18 pages × £20,000 = £4.32m (in current prices)

From sales of magazines = £2 per copy (in current prices)

Costs

Fixed running costs = £1m (in current prices)

Variable cost = £0.60 per copy (in current prices)

So, contribution per copy is £1.40 (in current prices)

After tax at 30%, contribution per copy is £0.98 (in current prices)
[£1.40 × 70% = £0.98]

Net present value calculation for fixed running costs, initial investment in printing equipment and computers, advertising revenue and tax saved due to capital allowances are:

Time	*0* £m	*1* £m	*2* £m	*3* £m	*4* £m
Investment	(10)				
Advertising revenue (inflated at 2% per annum)		4.41	4.49	4.58	4.68
Fixed running costs (inflated at 6% per annum)		(1.06)	(1.12)	(1.26)	(1.33)
		3.35	3.37	3.32	3.35
Tax at 30%		(1.01)	(1.01)	(1.00)	(1.01)
Capital allowances tax saved (W1)	—	0.38	0.28	0.21	0.63
Cash flows	(10)	2.72	2.64	2.53	2.97
DF at 12%	1.000	0.893	0.797	0.712	0.636
Present value	(10)	2.43	2.10	1.80	1.89

Net present value = (£1.78m)

Workings

W1: Tax saved due to capital allowances

Time		*Pool* £m	*Capital allowances*	*Tax saved at 30%*	*When saved*
0	Investment	5			
1	25% WDA	(1.25)	1.25	0.38	1
		3.75			
2	25% WDA	(0.94)	0.94	0.28	2
		2.81			
3	25% WDA	(0.70)	0.70	0.21	3
		2.11			
4	Balancing allowance	(2.11)	2.11	0.63	4

Net present value of contribution from sale of magazines (per copy)

Time		*1*	*2*	*3*	*4*
Contribution per copy (£) (inflated at 2% per annum)		1.428	1.456	1.486	1.515
DF at 12%		0.893	0.797	0.712	0.636
Present value (£)		1.275	1.160	1.058	0.964
Total	£4.457				

Present value of contribution from sale of magazines (per copy) over the four-year planning horizon = £4.457

Let number of magazines to be sold each year be *M*.

So sufficient magazines must be sold to generate £1.78 million as seen earlier.

So,

$$4.457 \times M = 1{,}780{,}000$$

$$M = \frac{1{,}780{,}000}{4.457}$$

$$M = 399{,}371 \text{ copies per annum.}$$

Conclusion

So Mags plc must sell just over 399,000 copies of the new magazine, Movies4U, each year in order to breakeven.

6.11

> *Topic being tested*
>
> Part (a) – Calculation of project NPV including taxation, several rates of inflation and use of the nominal cost of capital.
> Part (b) – Discussion of sensitivity analysis.
>
> *Approach*
>
> Set up a NPV proforma for the life of the project and enter on it the simple cash flows first – initial investment and disposal value.
> Ensure that you treat inflation correctly – since there are *several* inflation rates in this question it is necessary to *inflate up* the cash flows and discount them using the company's *nominal* cost of capital.
> Deal with the tax cash flows – 35% tax payable on the net cash flows and 35% tax saved on the capital allowances available on the buildings.

Solution

(a)

	0	*1*	2	3	4	5
Investment:	£'000	£'000	£'000	£'000	£'000	£'000
Machinery	(800)					
Land	(1,500)					
Buildings	(2,000)					
Disposal					2,850	
Sales		2,520	3,087	3,010	3,100	
Materials cost		(330)	(424)	(559)	(673)	
Labour cost		(262)	(364)	(417)	(511)	
Overheads		(252)	(298)	(333)	(365)	
Taxable		1,676	2,001	1,701	1,551	
Tax at 35%			(587)	(700)	(595)	(543)
Corporate allowances: tax saved (W1)			350	350		(280)
Cash flows	(4,300)	1,676	1,764	1,351	3,806	(823)
DF at 12%	1.000	0.893	0.797	0.712	0.636	0.567
Present value	(4,300)	1,497	1,406	962	2,421	(467)

Net present value is £1,519,000.

Since the NPV is positive, the proposed investment in the new manufacturing plant should be accepted.

Notes

The cost of gaining planning permission of £400,000 is non-relevant since it is a sunk cost.

Sales, labour costs and overhead costs have been inflated at 5% per annum.

Only 60% of overheads are relevant.

Materials costs have been inflated at 10% per annum.

Interest cost has been has been omitted since it is included in the cost of capital.

Depreciation has been omitted since it is not cash and so non-relevant.

The nominal cost of capital has been used to discount the cash flows since cash flows have been inflated up.

Workings

W1: Tax saved due to capital allowances

Time	*£'000*	*Pool*	*Corporate allowances*	*Tax saved at 35%*	*When saved*
0	Investment	2,000			
1	50% allowance	(1,000)	1,000	350	2
		1,000			
2	50% allowance	(1,000)	1,000	350	3
		–			
3	No allowance	–			
4	Disposal proceeds	(800)			
4	Balancing charge	800	(800)	(280)	5

(b) Sensitivity analysis involves estimating by how much cash flows can change before a worthwhile project should be rejected (or a non-worthwhile project should be accepted).

For example, in part (a) the NPV is positive and so the project should be accepted. However, if the actual sales revenues were to fall below the figures in the original forecasts, then the project might prove non-viable.

Sensitivity analysis should be undertaken since estimates of revenues, costs, tax rates, inflation rates and disposal values could easily change and affect the decision that should be taken with regard to the project. It is important that management are aware of the amount by which cash flows can change in £ or percentage terms.

One crucial problem when using sensitivity analysis is that only one variable can be changed at a time. In practice, several cash flows might change at the same time, for example, in response to economic conditions such as recession.

6.12

Topic being tested

Discussion questions relating to net present value calculations involving

Part (a) – Inflation
Part (b) – Taxation
Part (c) – A discussion question relating to the payback period.

Approach

This is a good opportunity to use your learned knowledge, however, it is still important to plan before you begin to write your answer.

For example, in Part (b) relating to taxation, taxation obviously affects the NPV negatively since tax is paid on the net cash flows so reducing the post-tax cash to be discounted.

But what about the tax effects of capital allowances?

Also the cost of capital will be reduced due to tax relief on any interest cost included in the cost of capital.

My plan would look like this:

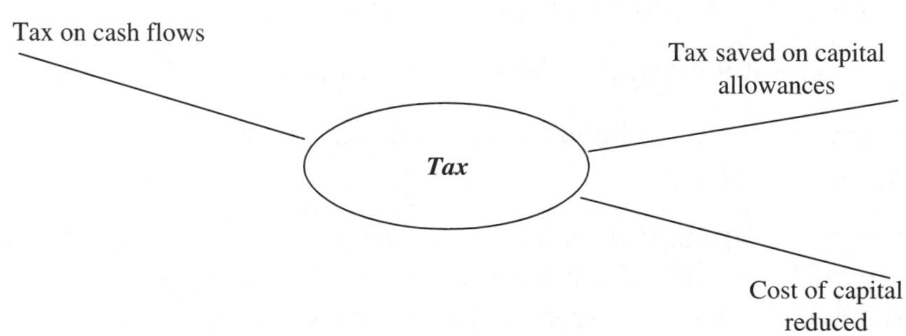

Solution

(a) *How inflation affects the NPV calculation.*

Inflation affects the cash flows to be used in the NPV calculation. Ideally, the cash flows which are subject to inflation should be *inflated up* at their specific rate of inflation and the net cash flows which result should be discounted at the company's *nominal* cost of capital.

However, if *all* of the cash flows inflate at the *same rate*, then the cash flows can be left *uninflated* (i.e. left in current value terms) and be discounted at the company's *real* cost of capital.

If, for example, selling prices are expected to inflate at a lower rate than the inflation rate for costs, perhaps due to the extent of competition in the market place, then margins will decline over time making the NPV lower than it would have been had there been no inflation.

The relationship between the nominal cost of capital (n), the general rate of inflation (i) and the real cost of capital (r) is given by the following equation:

$$\frac{1 + n}{1 + i} = 1 + r$$

For example, if the nominal cost of capital is 12% and the general rate of inflation is expected to be 4%, then the real cost of capital is:

$$\frac{1.12}{1.04} = 1.077$$

The real cost of capital is 7.7%.

The nominal cost of capital includes the inflation rate whereas the real cost of capital does not.

(b) *How taxation affects the NPV*

If tax exists, net cash flows will be subject to tax and this will decrease the cash available for discounting. This will reduce the NPV.

However, investment in fixed assets typically results in the availability of capital allowances. For example, 25% writing down allowances on expenditure on machinery.

The tax saved due to capital allowances will be:

amount of capital allowance × tax rate

Tax saved due to capital allowances therefore has a positive affect upon the NPV since tax is saved.

The cost of capital used to discount project cash flows typically includes the cost of any debt finance (the interest charge). Given that interest attracts tax relief, the cost of capital would be reduced by the existence of tax.

The overall impact of these tax effects could only be assessed by producing the NPV with and without tax.

(c) *Payback period*

The payback period is the time that the future project cash inflows are expected to take to pay off the initial investment.

Key advantages and disadvantages of the payback period method of investment appraisal are as follows:

Advantages	*Disadvantages*
Simple to calculate	Ignores the time value of money, unless cash flows are discounted to give the Discounted Payback Period
Simple for decision-makers to understand	
Concentrates on earlier cash flows which are easier to forecast	Once the payback period has been ascertained, any cash flows in later years are ignored
Is a measure of liquidity since it is based on cash flows	The payback period is set against a management target which may be set in an arbitrary way

6.13

(a)

REPORT

To: The Management

From: Management Accountant

Date: 20 November 2002

Re: Investment Appraisal

Payback method

The payback method, which is currently used, is one of the simplest methods to understand and apply to capital investment appraisal. It represents the length of time that is required for cash proceeds from an investment to recover the original cash outlay required by the investment.

The payback period for this investment is:

	Cumulative cash flows		
Initial outlay	*Years 1–3*	*Years 4–5*	
£'000	£'000	£'000	*Payback*
2,000	1,200	2,200	4 years 7 months

The company's target payback is four years and on this basis, as this project exceeds that target, it would be rejected.

It can be seen, therefore, that this method maintains the organisation's liquidity in that it favours projects with early cash inflow. While managers find this method easy to understand and apply it is flawed, as it does not take into account cash flows that are earned after the payback date which in the case of this project are quite significant. It also fails to take into account the differences in the timing of the proceeds that are earned before the payback date. Unlike discounted cash flow, the payback method ignores the importance of the time value of money, that is future cash receipts are not comparable to cash today. However, in order to overcome the problem associated with the time value of money, discounted payback could be used as an initial screening to assess the length of time the project will take to recoup the initial cash outlay. However, it should not be used as the only method as, unlike NPV, it is not an absolute measure as to whether or not the investment will maximise shareholders' wealth.

Accounting rate of return method

The ARR method expresses the annual average profit from a project as a percentage of the average annual investment in the project, in order to measure whether or not a project is worthwhile.

The ARR for this investment is:

	£'000
Total cash savings	4,350
Less: Depreciation	2,000
Accounting profit	2,350
Project life – years	10
Average annual accounting profit	235

ARR $\dfrac{235}{1{,}000} \times 100$

$= 23.5\%$

The company's target ARR is 25% and as this project only yields a return of 23.5%, it would be rejected.

As can be seen, this method uses annual accounting profits, rather than annual net cash flow, and while it allows for difference in the useful lives of the assets being compared, it ignores the time value of money. Also, when this method is used in investment appraisal, even if the benefits from a project come in later years, the averaging out of the profits and investment means that the same ARR will exist providing the cash inflows are the same. This method also measures the impact of the investment on the balance sheet and allows the organisation to select projects that maintain a strong balance sheet, rather than those that maximise shareholders' wealth. This method should not be used for project appraisal purposes as it can produce incorrect results.

Net present value method

I propose the use of the NPV method as it takes into account the time value of money, that is, it acknowledges that cash received in the future has less value than cash received today. With NPV, all future cash flows from the project will be discounted into present day values based on the company's cost of capital. If the discounted cash inflow exceeds the discounted cash outflow, a positive NPV will arise and the project would be accepted. A positive NPV means that the company has not only returned the desired cost of capital, but also an additional amount which will go towards maximising shareholders' wealth. When using the NPV method of investment appraisal, there are certain assumptions made:

1 Cash flows during a period are assumed to occur at the end of the period.
2 The discount rate is assumed to represent the company's cost of capital.
3 The initial cash outlay happens in Year 0, that is, now.

The NPV for this investment would be:

Cost of capital – 15%

Year	*Cash flow* £'000	*DF*	*PV* £'000
0	(2,000)	1.000	(2,000.00)
1–3	400	2.283	913.20
4–5	500	1.069	534.50
6–8	450	1.135	510.75
9–10	400	0.531	212.40
NPV			170.85

As the NPV is greater than zero, this means that the investment has returned the desired cost of capital, as well as an additional £170,850 and should, therefore, be undertaken as it increases shareholders' wealth.

Unlike the ARR and payback methods, the NPV method takes account of the time value of money and considers all relevant cash flows. The NPV model can also account for risk, taxation and inflation issues.

If we were to follow the target payback and ARR for the company as our methods of appraising capital investments we would have concluded that this investment should not be undertaken. This of course would have been the incorrect decision, as it can be clearly seen that the project's NPV is positive.

However, basing a decision only on a positive NPV does not take account of other factors such as the speed of repayments of the original investment, and therefore the discounted payback method should be incorporated in the decision-making process. Other difficulties encountered when applying NPV to this type of investment decision are:

The cost of capital being used may be set too high. This would result in a lower NPV, which may make the justification for the investment difficult. To overcome this difficulty the organisation should consider the rate used for similar projects with the same risk element.

The time horizons on this project may be too short. The outlay for the project is large and the benefits will probably come in the long term rather than the short/medium term. If the time horizon is too short, then the danger is that such future benefits are excluded from the calculation. I would recommend that the time horizon be reviewed and should be lengthened if appropriate.

It is sometimes difficult to quantify all of the benefits from this type of investment and therefore the resulting NPV may not be as high as expected and management may take the view not to undertake the investment. All benefits must be quantified, however crude. If there is significant difficulty in quantifying some of the benefits, then the non-quantifiable benefits should be detailed separately, but still considered in the decision-making process. Therefore, even if the NPV is zero or negative and the non-quantifiable benefits are significant, then the company should proceed with the investment.

As with all projects, there is always an element of uncertainty when predicting cash flows for a project. Such uncertainty needs to be built into the evaluation process and can be achieved through the use of probabilities. This could be incorporated in the next NPV calculation for this project.

As profits are reported annually to shareholders and yet it is cash flows for numerous projects extending over several years that we discount, this creates a problem for internal reporting purposes when reconciling the two.

I would recommend that this project be undertaken and that for the future we combine the discounted payback and NPV methods for capital investment decisions.

Signed: Management Accountant.

(b) **Post-completion appraisal**

A post-completion appraisal is "an objective and independent appraisal of the measure of success of a capital expenditure project in progressing the business as planned. The appraisal should cover the implementation of the project from authorisation to commissioning and its technical and commercial performance after commissioning. The information provided is also used by management as feedback which aids the implementation and control of future projects."

When P uses the NPV approach to appraise this investment, it will be highly dependent on accurate cash flow projections. If these projections are inaccurate, they may result in the acceptance of this project which could be undesirable and should probably not be pursued. In order to assess the accuracy of the projections made, P must follow-up on the results for this project. This procedure is called post-completion appraisal.

In order to undertake a post-completion appraisal, the management accountant of P must collect information about the actual cash flows plus the estimated cash flows for the remainder of the project's life. These cash flows should then be compared to the expected cash flows and should be based on the same method of evaluation as was used in making the original investment decision. If the outcome results in an unfavourable situation, then there must be an investigation as to why this has happened.

Such an investigation should indicate exactly what went wrong; for example, the predicted cash flows for the project might have been overstated. If the post-completion appraisal is undertaken during the project, it will allow for deviations from the plan to be identified and corrective action to be taken in order to place the project back on track. If the post-completion appraisal is carried out at the end of the project, it will then provide a mechanism whereby experience gained from the project can be fed into the organisation's decision-making process to aid decisions on future projects.

A post-completion appraisal can be a very difficult task. It must be remembered that capital investment decisions are made under uncertain conditions and, despite the use of various techniques to incorporate these conditions, what may have seemed like a good decision at the time may well turn out to be the wrong one.

Despite the difficulties encountered when undertaking a post-completion appraisal, it should be carried out, as it allows for past performance to be used to improve future decision-making.

Benefits

Under- or over-achieving projects can be rapidly modified.

Under-achieving projects can be terminated at an early stage.

Improvement in the quality of future decisions as the process provides valuable information on past projects. In other words, it aids organisational learning.

Managers are more realistic with their projections as they are aware that unrealistic projections will be highlighted through carrying out the post-completion appraisal.

Reasons for successful and unsuccessful projects are highlighted and can then be used in the appraisal of future projects.

Drawbacks

It is costly and time consuming to collect the information needed to carry out the post-completion appraisal.

Managers may perceive the post-completion appraisal as a policing exercise and this may discourage initiative and cause excessive caution. This may result in managers submitting only those projects that demonstrate a safe investment proposal.

It can be difficult to estimate the future cash flows expected from a project. This difficulty will be further compounded for P, as the costs and benefits from such a project will be experienced throughout the organisation.

6.14

(a) Whether a manufacturing organisation should have a general policy to carry out PCAs or not is a matter for debate – not all organisations do so.

The main argument in favour is that of organisational learning. Whether the project is successful or unsuccessful, it is likely that lessons will be learnt that can be applied to future projects, thus making them more successful. It is, of course, usually too late to take action to change the current project. Benefit will be gained therefore where lessons can be transferred. Some argue that lessons learnt from failings in one project are unlikely to be capable of being transferred to other projects because of their different nature. As JLX plc is a manufacturing organisation, it may well be able to transfer much of the knowledge gained to future projects, because the projects are likely to have many similar characteristics.

Another benefit of PCA is that it can control over-optimistic forecasts put forward by ambitious managers who may see prestigious projects as a way of advancing their own careers. This may well occur in a divisionalised organisation, such as JLX plc, where divisions may compete with each other. A PCA also stops managers viewing their pet projects in a favourable light, as they have to account for their over-optimistic forecasts.

This may be the moment for JLX plc to reassess the worth of PCAs in cost-benefit terms. It appears that the Group Finance Director did not really consider PCAs important, as he let the principle go because of the pressure of work in his department. Now, however, he appears to be using it as a lever to get more resources and/or staff. Is he genuinely arguing that a PCA is essential or is he using it as a lever to get staff and enhance his own position? The situation seems fraught with personal and behavioural issues.

(b) Assuming that an organisation does have a regime of PCA, all projects should be examined for two main reasons:

(i) An apparently unsuccessful project (i.e. where predicted returns have not materialised) may actually be performing quite successfully. A change in economic circumstances, which could not have been foreseen, may be the cause of its lower performance. Similarly, an apparently successful project, such as PRO35, may be showing good results only because economic circumstances have changed for the better. This is likely to be the case in the scenario, assuming PRO35 benefits from increased turnover because of favourable trading conditions. If a PCA is not carried out and changes in economic circumstances are not taken into account, complacency may creep in and optimum performance will not be obtained.

(ii) Knowledge can be gained and lessons learnt just as much from truly successful projects as from unsuccessful ones because methods of best practice and so on can be established and implemented when future projects are undertaken.

(c)

Tutorial note: The point this part of the question is that managers are using ROI (ROCE) to make decisions rather than NPV. Your answer could be structured around the disadvantages of ROI compared with NPV.

There are a number of problems with using ROI as a divisional performance measure:

Conflict between ROI and NPV
One of JLX plc's problems is likely to be because it uses NPV for assessing projects, and ROI for measuring divisional performance and calculating bonuses. In some circumstances, these two methods can give conflicting results and this will not assist in building good corporate morale. If too much pressure is put on achieving the divisional performance measure, managers may reject perfectly sound projects, yielding positive NPV's, if the projects are likely to decrease the divisional ROI on which the bonuses are based. NPV always provides the correct answer when making an investment decision, whereas ROI does not.

Short term versus long term
ROI will vary from year to year as assets are depreciated. This means that an investment that has a relatively large investment outlay in fixed assets will nearly always decrease the overall ROI in the initial years until the book value of the new investment has decreased. As JLX plc's divisional managers' bonuses rest on this, and if they are unlikely to be in that particular job for more than, say, three or four years, they will be reluctant to initiate large long-term investments which would ultimately be of great benefit to the company.

Percentage return versus size of investment
JLX plc would not wish its divisions to increase the ROI beyond a certain point as divisional growth is also important. The managers may restrict growth in order to be certain of future bonuses. For example, would JLX plc prefer a 15% return on £1m = £150,000 or a 20% return on £0.7m = £140,000? A growth target could be used with ROI, see below.

Using multiple measures
ROI is an encompassing measure and may hide a number of different factors, some of which can be good and others bad. It may be better to use a range of different measures, such as increase in sales revenue, market share, profit to sales ratio and so on. Alternatively, qualitative measures or the balanced scorecard approach could be used.

Massaging ROI
Any reward system that places too much emphasis on the achievement of a single, simple performance measure, such as ROI, is unlikely to be successful in the long term. In this case, JLX plc clearly places considerable emphasis on achieving the target ROI as bonuses depend on it. The managers of the divisions may spend a considerable amount of time "fixing" the performance measure and ensuring that it is satisfactory. This is likely to be to the detriment of the group. This could be the case with division X as its ROI is on target. On the other hand, if trading conditions are favourable, achieving the target ROI may not be so good as it seems and it may not indicate good divisional performance.

In favour of ROI is the fact that managers can easily understand the term and what affects its level, unlike some more complex measures. ROI is still widely used as a performance measure by external shareholders and stakeholders and the directors of JLX plc must consider the group's performance in this respect. Therefore, using the same measure at divisional level can be of assistance.

Advanced Investment Appraisal Techniques

7

Sensitivity analysis considers the degree of change in cash flows or profits that can occur, before a worthwhile investment becomes non-worthwhile.

A project with a positive NPV will have had its appraisal based on estimates. Any of the values used could change such that the NPV becomes negative rather than positive, meaning that the project should no longer go ahead.

> π To calculate the % sensitivity to an uncertain cash flow, use the following:
>
> $$\text{Sensitivity} = \frac{\text{NPV of project}}{\text{PV of uncertain cash flow}} \times 100\%$$

Mutually exclusive projects with unequal lives can have their NPVs compared in the normal way. If these projects are to be repeated for the foreseeable future (e.g. buying a machine that will last for three years before requiring replacement rather than one replaced every four years) then their *equivalent annual costs* must be compared.

> π Equivalent annual cost is calculated as
>
> $$\frac{\text{PV of one life cycle}}{\text{annuity factor}}$$

Capital rationing occurs when there is insufficient capital available to undertake all positive NPV projects.

The technique to decide which project to undertake depends on two factors:

- whether the projects are divisible
- whether the capital rationing is for one period or many.

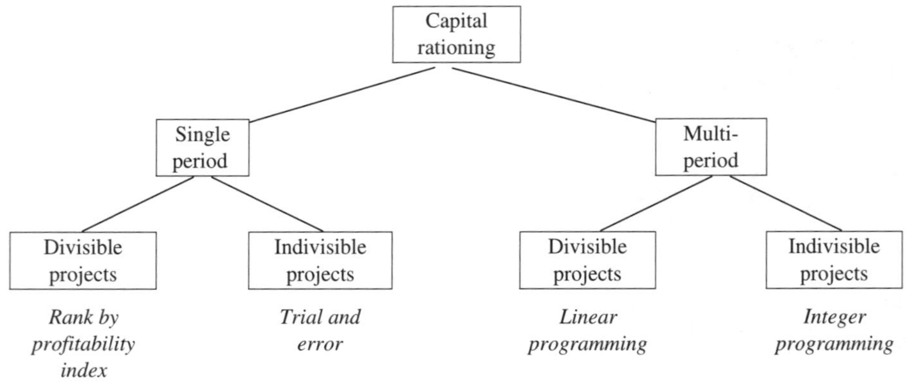

Questions

Use the following information to answer the next two questions.

An education authority is considering the implementation of a CCTV (closed circuit television) security system in one of its schools.

Details of the proposed project are as follows:

Life of project	5 years
Initial cost	£75,000
Annual savings:	
Labour costs	£20,000
Other costs	£5,000
Cost of capital	15% per annum

7.1 The IRR for this project is nearest to

A 10.13%
B 14.87%
C 15.64%
D 19.88%
E 20.13%

(2 marks)

7.2 The percentage change in the annual labour cost savings that could occur before the project ceases to be viable is

A 10.50%
B 11.73%
C 13.13%
D 35.20%
E 44.00%

(3 marks)

Use the following information to answer the next two questions.

A company is considering investing in a manufacturing project that would have a three-year life span. The investment would involve an immediate cash outflow of £50,000 and have a zero residual value. In each of the three years, 4,000 units would be produced and sold. The contribution per unit, based on current prices, is £5. The company has an annual cost of capital of 8%. It is expected that the inflation rate will be 3% in each of the next three years.

7.3 The NPV of the project (to the nearest £500) is

A £4,500
B £5,000
C £5,500
D £6,000
E £6,500

(3 marks)

7.4 If the annual inflation rate is now projected to be 4%, the maximum monetary cost of capital for this project to remain viable is (to the nearest 0.5%)

A 13.0%
B 13.5%
C 14.0%
D 14.5%
E 15.0%

(3 marks)

Use the following information to answer the next two questions.

A company is appraising an investment project with the following cash flows.

Initial investment £100,000

End of year inflows:

Year	£
1	34,000
2	25,000
3	30,000
4	40,000
5	28,000

The Year 5 inflow includes expected scrap proceeds of £10,000.

The cost of capital of the company is 12%.

7.5 Calculate the payback period and the NPV (to nearest £100).

	Payback period (years)	*NPV £*
A	2.275	12,963
B	3.275	12,963
C	2.275	15,963
D	3.275	15,963

(3 marks)

7.6 The cash inflow at the end of Year 2 is uncertain. What is the minimum possible value of the cash inflow for Year 2 such that the project is still viable?

A £6,750
B £8,750
C £12,750
D £18,750

(3 marks)

Use the following information to answer the next two questions.

A company is appraising five mutually exclusive projects. The following information relates to these five projects:

Project	*R*	*S*	*T*	*U*	*V*
Net present value (£)	8,000	10,000	6,000	12,000	14,000
Project life (years)	4	3	6	7	4
Initial investment (£)	20,000	24,000	16,000	26,000	40,000

The projects are all believed to be divisible. Each project can only be undertaken once.

7.7 Which project should the company undertake?

A Project R
B Project S
C Project T
D Project U
E Project V

(2 marks)

7.8 If the company subsequently finds out that it can invest in *all five* of the projects but only has £100,000 available for investment purposes, which is the best project to invest in?

A Project R
B Project S
C Project T
D Project U
E Project V

(3 marks)

7.9 Hurst plc makes "kiss-me-quick" hats which it sells to shops on the seafronts of most of the popular seaside towns around the UK.

Global warming has caused an increase in the number of people visiting the seaside in the UK and the directors of Hurst plc would like to take advantage of this upturn. They are contemplating building a new "kiss-me-quick" hat making factory just outside Blackpool which would be expected to have a six-year life.

If the new factory is built it is expected to have production capacity of 200,000 units per annum, although it is expected that demand for "kiss-me-quick" hats would only take up 85% of this capacity during the next six years. (The board are considering a larger factory than is strictly necessary because the marketing director, Mr N.O.T. Likely, would like to start marketing the hats in France and Belgium and would like to be able to increase production if such a campaign is successful.)

Information relating to each hat is as follows:

	£
Selling price	10
Variable costs:	
Materials	2
Labour	3
Overheads	1

Incremental fixed overheads are expected to be £110,000 per annum.

The cost of the new factory is expected to be:

Land and buildings	£1,500,000
Machinery	£900,000

The disposal value of the land and buildings is expected to be 50% of its original cost. Machinery is expected to have negligible scrap value.

All cash flows are expected to inflate at 5% per annum and the company's nominal cost of capital is 15.5% per annum.

Corporation tax is 20% payable in the same year as that in which the cash flows arise. Machinery attracts capital allowances at 33.33% straight line. No capital allowances are available on land and buildings.

Requirements

(a) Using real cash flows, calculate the NPV of the new factory. (*Note*: You may ignore the fact that inflation does not affect the capital allowances.)

(5 marks)

(b) Calculate the sensitivity of the decision to a change in the sales volume.

(5 marks)
(Total = 10 marks)

7.10 PI Limited has maximum capital of £1,400,000 to invest. Five capital projects have been identified which are of a similar degree of risk. The initial step of calculating the NPVs has been completed and the details are as follows:

Project	*Required initial outlay* £	*NPV* £
A	387,000	156,000
B	312,000	130,000
C	520,000	200,000
D	208,000	108,000
E	1,037,000	325,000

Projects cannot be postponed, all projects are *divisible* and multiples of the same projects are not allowed.

Requirements

(a) Calculate the Profitability index for each project and determine the optimal combination of projects to maximise NPV?

(5 marks)

(b) Explain what is meant by "hard" capital rationing and "soft" capital rationing and discuss why they might arise.

(3 marks)

(c) Outline the main limitations of using expected values when considering investment projects.

(2 marks)
(Total = 10 marks)

7.11 T Ltd (IMPM 11/03)

The management team of T Ltd, a small venture capital company, is planning its investment activities for the next five years. It has been approached by four start-up companies from the same industry sector which have presented their business plans for consideration. The forecast cash flows and resulting NPV for each start-up company are as follows:

			Operational cash flows				
Capital company	*Year 0* $'000	*Year 1* $'000	*Year 2* $'000	*Year 3* $'000	*Year 4* $'000	*Year 5* $'000	*NPV* $'000
A	(500)	(75)	(40)	50	400	650	60
B	(250)	(30)	(20)	(5)	250	247	0
C	(475)	(100)	(30)	(20)	400	750	77
D	(800)	(150)	(50)	50	900	786	80

The directors of T Ltd use a 12% cost of capital for appraising this type of investment.

You can assume that all investments are divisible and that they are not mutually exclusive.

Ignore tax and inflation.

Requirements

(a) Advise T Ltd which of the investments, if any, it should invest in.

(3 marks)

(b) If capital for investment now is limited to $700,000 but T Ltd can raise further capital in one year's time and thereafter at a cost of 12% per annum,

(i) Advise T Ltd how it should invest the $700,000.

(5 marks)

(ii) Discuss other factors which may affect the decision.

(4 marks)

(c) T Ltd has now found out that funds will also be restricted in future years and that the constraints are absolute and cannot be removed by project generated incomes. The present values of cash that will be available for future investment are as follows:

Year	*Present value* $'000
0	700
1	80
2	35

Formulate the linear programming model that will maximise NPV and explain the meaning of each variable and the purpose of each constraint you have identified.
(You are not required to attempt a solution.)

(10 marks)

(d) Briefly explain the benefits of using a linear programming format in this situation.

(3 marks)

(Total = 25 marks)

7.12 CAF plc (IDEC 5/02)

CAF plc is a large multinational organisation that manufactures a range of highly engineered products/components for the aircraft and vehicle industries. The directors are considering the future of one of the company's factories in the UK which manufactures product A. Product A is coming to the end of its life but another two years' production is planned. This is expected to produce a net cash inflow of £3 million next year and £2.3 million in the product's final year.

Product AA

CAF plc has already decided to replace product A with product AA which will be ready to go into production in two years' time. Product AA is expected to have a life of eight years. It could be made either at the UK factory under consideration or in an Eastern European factory owned by CAF plc. The UK factory is located closer to the markets and therefore if product AA is made in Eastern Europe, the company will incur extra transport costs of £10 per unit. Production costs will be the same in both countries. Product AA will require additional equipment and staff will need training; this will cost £6 million at either location. 200,000 units of product AA will be made each year and each unit will generate a net cash inflow of £25 before extra transport costs. If product AA is made in the UK, the factory will be closed and sold at the end of the product's life.

Product X

Now, however, the directors are considering a further possibility: product X could be produced at the UK factory and product AA at the Eastern European factory. Product X must be introduced in one year's time and will remain in production for three years. If it is introduced, the manufacture of product A will have to cease a year earlier than planned. If this happened, output of product A would be increased by 12.5% to maximum capacity next year, its last year, to build stock prior to the product's withdrawal. The existing staff would be transferred to product X.

The equipment needed to make product X would cost £4 million. 50,000 units of product X would be made in its first year; after that, production would rise to 75,000 units a year. Product X would earn a net cash flow of £70 per unit. After three years' production of product X, the UK factory would be closed and sold. (Product AA would not be transferred back to the factory in the UK at that stage; production would continue at the Eastern European site.)

Sale of factory

It is expected that the UK factory could be sold for £5.5 million at any time between the beginning of Year 2 and the end of Year 10. If the factory is sold, CAF plc will make redundancy payments of £2 million and the sale of equipment will raise by £350,000.

CAF plc's cost of capital is 5% each year.

Requirements

(a) Prepare calculations that show which of the three options is financially the best.

(15 marks)

(b) The directors of CAF plc are unsure whether their estimates are correct. Calculate and discuss the sensitivity of your choice of option in (a) to:

(i) Changes in transport costs.

(3 marks)

(ii) Changes in the selling price of the factory.

(3 marks)

(c) Briefly discuss the business issues that should be considered before relocating to another country.

(4 marks)
(Total = 25 marks)

✓ Answers

7.1 **D**

To calculate the IRR, we use two guesses.

Using 15% and 20% as our two guesses gives:

IRR calculation

Time	*Cash*	*DF at 15%*	*PV*	*DF at 20%*	*PV*
0	(75,000)	1	(75,000)	1	(75,000)
1–5	25,000	3.352	83,800	2.991	74,775
			8,800		(225)

$$IRR = a + \frac{N_a \times (b - a)}{N_a - N_b}$$

where,
a = lower %
b = higher %
N_a = NPV at a%
N_b = NPV at b%

$$IRR = a + \frac{N_a \times (b - a)}{N_a - N_b}$$

$$= 15 + \frac{8{,}800 \times (20 - 15)}{8{,}800 - (-225)}$$

$$= 15 + \frac{8{,}800 \times (20 - 15)}{8{,}800 + 225}$$

$$= 15 + 4.88$$

$$= 19.88\%$$

7.2 **C**

If the labour cost savings were to change there will be an impact upon the NPV of the project. As seen in the answer to question 1, at the company's cost of capital of 15% the NPV is £8,800.

If the labour cost savings were to fall, the NPV would fall. The NPV can fall to zero before the project ceases to be viable.

At present the NPV is:

Time	*Cash*	*DF at 15%*	*PV*
0	(75,000)	1	(75,000)
1–5	20,000	3.352	67,040
1–5	5,000	3.352	16,760
			8,800

The trick when answering this sensitivity analysis type of question is to look at the *current present value* of the cash flows. The present value of the labour savings is currently £67,040. This could fall by £8,800 (the current NPV) if the new NPV were to be zero.

This represents a percentage of:

$$\frac{£8,800}{£67,040} \times 100\% = 13.13\%$$

7.3 **A**

The cost of capital of 8% will be the *money* (or *nominal*) rate. The cost of capital is by definition the rate or return required by investors in the business, and if there is inflation in the economy, the rate or return that they require will reflect this inflation.

When calculating the NPV where a question includes inflation, we must discount the *inflated up* cash flows using the *money* rate, or discount the *uninflated* cash flows using the *real* cost of capital.

Both techniques should give the same answer.

Remember that the relationship between the money rate and the real rate is:

$$\frac{1+m}{1+i} = 1 + r$$

where,
m = money rate
i = inflation rate
r = real rate

Using the inflated up cash flows and the money rate:

Time		*Cash*	*DF at 8%*	*PV*
0		(50,000)	1	(50,000)
1	$4,000 \times 5 \times 1.03$	20,600	0.926	19,076
2	$4,000 \times 5 \times 1.03^2$	21,218	0.857	18,184
3	$4,000 \times 5 \times 1.03^3$	21,855	0.794	17,353
			NPV	4,613

Alternatively, using the uninflated cash flows and the real rate.

Real rate:

$$\frac{1+m}{1+i} = 1 + r$$

$$\frac{1.08}{1.03} = 1.0485$$

So real rate is 4.85%

Time		*Cash*	*DF at 4.85%*	*PV*
0		(50,000)	1	(50,000)
1	4,000 × 5	20,000	0.954	19,080
2	4,000 × 5	20,000	0.910	18,200
3	4,000 × 5	20,000	0.868	17,360
			NPV	4,640

The slight different between the NPVs is due to rounding of the discount factors.

Either way the answer is A.

7.4 C

The cost of capital at which the project is just still viable is the IRR.
(Remember that at the IRR, the NPV is zero, so the project is *just* still viable.)

The money cost of capital is required, so we must use the inflated up cash flows (using the revised inflation rate of 4%) and use them to calculate the IRR.

Using 10 and 15% as our two guesses gives:

Time		*Cash*	*DF at 10%*	*PV*	*DF at 15%*	*PV*
0		(50,000)	1	(50,000)	1	(50,000)
1	$4{,}000 \times 5 \times 1.04$	20,800	0.909	18,907	0.87	18,096
2	$4{,}000 \times 5 \times 1.04^2$	21,632	0.826	17,868	0.756	16,354
3	$4{,}000 \times 5 \times 1.04^3$	22,497	0.751	16,895	0.658	14,803
			NPV	3,670		(747)

$$\text{IRR} = a + \frac{N_a \times (b - a)}{N_a - N_b}$$

where,
a = lower %
b = higher %
N_a = NPV at a%
N_b = NPV at b%

$$\text{IRR} = a + \frac{N_a \times (b - a)}{N_a - N_b}$$

$$= 10 + \frac{3{,}670 \times (15 - 10)}{3{,}670 - (-747)}$$

$$= 10 + \frac{3{,}670 \times (15 - 10)}{3{,}670 + 747}$$

$$= 10 + \frac{3{,}670 \times (15 - 10)}{4{,}417}$$

$$= 10 + 4.15$$

$$= 14.15\%$$

7.5 **B**

Payback period:

Time	*Cash*	*Cumulative cash*
0	(100,000)	(100,000)
1	34,000	(66,000)
2	25,000	(41,000)
3	30,000	(11,000)
4	40,000	29,000
5	28,000	57,000

The project outflow is paid for by the end of Year 4. If we assume that the Year 4 cash is received evenly throughout the year:

$$\text{Payback period} = 3 \text{ years} + \frac{11{,}000}{40{,}000} \times 1 \text{ year}$$

Since only £11,000 of £40,000 of the Year 4 needs to be received to payback all of the initial investment.

So,
Payback period = 3 + 0.275 = 3.275 years

Net present value:

Time	*Cash*	*DF at 12%*	*PV*
0	(100,000)	1	(100,000)
1	34,000	0.893	30,362
2	25,000	0.797	19,925
3	30,000	0.712	21,360
4	40,000	0.636	25,440
5	28,000	0.567	15,876
			12,963

So NPV is £12,963.

7.6 **B**

If the Year 2 cash flow were to change it will have an impact upon the NPV of the project. In fact, if it were to fall the NPV will also fall.

If the NPV were to fall to zero, the project would be just still viable.

So we need to calculate the new value of the Year 2 cash inflow that would give us an NPV of zero:

At present the NPV is:

Time	*Cash*	*DF at 12%*	*PV*
0	(100,000)	1	(100,000)
1	34,000	0.893	30,362
2	25,000	0.797	19,925
3	30,000	0.712	21,360
4	40,000	0.636	25,440
5	28,000	0.567	15,876
		NPV	12,963

The trick when answering this sensitivity analysis type of question is to look at the *current present value* of the cash flow. The present value of the Year 2 cash flow is currently £19,925. This could fall by £12,963 (the current NPV) if the new NPV were to be zero.

This represents a percentage of:

$$\frac{£12,963}{£19,925} \times 100\% = 65\%$$

So the Year 2 cash flow must be at least 35% of its current value.

So the minimum value is £25,000 × 35% = £8,750.

7.7 **E**

If projects are mutually exclusive, the company can only invest in one project since doing so precludes investing in any of the other projects.

The company will therefore invest in project whichever generates the highest NPV.

This is Project V, so the answer is E.

Perhaps you did not read the question carefully and spot that the projects are mutually exclusive!

7.8 **D**

Now that all five projects can be undertaken, the company will have to decide which project is best, which is second best, which is third best, and so on.

It is tempting to rank the projects using highest NPV down to lowest NPV.

This would give the following ranking:

Project	*R*	*S*	*T*	*U*	*V*
NPV	£8,000	£10,000	£6,000	£12,000	£14,000
Ranking	4th	3rd	5th	2nd	1st

However, this would be the ranking of the projects if the company had sufficient capital to invest in all five projects at the same time.

The company has £100,000 available for investment purposes. Is this enough to be able to invest in all five projects at the same time, or does it represent a scarce resource which must be rationed carefully amongst the five projects?

Amount available: £100,000

Amount required: £20,000 + £24,000 + £16,000 + £26,000 + £40,000 = £126,000

The capital must be rationed:

To do this we must calculate NPV per pound to be invested in order to generate the best return possible from each pound to be invested.

Project	*R*	*S*	*T*	*U*	*V*
NPV	£8,000	£10,000	£6,000	£12,000	£14,000
Initial Investment	£20,000	£24,000	£16,000	£26,000	£40,000
NPV per pound invested	$\frac{8,000}{20,000}$	$\frac{10,000}{24,000}$	$\frac{6,000}{16,000}$	$\frac{12,000}{26,000}$	$\frac{14,000}{40,000}$
	= £0.40	= £0.42	= £0.375	= £0.46	= £0.35
Ranking using NPV per pound	3rd	2nd	4th	1st	5th

Notice that on the grounds of NPV per pound to be invested, project V is the worst performing project!

In fact, project U generated the highest NPV per pound to be invested and is therefore the best project to invest in.

7.9

> *Topic being tested*
>
> Part (a) – Net present value calculation using real (uninflated) cash flows which must be discounted at the *real* cost of capital.
> Part (b) – Sensitivity analysis to determine by how much the sales volume could change before the NPV falls to zero.
>
> *Approach*
>
> Part (a) – Calculate the NPV thinking carefully about the most efficient layout.
> Part (b) – Sensitivity analysis using the NPV calculated in Part (a) bearing in mind that a change in the sales volume will impact upon more than just sales revenue!

Solution

(a) Calculation of the project NPV using real cash flows and the real cost of capital.

The real cost of capital is calculated using:

$$\frac{1+n}{1+i} = 1 + r$$

where,
n = nominal cost of capital
i = general rate of inflation
r = real cost of capital

$$\frac{1.155}{1.05} = 1.10$$

The real cost of capital is 10%.

Net present value calculation

Number of units = 85% × 200,000 units
= 170,000 units

Contribution per unit = £10 − £2 − £3 − £1 = £4 per unit in real terms

Contribution per annum = 170,000 units × £4 = £680,000

Time	*Narrative*	*Cash flow*	*DF at 10%*	*PV*
0	Investment	(2,400,000)	1.000	(2,400,000)
1–6	Contribution	680,000	4.355	2,961,400
1–6	Fixed costs	(110,000)	4.355	(479,050)
1–6	Tax (W1)	(114,000)	4.355	(496,470)
1–3	Tax saved on capital allowances (W2)	60,000	2.487	149,220
6	Disposal value	750,000	0.564	423,000
			NPV	158,100

W1 20% × (680,000 − 110,000)
W2 20% × 33.33% × £900,000

The NPV of the project is £158,100.

(b) If the sales volume were to fall, the NPV of the project would fall.

Sensitivity analysis involves calculating the amount by which sales volume could change before the NPV falls to zero.

If the sales volume changes it will have an impact upon contribution and tax paid on the contribution. All other cash flows would be unaffected.

PV of the contribution (net of tax) = £2,961,400 × 80% = £2,369,120

This can fall by, at most, £158,100 (project NPV)

As a percentage = £158,100/£2,369,120 × 100% = 6.67%

This is the sensitivity of the decision to a change in sales volume.

(Note that sales would then be 100% − 6.67% = 93.33% of their existing value. Thus minimum sales = 93.33% × 170,000 = 158,661 units)

7.10

Topic being tested

Part (a) – Single period capital rationing for divisible projects using profitability index approach.
Part (b) – Discussion of reasons why capital available for investment purposes may be scarce – "hard" and "soft" capital rationing.
Part (c) – Discussion of expected value calculations.

Approach

Part (a) – Calculate the profitability index for each project and use to rank the projects from best to worst.
Part (b) – "Hard" and "soft" capital rationing should be easy to explain if you have the required knowledge!
Part (c) – Remind yourself how expected values are calculated and think what the problems may be.

Solution

(a) All five projects are worthwhile since they all have a positive NPV.

Total investment funds required to be able to undertake all five projects is £2,464,000. However, only £1,400,000 is available. We must ration this scarce capital by ranking the projects using their profitability index.

$$\text{Profitability index} = \frac{\text{PV of future cash flows (before deducting initial investment)}}{\text{PV initial investment}}$$

Project	*PV of future cash flows (1)*	*PV of investment (2)*	*Profitability index (1) ÷ (2)*	*Ranking*
A	156,000 + 387,000 = 543,000	387,000	1.403	3rd
B	130,000 + 312,000 = 442,000	312,000	1.417	2nd
C	200,000 + 520,000 = 720,000	520,000	1.385	4th
D	108,000 + 208,000 = 316,000	208,000	1.519	1st
E	325,000 + 1,037,000 = 1,362,000	1,037,000	1.313	5th

Optimal investment schedule

Project	*Investment* £		*NPV* £	
D	208,000		108,000	
B	312,000		130,000	
A	387,000		156,000	
	907,000			
C × 94.8%	493,000	(balancing amount)	189,600	(200,000 × 94.8%)
	1,400,000			
Maximum NPV			583,600	

493,000 ÷ 520,000 × 100% = 94.8%

(b) Both "soft" and "hard" capital rationing explain the situation where insufficient capital is available to a business to be able to undertake all investment projects that it would like to invest in.

"Soft" capital rationing describes the situation where capital is rationed due to *internal* factors such as unwillingness of management to issue new shares or to raise more debt finance.

"Hard" capital rationing describes the situation where capital is rationed due to *external* factors such as a depressed company share price or even a depressed stock market making a share issue difficult at present or ill-advised. Another reason could be that the company already has a high degree of gearing (debt compared to the size of the company), and banks are not prepared to lend more money to the company.

(c) The major limitations of the use of expected values to arrive at project cash flows follow.

Deciding upon the possible outcomes, for example, the possible different level of sales revenue for a particular year, can be difficult in practice.

Assigning probabilities to those outcomes can be difficult and may be arrived at in an arbitrary way.

The expected value arrived at may not even be one of the possible outcomes predicted.

7.11

(a)

Company	*NPV* $'000
A	60
B	0
C	77
D	80

The management team of T Ltd should invest in Companies D, C and A as they generate a positive NPV. The positive NPV forecast to be generated by Companies D, C and A means that T Ltd would not only be returned the desired cost of capital (12%), but also an additional amount of $80,000 in the case of Company D; $77,000 in the case of Company C; and $60,000 in the case of Company A. These amounts will go towards maximising shareholders' wealth.

T Ltd will be indifferent as to whether to invest in Company B as it generates a zero NPV. The zero NPV forecast to be generated by Company B means that T Ltd would only return the desired cost of capital (12%) and no more.

(b) (i)

Company	*A* $'000	*B* $'000	*C* $'000	*D* $'000
NPV	60	0	77	80
Investment	500	250	475	800
NPV/$1	0.12	0	0.162	0.10
Ranking	2nd	4th	1st	3rd

Invest $475,000 in Company C and $225,000 in Company A.

(ii) *The riskiness of the product/service that Company C and A wish to offer*
If it is very innovative and untested, there will be a higher amount of risk than a product/service being launched which is competitive with another product/service already in the market. For example, Company D may be launching a competitive product/service and be less risky than Companies C and A.

The experience of the management staff within Companies C and A will be important
If the start-up team has specific and relevant commercial experience within their industry then this will ensure that the investment will be carefully managed.

T Ltd's attitude to risk will be an important element
This will probably depend on their current portfolio of investments. If there is a large amount already invested in high-risk projects they may decide to lower their exposure by investing in a more reliable, less risky venture.

The speed of the payback period on these investments will also be important
The sooner the funds are repaid, the sooner the funds will be available for investment in other projects. This may be a factor that T Ltd will consider when finalising their decision.

(c) Let X_1 = Proportional investment in Company A
Let X_2 = Proportional investment in Company B
Let X_3 = Proportional investment in Company C
Let X_4 = Proportional investment in Company D

Maximise $= 60X_1 + 0X_2 + 77X_3 + 80X_4$

Subject to:

$500X_1 + 250X_2 + 475X_3 + 800X_4 + S_1 = 700$	(Period 0 Constraint)
$75X_1 + 30X_2 + 100X_3 + 150X_4 + S_2 = 89.60$	(Period 1 Constraint)
$40X_1 + 20X_2 + 30X_3 + 50X_4 + S_3 = 43.91$	(Period 2 Constraint)

$0 \leq X_j \leq 1 \ (j = 1 \ldots 3)$

Our objective function seeks to maximise the NPV from our investment, subject to the investment constraints for each of the three periods. S_1, S_2 and S_3 represent the slack variables (i.e. the unused funds for each of the three periods). Xj may take a value from 0 to 1 and ensures that none of the investments can be undertaken more than once, but allows for partial investments to be undertaken.

(d) Benefits
With computer programs, a complex investment decision like this can be quickly and efficiently solved. It is also usual for these computer programs to provide a sensitivity analysis of the problem, allowing the decision-makers to identify by how much key variables can change without changing the solution.

Once the final tableau for this investment decision has been established, the output will provide details of the opportunity costs and the marginal rates of substitution for the scarce resources which is useful for decision-making, planning and control purposes.

Provides a clear plan of action.

7.12

(a) *NPV of planned sales of A at 5%*

Year		£m
1	£3.0m × 0.952	2.856
2	£2.3m × 0.907	2.085
		4.942

Net revenue from sale of factory:

Redundancy £m	*Factory and Equipment sale* £m	*Total* £m	*Year*	*Disc rate* 5%	*NPV* £m
(2)	5.5 + 0.35	3.85	2	0.907	3.492
			4	0.823	3.169
			10	0.614	2.364

Options:

(i) Produce product A, then replace it with AA at the UK factory.
(ii) Produce product A, then sell the UK factory in Year 2 and make AA in Eastern Europe for eight years.
(iii) Produce a limited number of product A, then product X and sell the UK factory in Year 4 and make product AA in Eastern Europe for eight years.

Option (i)

Year(s)		*NPV* £m
1–2	Normal sales of product A	4.942
2	Equipment and training cost for product AA £(6)m × 0.907	(5.442)
3–10	Product AA 200,000 × £25 = 5,000,000 × (7.722 − 1.859) = 5,000,000 × 5.863	29.315
10	Sale of factory	2.364
		31.179

Option (ii)

Year(s)		*NPV* £m
1–2	Normal sales of product A	4.942
2	Sale of factory	3.492
2	Equipment and training cost for product AA	(5.442)
3–10	Product AA with additional transport costs 200,000 × £15 = 3,000,000 × (7.722 − 1.859) = 3,000,000 × 5.863	17.589
		20.581

Therefore, it would be better to produce product AA at the UK factory.

Option (iii)

Year(s)		£m
1	Purchase equipment for X and produce A £(4m) − £3m × 0.952	(0.952)
2	Sales of A (see note below) £0.375 × 0.907	0.340
	Inflow from X = 50,000 × £70 = £3.50m × 0.907	3.175
3	Inflow from X = 75,000 × £70 = £5.25m × 0.864	4.536
4	Inflow from X = 75,000 × £70 = £5.25m × 0.823	4.321
	Sale of factory	3.169
2	Equipment and training cost for product AA	(5.442)
3–10	Product AA with additional transport costs	17.589
		26.736

Note: Answers which included all sales of A in Year 1 were accepted.

The first option is the best.

(b) (i) **Changes in transport costs**

Transport costs are the same in options (ii) and (iii), therefore the comparison is made between options (i) and (iii) [the better option of (ii) and (iii)]. The incremental NPV of option (i) over option (iii) is £31.179m − £26.736m = £4.443m

Extra transport costs for product AA:

		£m
Years 3–10	200,000 × £10 = £2m × (7.722 − 1.859)	11.726
They could drop by (38% of 11.726)		4.443
		7.283

£7,283,000 ÷ 5.863 = £1,242,000

Therefore, the transport costs would have to fall by £758,000 per annum (or 38%) before the choice was invalid – this is not sensitive.

As transport costs do not affect the decision, it underlines the choice of option (i). Product X does not generate enough income to cover the extra transport costs of producing product AA in Eastern Europe.

(ii) **Changes in the selling price of the factory**

On the figures given, closing the factory in Year 2, option (ii) is by far the worst option and so the selling price is irrelevant as any change would have to be colossal.

The decision between options (i) and (iii) does not depend on the price of the factory either. This is because the incremental NPV of option (i) is £4.443 million compared to the net difference in the present value of the sale price of £5.5m × (0.823 − 0.614) = £5.5m × 0.209 = £1.150m.

£1.150m + £4.443m = £5.593m – a 386% increase. This means that the selling price would have to be £26.7 million, before option (iii) was preferred.

(c) The decision to consider relocation will usually be based on several major issues. These may include the following.

- Situating the business closer to the market it serves, in order to respond quickly to changes in customer needs.
- The availability of skilled labour in the locality.
- Lower taxation rates.

However, there are likely to be a number of additional difficulties which should be considered and weighed against the benefits. These include the following.

- The difficulty in running a business that is geographically widely spread. This is particularly true if the nature of the business requires control from the centre.
- The problem of dealing in different currencies together with the risk attached to this.
- Management problems caused by different cultural habits.

Expected Values and Decision Trees

8

Expected values and the term *uncertainty* are often used in the same breath.

When making decisions, the level of profit for a particular year or the amount of a cash flow are unlikely to be known with certainty.

It may be possible to estimate several possible values for a profit figure or particular cash flow and then assign probabilities to those values.

For example, the amount of sales revenue for the first year of a new project may be estimated to be at a level of £250,000 or £340,000 or £470,000.

If probabilities of 0.5, 0.3 and 0.2 are assigned to those values, the expected sales revenue figure will be:

£250,000 × 0.5 + £340,000 × 0.3 + £470,000 × 0.2 = £321,000

This amount of £321,000 can now be used as the first-year revenue figure in a NPV calculation, for example.

Note that the probabilities of the possible values have to add to one.

Expected value calculations are also an integral part of drawing and using a *decision tree.*

Decision trees are a useful way of determining what decision should be taken where a decision results in several possible outcomes and also results in further decisions having to be taken as a result of the initial decision.

The *approach* for decision tree questions is to:

Draw the decision tree from left to right.
Ensure that you distinguish between decision points and chance points on the tree.
For example, you could use:

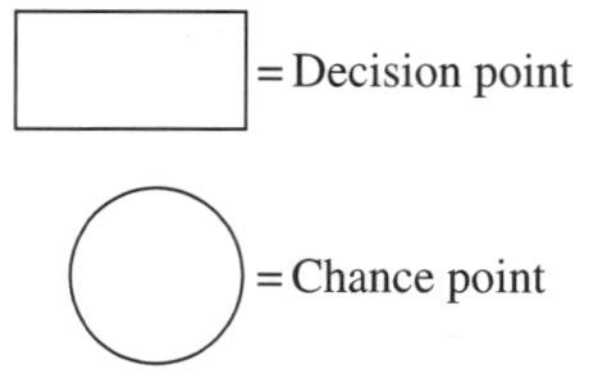

Place revenues, costs and probabilities onto the tree.
Use letters to denote the decision and chance points for referencing purposes.
Work backwards, that is, from far right to far left calculating expected values at the chance points and stating the decision to be made at decision points.
State your conclusion, that is, what decision should the business take.

? Questions

8.1 Expected values are often used in decision-making. The option with the highest expected value is usually chosen. However, which of the following are weaknesses associated with the decision to choose the option with the highest expected value.

(i) It ignores risk aversion.
(ii) Probabilities used can be difficult to derive.
(iii) It ignores negative values.
(iv) It cannot be used as a decision-making tool if the expected value gives a loss.

A (i), (ii), (iii) and (iv)
B (i), (ii) and (iii) only
C (i) and (iv) only
D (i) and (ii) only
E (ii) and (iii) only

(2 marks)

8.2 HED Ltd is using the NPV technique to appraise a new investment but is unsure as to the likely scrap proceeds to expect when the asset to be used in the project will be disposed of at the end of the project life.

An independent valuer of this type of asset has suggested the following possible scrap values and their associated probabilities.

Scrap value £	*Probability*
40,000	0.3
50,000	0.4
65,000	0.2
78,000	0.1

What is the expected scrap proceeds to be used in the NPV calculation?

A £63,300
B £58,250
C £54,100
D £52,800
E £51,800

(2 marks)

8.3 HJD plc had been selling clothes for some time but has decided to diversify its activities by selling footwear as well.

Its new products are to be boots, sandals and shoes. Budgeted sales revenue for the forthcoming year for each type of product is uncertain, so the company has paid for a market research report which has given the following likely sales revenue figures together with their respective probabilities.

Boots	*Probability*	*Sandals*	*Probability*	*Shoes*	*Probability*
40,000	0.20	28,000	0.10	32,000	0.45
50,000	0.50	37,000	0.10	42,000	0.35
65,000	0.10	59,000	0.05	52,000	0.05
78,000	0.20	95,000	0.75	62,000	0.15

The company wishes to maximise revenue. In which order should the company produce the three new products in the order of highest revenue to lowest revenue?

A Boots then Sandals then Shoes
B Boots then Shoes then Sandals
C Sandals then Boots then Shoes
D Sandals then Shoes then Boots
E Shoes then Sandals then Boots

(3 marks)

8.4 Which of the following statements with respect to expected values is correct?

A The expected value will always equal one of the possible outcomes.
B The expected value is a weighted average of the possible outcomes.
C The expected value will never equal one of the possible outcomes.
D The expected value takes into account the risk averse nature of the decision-maker.
E The expected value is a simple average of the possible outcomes.

(2 marks)

Use the following information to answer the next two questions.

X Ltd can choose from five mutually exclusive projects. The projects will each last for one year only and their net cash inflows will be determined by the prevailing market conditions. The forecast annual cash inflows and their associated probabilities are shown below.

Market conditions	*Poor*	*Good*	*Excellent*
Probability	0.20	0.50	0.30
	£'000	£'000	£'000
Project L	500	470	550
Project M	400	550	570
Project N	450	400	475
Project O	360	400	420
Project P	600	500	425

8.5 Based on the expected value of the net cash inflows, which project should be undertaken?

A L
B M
C N
D O
E P

(2 marks)

8.6 The value of perfect information about the state of the market is

A £0
B £5,000
C £26,000
D £40,000
E £128,000

(3 marks)

8.7 When using the expected value technique it is necessary to

(i) estimate all possible financial outcomes of the decision
(ii) consider non-financial issues such as reaction of customers and competitors
(iii) assign probabilities to all financial outcomes of the decision
(iv) consider how sensitive to changes in financial outcomes the decision is

A (i) and (ii) only
B (i) and (iii) only
C (ii) and (iii) only
D (i), (ii) and (iii) only
E (i), (ii), (iii) and (iv)

(2 marks)

Use the following information to answer the next two questions.

P Ltd sells 90,000 units of product Y per annum. At this level of sales and output, the selling price and variable cost per unit are £50 and £21 respectively. The annual fixed costs are £1,200,000. The management team is considering lowering the selling price per unit to £45.

The estimated levels of demand at the new price and the probabilities of them occurring are:

Demand	*Probability*
100,000 units	0.45
120,000 units	0.55

It is thought that at either of the higher sales or production levels the variable cost per unit and the probability of it occurring will be as follows:

Variable cost per unit	*Probability*
£20	0.40
£18	0.60

8.8 The probability that lowering the selling price to £45 per unit would increase profit is

A 0.18
B 0.21
C 0.25
D 0.33
E 0.82

(4 marks)

8.9 The expected value of the company profit if the selling price is reduced to £45 per unit is

A £639,000
B £1,069,200
C £1,708,200
D £2,040,000
E £3,652,000

(4 marks)

8.10 When drawing a decision tree, set steps should be followed.

Which of the following are steps involved in drawing a decision tree?

(i) Using different symbols to denote decision points and outcome points.
(ii) Draw the tree working from left to right.
(iii) Assign probabilities to the options at a decision point.
(iv) Calculate the expected value for the decision to be made, working from right to left.

A (i), (ii), (iii) and (iv)
B (i), (ii) and (iii) only
C (i), (iii) and (iv) only
D (i) and (iii) only
E (i), (ii) and (iv) only

(2 marks)

8.11 A company is about to make a decision using the decision tree technique. The decision tree has already been drawn and is as follows:

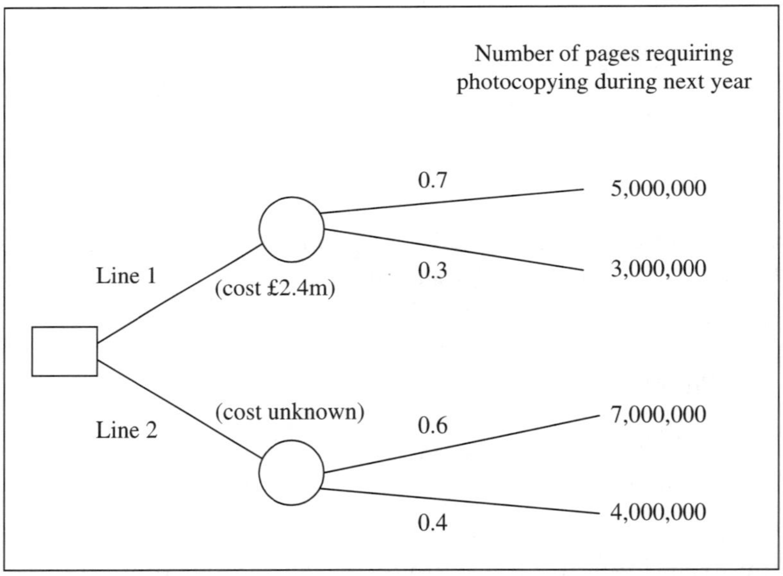

Line 1 represents investment in new photocopiers at a cost of £2.4 million. The expected life of the photocopiers is only one year due to expected heavy usage. Scrap value is expected to be negligible. The company would also have to purchase ink (toner) and pay for maintenance of the copiers which they believe would cost five pence per page copied.

Line 2 represents using an external copying company to do any photocopying work that the company requires. The cost of using the external copying company is expected to be on a "per page copied" basis. This will be an inclusive cost, that is, no other charges will be made by the external company.

Because of quality differences the number of copies done internally and externally would not be the same.

What is the maximum price that the external copying company could charge per page to be copied?

A 41.4 pence
B 45.2 pence
C 47.6 pence
D 54.5 pence
E 59.5 pence

(4 marks)

8.12 The decision tree that a company is to use for decision-making purposes is set out below.

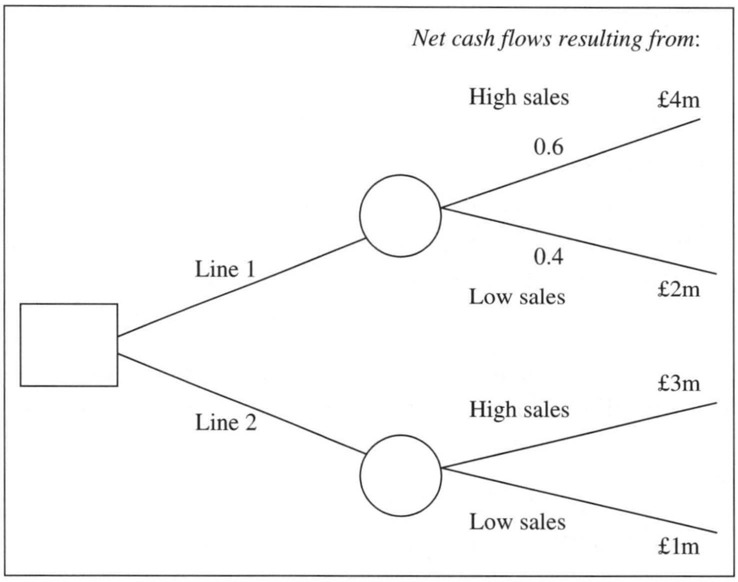

Line 1 represents the decision to invest in new premises. This would cost £2 million.
Line 2 represents spending money to upgrade the existing premises which are slightly smaller than the new premises being considered. This would cost £1.5 million.

The probabilities of high sales and low sales if money were to be spent on upgrading the existing premises are not known.

What is the lowest possible value for the probability of *high sales* if money were to be spent on upgrading the existing premises?

A 0.15
B 0.40
C 0.60
D 0.85
E 0.90

(4 marks)

8.13 Biggles uses decision tree analysis in order to make decisions relating to market research as to potential demand for new products.

It has developed a product which is the brainchild of the production director, however, no market research has yet been undertaken to establish the extent of consumer demand.

If the product is sold without market research being undertaken first, it is believed that contribution of £3 million could be achieved with a probability of 0.6. Otherwise, contribution will be £1.8 million.

However, it is believed that if market research *were undertaken*, the useful feedback and potential for product modification to better meet consumers' needs would increase the probability of the higher level of contribution to 0.85. The two possible levels of contribution would remain unchanged.

What is the maximum amount that the company should be prepared to spend on market research?

A £0
B £100,000
C £200,000
D £300,000
E £400,000

(3 marks)

8.14 The owner of a boat-building company is deciding whether or not to exhibit at a particular boat show, which is to be held early in the season. The total cost of exhibiting at the show will be £6,000. Sales will be dependent on the weather; there is a 0.3 chance that the weather will be dry and a 0.7 chance that the weather will be wet.

If the weather is dry, the owner expects to sell six yachts at the show. If the weather is wet, he expects to sell only two yachts at the show. The contribution per yacht sold is £10,000.

If the owner does not exhibit at the show, he believes that two of the yachts he expects to sell at this show would be sold at another show later in the year.

The expected net gain from exhibiting at the show is

A £0
B £6,000
C £12,000
D £26,000
E £32,000

(2 marks)

8.15 Oil plc is an oil exploration company. It undertakes geological surveys of land which it feels may bear oil. If the survey suggests that oil is present, Oil plc drills the land, extracts the oil and then sells it to an oil refining company.

Based on past experience, the probability of a survey predicting that oil is present underground is 0.6. When Oil plc has subsequently drilled for oil, it has been present 80% of the time. Currently surveys are undertaken using seismology equipment which was purchased by Oil plc four years ago at a cost of £1.4 million and currently has a disposal value of £0.3 million.

A new piece of equipment has been designed by Seismik plc which would cost £2.0 million if purchased by Oil plc. It includes a system which gives a better indication of where surveys should be undertaken. This leads to much greater accuracy. In tests, this new equipment has been shown to predict the existence of oil 85% of the time with an accuracy level of 92% (i.e. in tests of the new equipment, when the survey suggested oil was present and the land was drilled, oil was actually present 92% of the time).

Each time a survey is undertaken using Oil plc's existing equipment, the cost of labour, materials and other variable costs is £40,000.

With the new equipment designed by Seismik plc, these costs would total £15,000 per survey.

If Oil plc decides to drill for oil, the drilling cost is £17,500.

During the forthcoming year, Oil plc would expect to undertake around 20 surveys.

When oil is found to be present, it can be sold to the refining company for £20 per barrel. On average, the amount of oil extracted is 10,000 barrels. It is the policy of the company not to drill if a survey result is negative.

If no oil is found to be present, the sales revenue is obviously zero.

Requirements

(a) Assuming that 20 surveys are undertaken during the next year, use a decision tree to determine whether Oil plc should continue to use its existing survey equipment or buy the new equipment available from Seismik plc.

(8 marks)

(b) If the cost of buying the new equipment from Seismik plc were to change, of what price would the equipment need to be in order for Oil plc to be indifferent between using its existing equipment and buying the new equipment?

(2 marks)
(Total = 10 marks)

8.16 NP plc (IDEC 5/02 (Amended))

NP plc is a company that operates a number of different businesses. Each separate business operates its own costing system, which has been selected to suit the particular needs of that business. Data is transferred to Head Office for weekly management control purposes.

NP plc is considering investing in a project named Fantazia, which is a pleasure park consisting of a covered dome and external fun rides. The cost of the dome, which is a covered frame that can be dismantled and erected elsewhere or stored, is £20 million. NP plc is considering two sites for the dome: London or Manchester. The cost of acquiring the land and installing the equipment is expected to be £20 million for the London site and £9 million for the Manchester site.

A market research survey shows that if Fantazia were to be situated in London, there is a 0.5 chance of getting 1.2 million visitors a year for the next four years and a 0.5 chance of getting only 0.8 million visitors a year. Each visitor to the London site is expected to spend £25 on average. This comprises a £10 entrance fee which includes access to fun rides, £10 on souvenir merchandise and £5 on food and drink.

If Fantazia were to be situated in Manchester, there is a 0.4 chance of getting 1.2 million visitors a year for the next four years and a 0.6 chance of getting only 0.8 million visitors. Each visitor to the Manchester site is expected to spend £23 on average. This comprises £9 entrance fee, £10 on merchandise and £4 on food and drink.

The average cost of servicing each visitor (i.e. providing rides, merchandise and food and drink) at both sites is estimated to be £10.

After four years, the dome could be kept in operation for a further four years or dismantled. If the dome is kept on the same site, it is estimated that visitor numbers will fall by 0.1 million a year. This means that London would have a 0.5 chance of 1.1 million visitors and a 0.5 chance of 0.7 million visitors in each of Years 5 to 8, and Manchester a 0.4 chance of 1.1 million visitors and a 0.6 chance of 0.7 million visitors.

If the dome were to be dismantled after four years, it could be stored at a cost of £0.5 million a year, sold for £4 million or transferred to the other site. The number of visitors and revenue received at this site would be as predicted for Years 1 to 4.

The cost of dismantling the dome and equipment would be £3 million and the cost of moving and re-erecting it would be £9 million.

The purchase or sale price of the land at the end of Year 4 would be: London £14 million and Manchester £10 million. At the end of Year 8, the dome's resale value would be zero and all land values would be as four years previously.

The final cost of dismantling the dome and equipment would be £2 million.

NP plc uses a discount rate of 10% when evaluating all projects.

Requirements

(a) Assuming that NP plc intends to terminate the Fantazia project *after four years*:

(i) Draw a decision tree to show the options open to NP plc.

(3 marks)

(ii) Calculate which option would generate the highest NPV. (Use either the decision tree or another method.)

(5 marks)

(b) Assuming that NP plc chose the most advantageous option for Years 1 to 4, determined in your answer to (a)(ii) above,

(i) Draw a decision tree for Years 5 to 8, showing the options open to NP plc if Fantazia is not terminated after four years.

(3 marks)

(ii) Calculate which of these options generates the highest NPV over Years 5 to 8.

(5 marks)

(c) Advise the company which options it should select in order to maximise NPV over the full eight years of the project. State what that NPV would be.

(5 marks)

(d) Discuss how customer profitability analysis could be used by Fantazia in order to assess visitor profitability.

(4 marks)

(Total = 25 marks)

✓ Answers

8.1 **D**

(i) Is correct. Even if an expected value is a small positive result, some businesses might still not go ahead with the decision due to their risk-averse nature. They may wish to see a fairly large positive expected value in order to go ahead.

(ii) Is correct. A weakness of using expected values for decision-making is that the expected value and hence the decision being made are sensitive to the probabilities being used and these can be difficult to derive in practice.

(iii) Is incorrect. Negative values, such as negative cash flows if calculating an expected cash flow for NPV purposes, can be used. A negative value will have an impact upon the overall value that results.

(iv) Is incorrect. Even if the expected value is a loss it can still be used for decision-making purposes. In fact most businesses would decide not to go ahead (subject to any other non-financial considerations such as reaction of customers, reaction of competitors, etc.).

8.2 **D**

The expected value is arrived at by multiplying each scrap value by its probability and then add up the resulting figures as follows:

(1) Scrap value £	*(2)* Probability	*(1) × (2)* £
40,000	0.3	12,000
50,000	0.4	20,000
65,000	0.2	13,000
78,000	0.1	7,800
	Total	52,800

8.3 **C**

The expected value should be calculated for each product, and is arrived at by multiplying each sales revenue value by its probability and then add up the resulting figures as follows:

Boots

(1) £	*(2)* Probability	*(1) × (2)* £
40,000	0.20	8,000
50,000	0.50	25,000
65,000	0.10	6,500
78,000	0.20	15,600
	Total	55,100

Sandals

(1)	*(2)*		*(1) × (2)*
£	*Probability*		£
28,000	0.10		2,800
37,000	0.10		3,700
59,000	0.05		2,950
95,000	0.75		71,250
		Total	80,700

Shoes

(1)	*(2)*		*(1) × (2)*
£	*Probability*		£
32,000	0.45		14,400
42,000	0.35		14,700
52,000	0.05		2,600
62,000	0.15		9,300
		Total	41,000

So highest expected revenue is generated by Sandals followed by Boots.

The lowest expected revenue is generated by Shoes.

So the order of production should be:

Sandals then Boots then Shoes.

8.4 **B**

Answer A is incorrect. The expected value might be equal to one of the possible outcomes, but this is unlikely to be the case.

Answer B is correct. The expected value is calculated by multiplying each possible outcome by its probability and adding the resulting amounts together. It is an average where probabilities are used as weighting factors.

Answer C is incorrect. The expected value might be equal to one of the possible outcomes but this is unlikely to be the case.

Answer D is incorrect. Even if an expected value is a small positive result, some businesses might still not go ahead with the decision due to their risk averse nature. They may wish to see a fairly large positive expected value in order to go ahead.

Answer E is incorrect. The expected value is a weighted average NOT a simple average.

8.5 **B**

We need to find the Project with the highest expected value. The expected values are as follows:

£'000:

Project L
$0.2 \times 500 + 0.5 \times 470 + 0.3 \times 550 = 500$

Project M
$0.2 \times 400 + 0.5 \times 550 + 0.3 \times 570 = 526$

Project N
$0.2 \times 450 + 0.5 \times 400 + 0.3 \times 475 = 432.5$

Project O
$0.2 \times 360 + 0.5 \times 400 + 0.3 \times 420 = 398$

Project P
$0.2 \times 600 + 0.5 \times 500 + 0.3 \times 425 = 497.5$

Project with the highest expected value should be undertaken, and this is project M.

8.6 **D**

If X Ltd had perfect information about market conditions, that is, if it knew with certainty what the market conditions were going to be, it could make better decisions. In fact, if it knew what the market conditions were going to be, it could choose the best option for those conditions. It would be prepared to pay for this perfect information an amount up to the financial benefit it derives from having the information.

If the company knew that market conditions were going to be *poor*, of all the projects available, project P gives the best result with cash inflows of £600,000.

Similarly, if the company knew that market conditions were going to be *good*, of all the projects available, project M gives the best result with cash inflows of £550,000.

And if the company knew that market conditions were going to be *excellent*, of all the projects available, project M once again gives the best result with cash inflows of £570,000.

So we have the following cash inflows for the different market conditions:

Market conditions	*Cash inflows* £'000
Poor	600
Good	550
Excellent	570

However, the company will only know that conditions will be poor 20% of the time (probability of it happening is 0.2). It will only know that conditions will be good 50% of the time (probability of it happening is 0.5), and that conditions will be excellent 30% of the time (probability of it happening is 0.3).

So even with perfect information there is an expected value, which is:

$0.2 \times 600 + 0.5 \times 550 + 0.3 \times 570 = 566$

From the previous question, without perfect information the highest expected value was £526(000).

So the benefit or value of the perfect information to the company is

£566,000 − £526,000 = £40,000

8.7 **B**

(i) Is correct. It is an integral part of the expected value technique.
(ii) Is incorrect. It is important to consider non-financial issues such as reaction of customers and competitors when making the final decision. However, the

expected value technique does not take account of these non-financial issues. That is why they must be considered separately.

(iii) Is correct. It is an integral part of the expected value technique.

(iv) Is incorrect. It is important to consider sensitivity of cash flows and probabilities when making the final decision. However, the expected value technique does not take account of these sensitivities. Sensitivity analysis is undertaken after the expected value has been calculated based upon a set of financial outcomes and probabilities. These financial outcomes and probabilities can then be altered to see what effect such alterations would have on the expected value and the decision to be made.

8.8 **E**

We need to calculate the existing level of profit and then calculate the possible levels of profit after the change in selling price, so that we can see under which circumstances the profit will have increased.

Existing level of profit before change in selling price:

Sales revenue	(90,000 units × £50)	£4,500,000
Less:		
Variable costs	(90,000 units × £21)	£1,890,000
Less:		
Fixed costs		£1,200,000
Profit		£1,410,000

If the price is reduced, the following table sets out the possible price and variable cost combinations and their probabilities:

Sales demand	*Variable cost per unit*	*Probability*	*Contribution*	*Fixed cost*	*Profit*
Units			(£45 − VC) × number of units		
100,000	£20	0.45 × 0.40 = 0.18	£2,500,000	£1,200,000	£1,300,000
100,000	£18	0.45 × 0.60 = 0.27	£2,700,000	£1,200,000	£1,500,000
120,000	£20	0.55 × 0.40 = 0.22	£3,000,000	£1,200,000	£1,800,000
120,000	£18	0.55 × 0.60 = 0.33	£3,240,000	£1,200,000	£2,040,000

So the profit will increase when sales are 100,000 units and variable cost is £18, and when sales are 120,000 units and variable cost is £20, and when sales are 120,000 units and variable cost is £18.

The probability of increase in profit is therefore:

0.27 + 0.22 + 0.33 = 0.82

8.9 **C**

Using the probability table we produced in the answer to question 8.8 above

Level of profit	*Probability*		*Expected value*
£1,300,000	0.18		£234,000
£1,500,000	0.27		£405,000
£1,800,000	0.22		£396,000
£2,040,000	0.33		£673,200
		Total	£1,708,200

8.10 **E**

(i) Is correct.
(ii) Is correct.
(iii) Is incorrect. Probabilities are assigned to each OUTCOME point.
(iv) Is correct.

8.11 **B**

We must compare the expected cost of purchasing the photocopiers with the expected cost of using the external copying company.

The maximum that the external copying company charges will be the cost per page copied such that these two options have the same overall cost.

Expected cost of investing in new photocopiers:

Cost of photocopiers = £2,400,000

Expected cost per page for toner and maintenance
(5,000,000 × 0.7 + 3,000,000 × 0.3) × 5 pence = 22,000,000 pence = £220,000

So, total cost of investing in new photocopiers:
£2,400,000 + £220,000 = £2,620,000

If the photocopying is undertaken by the external copying company, the cost for all pages to be copied cannot exceed £2,620,000.

Expected number of copies to be made:
7,000,000 × 0.6 + 4,000,000 × 0.4 = 5,800,000

Therefore, maximum charge per page:
£2,620,000 ÷ 5,800,000 per page = 45.2 pence per page

8.12 **D**

To calculate the lowest possible value for the probability of *high sales* if money were to be spent on upgrading the existing premises, we must first calculate the expected value for investing in new premises.

We can work out the missing probability knowing that the expected value when upgrading the existing premises must be at least the same as the expected value for investing in new premises.

Expected value for investing in brand new premises:
(£4m × 0.6 + £2m × 0.4) less cost of £2m
= £3.2m − £2m
= £1.2m

Expected value if existing premises are upgraded:
Let us say that the probability of high sales is "P"
Then the probability of low sales will be "1 − P"

So the expected value will be
$3,000,000 \times P + 1,000,000 \times (1 - P)$ less cost of £1,500,000
$= 3,000,000 \times P + 1,000,000 - 1,000,000 \times P - 1,500,000$
$= 2,000,000 \times P - 500,000$

For the two expected values to be equal to each other:

$1,200,000 = 2,000,000 \times P - 500,000$

So,
$1,700,000 = 2,000,000 \times P$

$P = 1,700,000 \div 2,000,000 = 0.85$

8.13 **D**

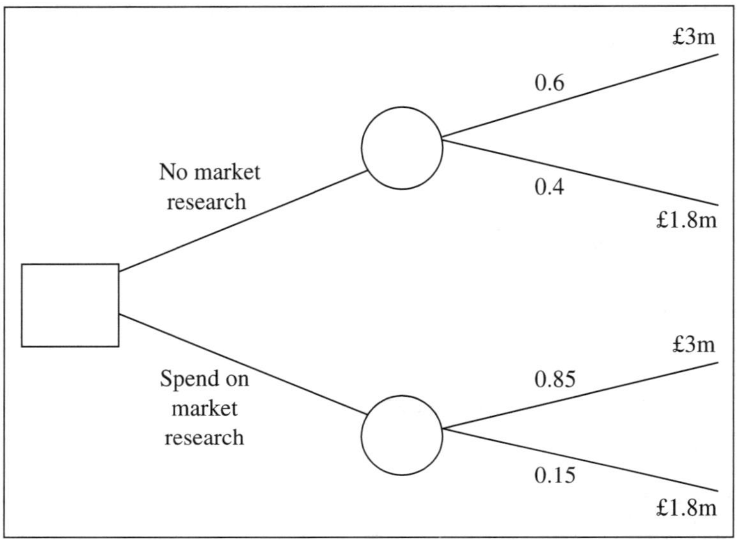

Expected value *if not* spent on market research is:
$0.6 \times 3,000,000 + 0.4 \times 1,800,000 =$ £2,520,000

Expected value *if* spent on market research is:
$0.85 \times 3,000,000 + 0.15 \times 1,800,000 =$ £2,820,000

Biggles will be better of by £300,000 if it undertakes market research.

This is therefore the maximum it should be prepared to pay for the market research.

8.14 **B**

If the owner does NOT attend the exhibition:

Sales revenue = £20,000

If the owner does attend the exhibition:

expected value of sales revenue is: $0.3 \times 60,000 + 0.7 \times 20,000 =$ £32,000

But the cost of attending the exhibition is £6,000

so expected profit if the owner attends exhibition = £32,000 − £6,000 = £26,000

Therefore, by attending the exhibition the owner will be better off by:

£26,000 − £20,000 = £6,000

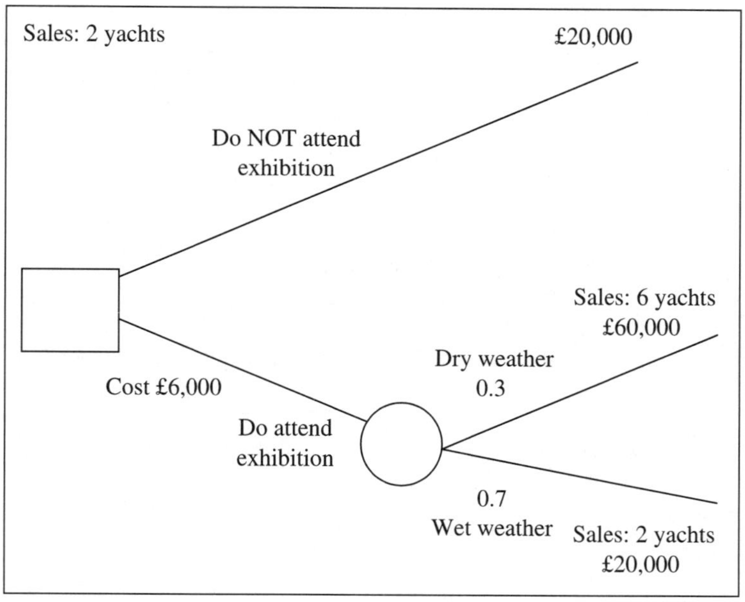

8.15

Topic being tested

Making decisions using decision tree analysis.

Approach

Draw the decision tree from left to right.
Ensure that you distinguish between decision points and chance points on the tree.
Place revenues, costs and probabilities onto the tree.
Use letters to denote the decision and chance points for referencing purposes (A to I in this example – see solution).
Work backwards, that is, from far right to far left calculating expected values at the chance points and stating the decision to be made at decision points.
Draw a conclusion.

Solution

(a) The company needs to decide whether to survey for oil using its existing survey equipment or buy new equipment that has become available.

Decision tree:

Notation:

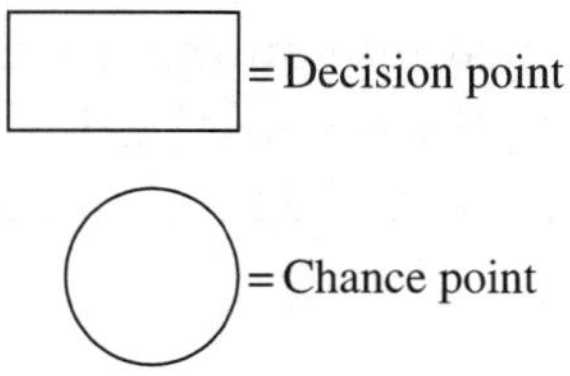

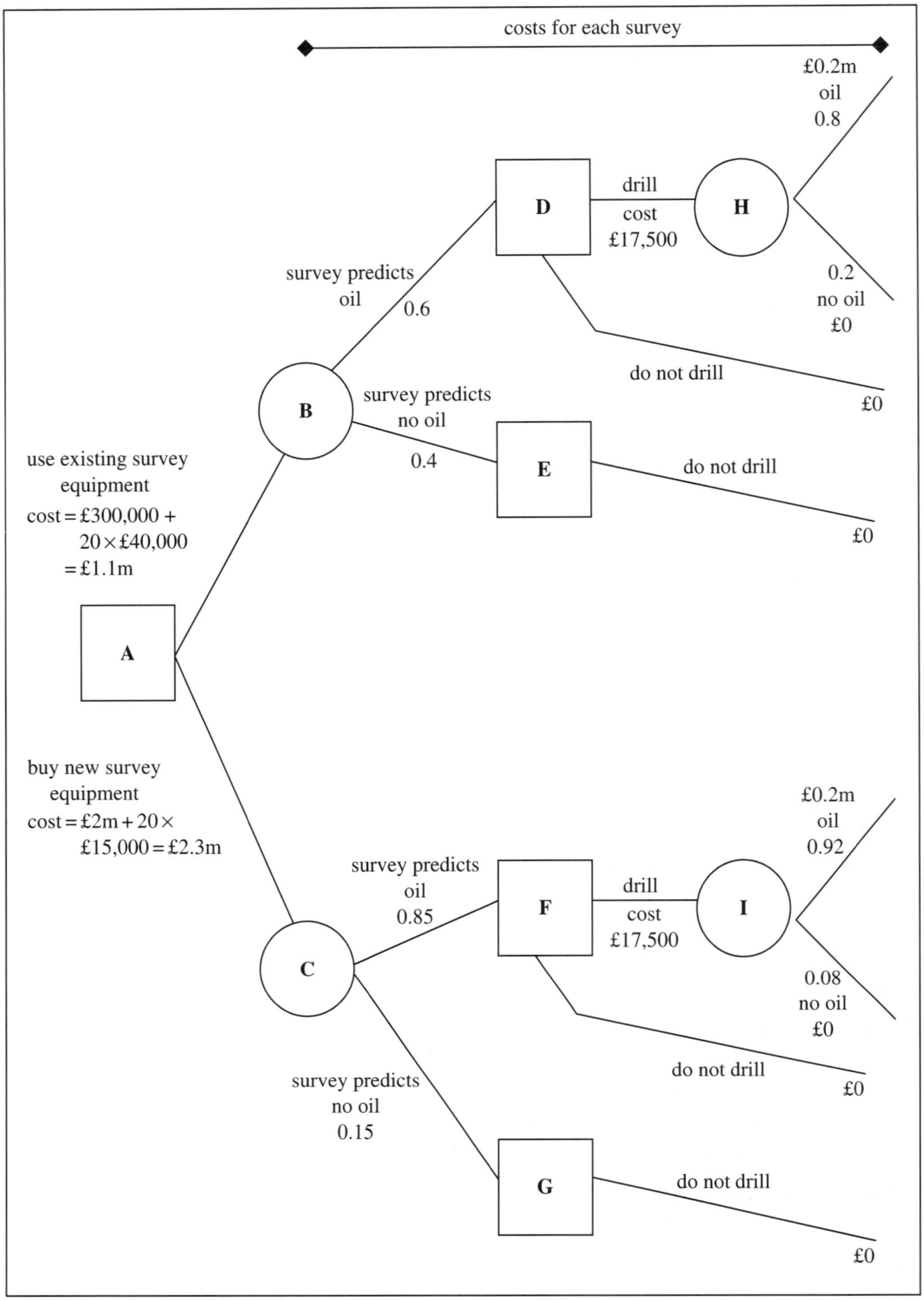

Note: Strictly speaking decision boxes E and G could be omitted from the diagram as there is no decision to be made.

The original cost of the existing equipment of £1.4 million is non-relevant since it is a sunk cost. However, the disposal value of £300,000 is relevant since this is the disposal proceeds that would be forgone if the existing equipment is continued to be used for surveys.

Calculation of expected values and discussion of decisions to be made:

Expected value at chance Point H

$0.8 \times £0.2m + 0.2 \times £0 = £160{,}000$ per survey

Expected value at chance Point I

$0.92 \times £0.2m + 0.08 \times £0 = £184{,}000$ per survey

Decision at D is to drill for oil since net revenue will be £160,000 − £17,500 = £142,500 per survey. The decision at E is not to drill for oil.

Decision at F is to drill for oil since net revenue will be £184,000 − £17,500 = £166,500 per survey. The decision at G is not to drill for oil.

Expected value at chance Point B

$$\begin{aligned}0.6 \times \text{value at D} + 0.4 \times \text{value at E} &= 0.6 \times £142{,}500 + 0.4 \times £0 \\ &= £85{,}500 \text{ per survey}\end{aligned}$$

Expected value at chance Point C

$$\begin{aligned}0.85 \times \text{value at F} + 0.15 \times \text{value at G} &= 0.85 \times £166{,}500 + 0.15 \times £0 \\ &= £141{,}525 \text{ per survey}\end{aligned}$$

So value at B for 20 surveys is:
20 surveys × £85,500 = £1,710,000

And value at C for 20 surveys is:
20 surveys × £141,525 = £2,830,500

Decision at A is:

Either
continue to use existing equipment – cost £1.1 million
Expected value at B of £1,710,000
so expected future profit of £610,000

or
buy new equipment – cost £2.3 million
Expected value at C of £2,830,500
so expected future profit of £530,500

Conclusion

The company should continue to use the existing equipment, on the grounds of expected values, since the company will be £79,500 better off by doing so.
(This is the same as almost £4,000 per survey (£79,500 ÷ 20 surveys).)

(b) The company would be indifferent between buying the new survey equipment and continuing to use the existing equipment if the future profit were the same for each option.

Future profit if it uses the existing equipment (from solution for Part (a)) is £610,000.

Let the cost of the new equipment be £*N*, then future profit with the new equipment would be

Cost of new equipment	(*N*)
Cost of 20 surveys	(300,000)
Expected value at Point C	2,830,500
	2,530,500 − *N*

So to be indifferent, the cost of new equipment woule be:
$2{,}530{,}500 - N = 610{,}000$

So,
$N = 2{,}530{,}500 - 610{,}000 = 1{,}920{,}500$

So the maximum cost of the new survey equipment is £1,920,500

(Alternative approach: It is currently better to continue to use the existing equipment by £79,500. So the cost of the new equipment would have to fall by £79,500 to a new price of £2,000,000 − £79,500 = £1,920,500

This approach is obviously a lot quicker!)

8.16

Cumulative discount rate
- Years 1 to 4 = 3.169
- Years 5 to 8 = 2.165

Contribution

– London	£25 − £10 = £15
– Manchester	£23 − £10 = £13

(a) (i) Ignoring the time value of money.

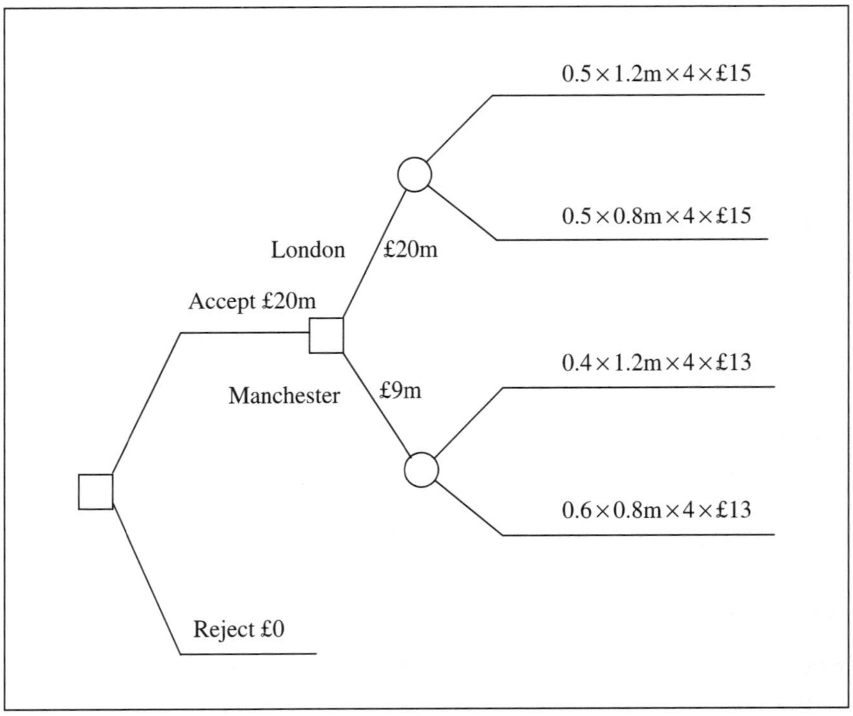

(ii)

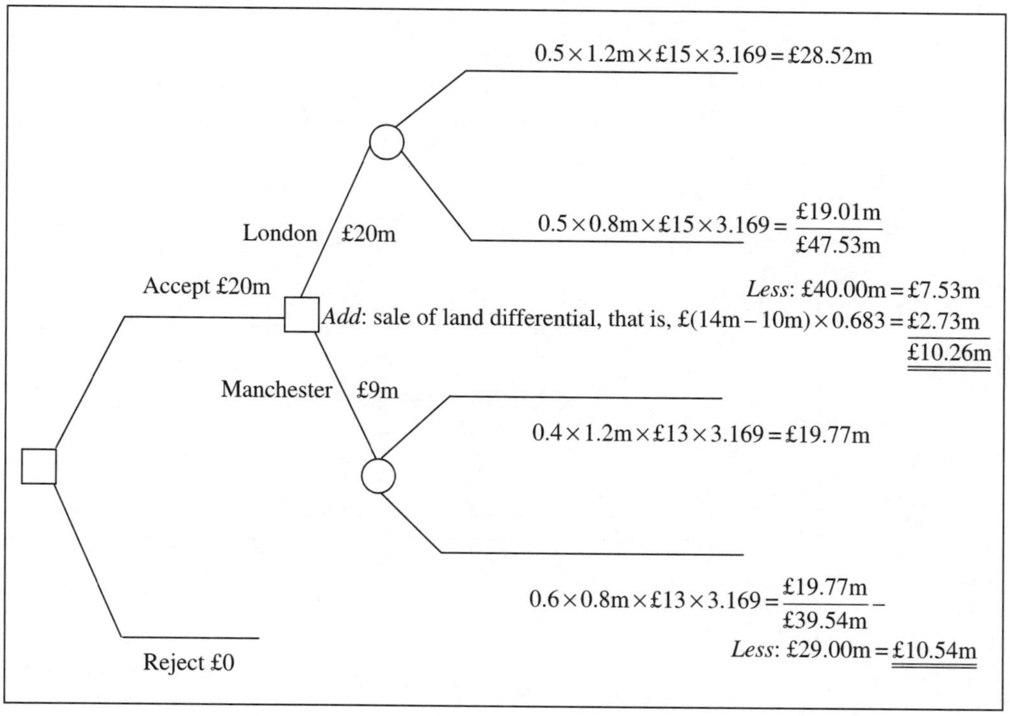

Therefore, Manchester is just the better option by £0.28m

(b) (i) Ignoring the time value of money.

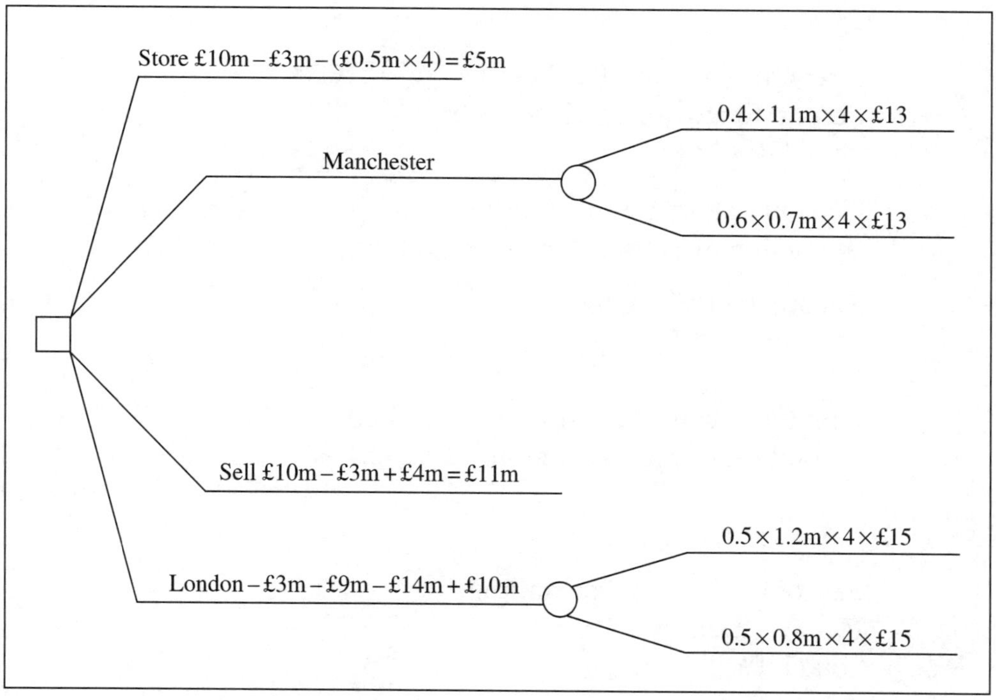

(ii)

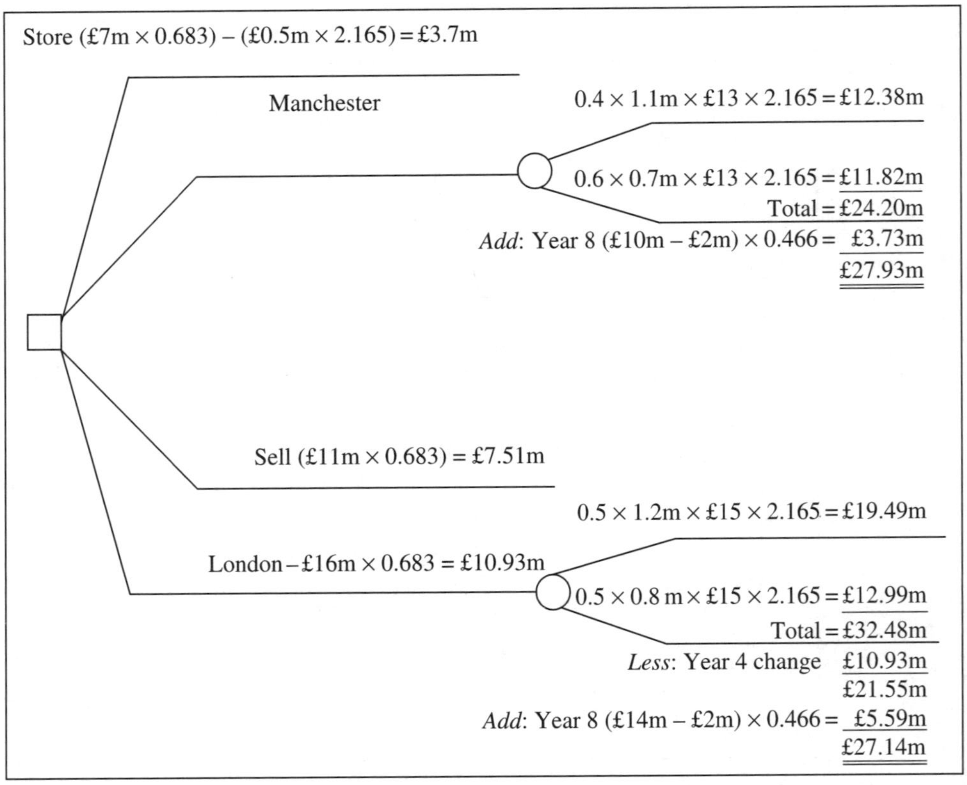

Therefore, keeping Fantazia in Manchester generates the higher NPV by a small margin.

(c) Based on *requirement* (b), NP plc should site Fantazia in Manchester for eight years.

The total NPV will be:

	£m
First four years at Manchester	10.54
Second four years at Manchester	27.93
Total NPV	38.47

The only alternative option that may produce a greater NPV is to site Fantazia in London in Years 1–4 and keep it there during Years 5–8:

The total NPV will be:

	£m		
First four years at London	7.53		
Second four years at London	29.23 ←	0.5 × 1.1 × £15 × 2.165	17.86
		0.5 × 0.7 × £15 × 2.165	11.37
			29.23
Sale of land net of dismantling:			
(£14m − £2m) × 0.466 =	5.59		
Total NPV	42.35		

The best option is to site Fantazia in London.

(d) Fantazia may use customer profitability analysis (CPA). Visitors should be divided into a number of different categories/market segments, such as family card, parties, teenagers, and their selection of rides and spending on merchandise and food monitored and a profitability per segment calculated. This information could be used to identify which rides appeal to which segment and promotion policies could be based on this.

In order to get the information required for CPA, activity based costing could be used to cost the different activities that different types of customer use to a greater or lesser extent. As rides are not priced individually, their profitability cannot be assessed, but their popularity and "cost" can be. However, this "cost" is likely to be based on marginal, rather than total cost because it is unlikely that many fixed costs could be apportioned accurately using cost drivers.

It is the type of visitor/entrance ticket attracted that will increase profitability. Therefore, it is recommended that Fantazia assesses its requirements in order to determine customer profitability and selects the costing system on that basis.

In order to increase profitability by controlling/reducing costs, each ride will need to be assessed in terms of opening hours and staff involved and this should be compared with a measure of visitor appeal.

Costing

9

Costing involves the calculation of cost per unit for the range of a company's goods and services. In addition to the traditional absorption and marginal costing, there are a number of newer alternatives.

> *Activity based budgeting/costing*
>
> A form of management that tries to establish the links between costs and units by examining the activities that cause those costs, improving control.
>
> Decisions are of better quality since cost information reflects resource usage, and performance should be enhanced since control is emphasised through management structures.

> *Target costing*
>
> This is a reversal of the traditional cost plus pricing system where the selling price is based on existing cost levels plus a mark-up. In target costing the starting point is the selling price, appropriate profits are then deducted and the result is the target cost.
>
> The company should improve its customer focus (by starting with the customer) as well as improving cost control (costs increases cannot be passed on to the customer). In essence the product is designed around the cost.

> *Life cycle costing*
>
> Increasingly companies are finding that costs of new products are incurred in the early stages of the life cycle. Traditional reporting systems tend to use arbitrary time periods to match costs and revenues. Life cycle costing attempts to match costs with revenues over whatever time period is appropriate.
>
> Making this link enables a company to properly ascertain the overall profitability of a product and improve future decision-making.

Questions

9.1 A laboratory which does blood testing is intending to use ABC system to obtain accurate information regarding the three tests undertaken.

It has maintenance costs of £93,840 which are related to the equipment used for the testing of the blood. The cost driver for the maintenance expenditure is taken as the number of stages in tests undertaken.

Information about each test and the number of stages required is given below.

Test	*GL*	*BD*	*XS*
Total tests undertaken	8,000	3,000	5,000
Number of stages	3	4	2

What is the maintenance cost for each test of type BD?

A £2.04
B £5.87
C £8.16
D £10.43

(2 marks)

9.2 Grant plc has struggled with low profits in recent years and so is undertaking a major overhaul of its systems. It is replacing its production process with a more highly automated one and adopting a target costing approach.

A summary of the changes is given below.

	Current system	*New system*
Selling price	£41	£35
Variable cost per unit	£26	£8
Fixed cost per annum (excluding depreciation)	£185,000	?
Capital equipment	£1.7m	£4.4m
Life expectancy	5 years	8 years
Sales volume	40,000 per annum	90,000 per annum

The company holds no stock and uses straight line depreciation.

What is the target fixed cost (excluding depreciation) for annual production if the company intends to achieve five times its current profit?

A £355,000
B £925,000
C £1,505,000
D £2,055,000

(3 marks)

9.3 A company is changing its costing system from traditional absorption costing (AC) based on labour hours to ABC system.

It has overheads of £156,000 which are related to taking material deliveries.

The delivery information about each product is given below.

Product	X	Y	Z
Total units required	1,000	2,000	3,000
Delivery size	200	400	1,000

Total labour costs are £360,000 for 45,000 hours. Each unit of each product takes the same number of direct hours.

Assuming that the company uses the number of deliveries as its cost driver, calculate the increase or decrease in unit costs for Z arising from the change from AC to ABC.

A £0.50 increase
B £0.50 decrease
C £14.00 increase
D £14.00 decrease

(3 marks)

9.4 The following statements relate to the justification of the use of life cycle costing.

(i) Product life cycles are becoming increasingly short. This means that the initial costs are an increasingly important component in the product's overall costs.
(ii) Product costs are increasingly weighted to the start of a product's life cycle, and to properly understand the profitability of a product these costs must be matched to the ultimate revenues.
(iii) The high costs of (for example) research, design and marketing in the early stages in a product's life cycle necessitate a high initial selling price.

Which of these statements are substantially true?

A (i) and (ii) only
B (ii) and (iii) only
C (i) and (iii) only
D all of them

(2 marks)

9.5 A company is designing a new version of its best selling product, to be called "Widget4u". Estimated information regarding this product is shown below.

Design costs (viewed as capital)	£158,000
Production equipment costs	£982,000
Annual fixed costs (excluding depreciation)	£28,000
Variable costs	£8 per unit
Selling price	£34 per unit
Target sales	10,000 units per annum
Life	5 years
Required return on capital	15%

What is the target cost for annual production?

A £80,000
B £112,000
C £169,000
D £336,000

(3 marks)

9.6 LM Hospital (IDEC 5/01 (Amended))

LM Hospital is a private hospital, whose management is considering the adoption of an ABC system for the year 2001/02. The main reason for its introduction would be to provide more accurate information for pricing purposes. With the adoption of new medical technology, the amount of time that some patients stay in hospital has decreased considerably, and the management feels that the current pricing strategy may no longer reflect the different costs incurred.

Prices are currently calculated by determining the direct costs for the particular type of operation and adding a mark-up of 135%. With the proposed ABC system, the management expects to use a mark-up for pricing purposes of 15% on cost. This percentage will be based on all costs except facility sustaining costs. It has been decided that the hospital support activities should be grouped into three categories – admissions and record keeping, caring for patients and facility sustaining.

The hospital has four operating theatres that are used for 9 hours a day for 300 days a year. It is expected that 7,200 operations will be performed during the coming year. The hospital has 15 consultant surgeons engaged in operating theatre work and consultancy. It is estimated that each consultant surgeon will work at the hospital for 2,000 hours in 2001/02.

The expected costs for 2001/02 are:

	£
Nursing services and administration	9,936,000
Linen and laundry	920,000
Kitchen and food costs (3 meals a day)	2,256,000
Consultant surgeons' fees	5,250,000
Insurance of buildings and general equipment	60,000
Depreciation of buildings and general equipment	520,000
Operating theatre	4,050,000
Pre-operation costs	1,260,000
Medical supplies – used in the hospital wards	1,100,000
Pathology laboratory (where blood tests etc. are carried out)	920,000
Updating patient records	590,000
Patient / bed scheduling	100,000
Invoicing and collections	160,000
Housekeeping activities, including ward maintenance, window cleaning, etc.	760,000

Other information for 2001/02:

Nursing hours	480,000
Number of pathology laboratory tests	8,000
Patient days	44,000
Number of patients	9,600

Information relating to specific operations for 2001/02:

	ENT (Ear, nose and throat)	*Cataract*
Time of stay in hospital	4 days	1 day
Operation time	2 hours	0.5 hour
Consultant surgeon's time (which includes time in the operating theatre)	3 hours	0.85 hour

Requirement

Before making the final decision on the costing/pricing system, management has selected two types of operation for review: an ENT operation and a cataract operation.

Calculate the prices that would be charged under each method for the two types of operation. (Your answer should include an explanation and calculations of the cost drivers you have used.)

(10 marks)

9.7 Exe plc is a motor car manufacturer. Exe plc has been in business for many years, and it has recently invested heavily in automated processes. It continues to use a total costing system for pricing, based on recovering overheads by a labour hour absorption rate.

Exe plc is currently experiencing difficulties in maintaining its market share. It is therefore considering various options to improve the quality of its motor cars, and the quality of its service to its customers. It is also investigating its present pricing policy, which is based on the costs attributed to each motor car.

Requirement

Explain the benefits (or otherwise) that an ABC system would give Exe plc.

(10 marks)

9.8 S&P Products plc (IDEC 11/01 (Amended))

S&P Products plc purchases a range of good quality gift and household products from around the world; it then sells these products through "mail order" or retail outlets. The company receives "mail orders" by post, telephone and Internet. Retail outlets are either department stores or S&P Products plc's own small shops. The company started to set up its own shops after a recession in the early 1990s and regards them as the flagship of its business; sales revenue has gradually built up over the last 10 years. There are now 50 department stores and 10 shops.

The company has made good profits over the last few years but recently trading has been difficult. As a consequence, the management team has decided that a fundamental reappraisal of the business is now necessary if the company is to continue trading.

Meanwhile the budgeting process for the coming year is proceeding. S&P Products plc uses an ABC system and the following estimated cost information for the coming year is available:

Retail outlet costs:

Activity	Cost driver	Rate per cost driver (£)	Number per annum	
			Department store	Own shop
Phone queries and requests to S&P	Calls	15	40	350
Sales visits to shops and stores by S&P sales staff	Visits	250	2	4
Shop orders	Orders	20	25	150
Packaging	Deliveries	100	28	150
Delivery to shops	Deliveries	150	28	150

Staffing, rental and service costs for each of S&P Products plc's own shops cost on average £300,000 a year.

Mail order costs:

		Rate per cost driver (£)		
Activity	**Cost driver**	**Post**	**Phone**	**Internet**
Processing "mail orders"	Orders	5	6	3
Dealing with "mail order" queries	Orders	4	4	1
Number of packages per order				
Packaging and deliveries for "mail orders" – cost per package £10	Packages	2	2	1

The total number of orders through the whole "mail order" business for the coming year is expected to be 80,000. The maintenance of the Internet link is estimated to cost £80,000 for the coming year.

The following additional information for the coming year has been prepared:

	Department store	Own shop	Post	Phone	Internet
Sales revenue per outlet	£50,000	£1,000,000			
Sales revenue per order			£150	£300	£100
Gross margin: mark-up on purchase cost	30%	40%	40%	40%	40%
Number of outlets	50	10			
Percentage of "mail orders"			30%	60%	10%

Expected head office and warehousing costs for the coming year:

	£
Warehouse	2,750,000
IT	550,000
Administration	750,000
Personnel	300,000
	4,350,000

Requirements

(a) (i) Prepare calculations that will show the expected profitability of the different types of sales outlet for the coming year.

(13 marks)

(ii) Comment briefly on the results of the figures you have prepared.

(3 marks)

(b) In relation to the company's fundamental reappraisal of its business,

(i) Discuss how helpful the information you have prepared in (a) is for this purpose, and how it might be revised or expanded so that it is of more assistance.

(7 marks)

(ii) State whether you think the profitability figures you have obtained are suitable for deciding whether part of the business should be discontinued.

(2 marks)
(Total = 25 marks)

9.9 MANPAC (IDEC 11/03)

SY Ltd, a manufacturer of computer games, has developed a new game called the MANPAC. This is an interactive 3D game and is the first of its kind to be introduced to the market. SY Ltd is due to launch the MANPAC in time for the peak selling season.

Traditionally SY Ltd has priced its games based on standard manufacturing cost plus selling and administration cost plus a profit margin. However, the management team of SY Ltd has recently attended a computer games conference where everyone was talking about life cycle costing, target costing and market-based pricing approaches. The team has returned from the conference and would like more details on the topics they heard about and how they could have been applied to the MANPAC.

Requirements

As Management Accountant of SY Ltd,

(a) Discuss how the following techniques could have been applied to the MANPAC:

- life cycle costing
- target costing.

(8 marks)

(b) Evaluate the market-based pricing strategies that should have been considered for the launch of the MANPAC and recommend a strategy that should have been chosen.

(6 marks)

(c) Explain each stage in the life cycle of the MANPAC and the issues that the management team will need to consider at each stage. Your answer should include a diagram to illustrate the product life cycle of the MANPAC.

(11 marks)
(Total = 25 marks)

9.10 Standard (IDEC 5/02)

Standard costing and target costing have little in common for the following reasons:

- the former is a costing system and the latter is not
- target costing is proactive and standard costing is not
- target costs are agreed by all and are rigorously adhered to, whereas standard costs are usually set without wide consultation.

Requirements

(a) Discuss the comparability of standard costing and target costing by considering the validity of the statements above.

(18 marks)

A pharmaceutical company, which operates a standard costing system, is considering introducing target costing.

(b) Discuss whether the company should do this and whether the two systems would be compatible.

(7 marks)
(Total = 25 marks)

Answers

9.1 **C**

ABC	Number of stages for GL	8,000 × 3	24,000
	Number of stages for BD	3,000 × 4	12,000
	Number of stages for XS	5,000 × 2	10,000
	Total		46,000

Cost per stage	£93,840 ÷ 46,000	£2.04
Cost per test of BD	£2.04 × 4 stages	£8.16

9.2 **C**

First we will calculate existing profit and multiply by 5. We can then look at the contribution required. Fixed costs need to include depreciation when calculating profit.

	£
Current contribution (41 − 26) × 40,000	£600,000
Current fixed costs £185,000 + £1.7m ÷ 5 years	£525,000
Current profit	£75,000
Expected contribution (35 − 8) × 90,000	£2,430,000
Target profit 5 × £75,000	£375,000
Target fixed costs	£2,055,000
Depreciation £4.4m ÷ 8 years	£550,000
Target fixed costs	£1,505,000

9.3 **D**

It is worth noting that the labour cost is not needed here: it is a direct cost and will not change, regardless of the method used.

We will calculate the overhead cost per unit under both systems and calculate the difference.

AC since the time per unit is the same for each product, the overheads per unit will also be the same.

£156,000 ÷ 6,000 units			£26
(you would get the same answer using labour hours)			

ABC	Number of deliveries for X	1,000 ÷ 200	5
	Number of deliveries for Y	2,000 ÷ 400	5
	Number of deliveries for Z	3,000 ÷ 1,000	3
	Total		13

Cost per delivery	£156,000 ÷ 13	£12,000	
Cost per unit of Z	£12,000 ÷ 1,000 units		£4
Decrease	£26 − £12		£14

9.4 **A**

(i) This is true, justifying the time and effort of life cycle costing.
(ii) As above.
(iii) This is not true: life cycle costing is not about setting selling prices, it is about linking total revenues to total costs. Even if it were about setting a selling price, the early sales may well be at a loss since it is TOTAL revenues and costs that are considered. Furthermore, the pre-launch costs are sunk at launch and are therefore irrelevant when setting a selling price.

9.5 **C**

The target cost is the expected sale proceeds less required profit. Note that the annual cost information (and depreciation) given is irrelevant.

		£
Expected revenue	£34 × 10,000	£340,000
Required profit	15% × (158,000 + 982,000)	£171,000
Target cost		£169,000

9.6

Direct costs:

Number of theatre hours	300 days × 4 theatres × 9 hours	10,800
Theatre cost per hour	£4,050,000 ÷ 10,800	£375
Pre-operation cost per operation	£1,260,000 ÷ 7,200	£175
Consultants' fees per hour	£5,250,000 ÷ (2,000 hours × 15)	£175

Indirect costs:

Caring for patients:	£'000
Nursing	9,936
Linen and laundry	920
Kitchen and food	2,256
Medical supplies	1,100
Pathology laboratory	920
	15,132

Patient care cost per day = £15,132,000 ÷ 44,000 days = £343.91

Admissions and record keeping:	£'000
Updating records	590
Patient/bed scheduling	100
Invoicing	160
	850

Admission costs per patient = £850,000 ÷ 9,600 patients = £88.54

Facility sustaining costs:	£'000
Housekeeping	760
Insurance of buildings etc.	60
Depreciation of buildings etc.	520
	1,340

> ! The indirect costs have been split into the three categories indicated in the question. The chosen cost driver for caring for patients is patient days, on the grounds that most of the costs placed in this category are dependent on the length of patient stay. Medical supplies and pathology laboratory do not fit well into this category and a more accurate accounting treatment would have been given if the information had been available.
>
> The chosen cost driver for admissions and record keeping is number of patients, on the grounds that these costs vary with the number of patients rather than their length of stay or type of illness.
>
> Facility sustaining costs have not been given a cost driver because the question says that the mark-up is to cover these costs. Either treatment is acceptable under ABC.

Price for an ENT operation:

	Existing method	*ABC*	
	£	£	£
Direct costs:			
Operation £375 × 2 hours	750.00		
Pre-operation costs	175.00		
Consultant's fee £175 × 3 hours	525.00		
	1,450.00		1,450.00
Mark-up on direct costs 135%	1,957.50		
ABC (Support costs):			
Patient care cost £343.91 × 4 days		1,375.64	
Admission costs		88.54	
			1,464.18
			2,914.18
Mark-up 15%			437.13
Price	3,407.50		3,351.31

Price for a cataract operation:

	Existing method	*ABC*	
	£	£	£
Direct costs:			
Operation £375 × 0.5 hour	187.50		
Pre-operation costs	175.00		
Consultant's fee £175 × 0.85 hour	148.75		
	511.25		511.25
Mark-up on direct costs 135%	690.19		
ABC (Support costs):			
Patient care cost £343.91 × 1 day		343.91	
Admission costs		88.54	
			432.45
			943.70
Mark-up 15%			141.56
Price	1,201.44		1,085.26

9.7 An ABC system is a form of absorption costing that dispenses with the arbitrary labour hours (or similar) as a basis for absorption and replaces it with a more realistic system based on the activities that cause the costs.

The benefits of this to Exe plc are set out below.

The cost split between products should be more realistic, helping to inform Exe plc's management as to which products are using more of the company's productive resources.

An understanding of the activities that cause costs should help the management of Exe plc to exercise better control over those activities and hence the costs.

Selling prices based on cost will now more realistically reflect the resources that went into producing the car being sold, helping to ensure that Exe plc becomes (more) profitable.

The adoption of ABC system can be part of a wider scheme encouraging everyone to focus on their customer, as required by TQM and similar approaches. It is clear that sales staff have customers but it should also be apparent that the Management Accountant has customers: managers. Managers need accurate reliable relevant information to help them fulfil their roles, ABC system should help provide this.

An ABC system will reflect the change in the nature of production: traditional manufacturing had a large direct labour component and thus using labour hours to absorb overheads was realistic, a change to ABC system will reinforce to management the changes in the company.

As car production becomes more customer focused, and customers demand ever more personalised products the complexity and diversity inherent in the system will be captured by the costing information.

Unfortunately ABC system suffers from some drawbacks.

It implies more than it can deliver: ABC system is still somewhat arbitrary. Managers may feel that this is the "correct" cost and make incorrect decisions because of this.

Activity based costing is more complex and time consuming than traditional approaches. It is not clear that its benefits are sufficiently high to ensure that it covers its own costs.

On balance an ABC system will probably benefit the company but it would become much more powerful if combined with JIT and TQM production systems.

9.8

(a) (i) *Calculation of net margin per type of outlet:*

	Department store £	*Own shop* £	*Post* £	*Mail order phone* £	*Internet* £
Sales revenue	50,000	1,000,000	150.00	300.00	100.00
Gross margin* (50,000 ÷ 1.30, etc.)	11,538	285,714	42.86	85.71	28.57
Less:					
Telephone queries		300,000			
Sales contacts (£15 × 40, etc.)	600	5,250			
Sales visits (£250 × 2, etc.)	500	1,000			
Orders (£20 × 25, etc.)	500	3,000			
Packaging (£100 × 28, etc.)	2,800	15,000			
Delivery (£150 × 28, etc.)	4,200	22,500			
Order cost			5.00	6.00	3.00
Queries			4.00	4.00	1.00
Packing, etc. (£10 × 2, etc.)			20.00	20.00	10.00
Internet cost					10.00
	8,600	346,750	29.00	30.00	24.00
Net margin	2,938	(61,036)	13.86	55.71	4.57
Net margin / sales	5.9%		9.2%	18.6%	4.6%

* Gross margin calculation for 30% of purchase cost: 100 = 0.3X + X

X = 76.92%

0.3X = 23.076%

£50,000 × 23.076% = £11,538

Tutorial note: You may prefer to take the view that if the margin is 30/100 of cost it must be 30/130 of sales, that is, 23.076%

Calculation of total margin for each type of outlet:

	Department stores £'000	*Own shops* £'000	*Post* £'000	*Mail order phone* £'000	*Internet* £'000	*Total* £'000
Total revenue	2,500	10,000	3,600	14,400	800	31,300
Total net margin	146.90	(610.36)	332.64	2,674.08	36.56	2,579.82

(ii) The calculations on the previous page show the following:

S&P's own shops will make a considerable "loss".

The department store sales will not generate as good a profit as the "mail order" side.

The telephone mail order, that is 46% of the business, will generate 104% of the current total profit.

The Internet business is not particularly profitable in the coming year, but it will presumably grow quite quickly. If this happens, the charge for maintaining the Internet, which is expressed by each order, will presumably decline as it is likely to be a semi-fixed cost.

Requirements

(b) (i) The calculations show the profitability of the different types of outlet for the coming year only, which is of some use. For example, it shows that S&P's own shops make a considerable loss and it would appear, on the surface, that the company would be better off without them, perhaps transferring the business to franchises within department stores. It also indicates that the emphasis of the business should be switched to the "mail order" side, as it is more profitable and, in particular, to the telephone section.

However, the latter shows how dangerous this kind of assumption can be because the telephone section may have peaked and, in future, growth in the Internet section may be at the expense of the telephone section. Therefore, decisions about future strategies cannot be made on predicted short-term costs and revenues. Any attempt to do so could prove disastrous. Growth in the market, competitors' moves, customers' needs and requirements must be the basis for any decisions.

The ABC costs could, however, be used to highlight areas for cost reduction and procedural changes which could assist longer-term profitability. ABC is a method for apportioning costs and it suffers from the same defects as every absorption method. In S&P's case, the analysis does not look very detailed/accurate and so may be little better than a traditional absorption system.

The head office and warehousing costs need to be examined in detail to determine which type of outlet incurs what part of the cost, as these costs may be caused and used more by some types of outlets than others. If this is so, what would happen to cost if one type of outlet was abandoned and others increased in size?

(ii) The decision to close operations should not be based on an apportionment of fixed costs since this is bound to be somewhat arbitrary (although ABC system is generally considered more informative than traditional system, as it still contains a degree of arbitrariness).

Generally incremental costs and revenues should be used, requiring the use of marginal costing.

9.9

Tutorial note: This answer is not only longer than would be expected of students in the time available, but illustrates the main issues that should be addressed.

(a) *Life cycle costing*

Life cycle costing involves identifying the costs and revenues over a product's life, that is, from inception to decline. Life cycle costing aims to maximise the profit generated from a product over its total life cycle. Studies show that 80 to 90% of a product's costs are incurred or committed during the planning and design stage and any increase in time during these stages means an increase in cost and a reduction in profit. The life cycle costing's view is that the revenue generated from a product must not only cover the production costs, but must also cover the costs incurred in the pre- and post-production stages of planning and concept design, preliminary design, detailed design and testing and the distribution and customer service costs. The product design and production process is determined at an early stage and provides the basis of the production costs. These costs effectively become "locked in" early in the product's life and it is at these early stages that cost management can be most effectively exercised.

This is unlike the current system that SY Ltd uses in that the standard manufacturing cost, once established, is uplifted by adding an amount to cover the selling and administration costs as well as a profit margin. The costs incurred during the planning and design stages are therefore ignored when pricing the MANPAC and these will be a significant element of the cost. Also, this approach reports costs and revenues on a periodic basis and actually ignores the total profitability of the MANPAC over its total life cycle. Therefore, the current approach used by SY Ltd does not provide a complete overview of the return generated over the MANPAC's life.

If SY Ltd were to implement life cycle costing, it would provide an overview of the MANPAC's performance. This would provide vital information when assessing potential cost reduction opportunities as well as revenue extension opportunities for the game.

Target costing

Target costing is effectively part of a strategic profit planning system in that it seeks to control costs and manage profit over a product's life cycle. Unlike standard costing, it is not a costing system. The main objective of target costing is to minimise costs over the life cycle of a product without compromising quality, reliability and other customer requirements. SY Ltd currently uses standard costing which is a system whereby a predetermined cost is established for the MANPAC. Once the MANPAC goes into production, any deviations from the standard cost are measured through variance analysis. SY Ltd also uses the standard cost information to determine the standard selling price. Unlike target costing, the standard costing method used by SY Ltd is taking an inward-looking approach for both pricing and cost control which focuses attention on the short term rather than the long term.

If SY Ltd were to implement target costing, the development and design stages for the MANPAC would be used to determine the target selling price. In order to identify the target cost for the MANPAC, SY Ltd must first undertake some market research to determine the target selling price for the MANPAC. From this, a desired margin would be deducted in order to arrive at a target cost. If the target cost is less than the predicted actual cost, the MANPAC will go through a redesign stage until such time as the MANPAC can be delivered within the target cost. Ultimately, SY Ltd must be able to manufacture and deliver the MANPAC at a cost that will enable the desired profit margin to be achieved, that is, the target profit. SY Ltd should then continue to revise the target cost over the life of the MANPAC and therefore make an ongoing effort to reduce costs and maintain profit. Continually revising the target cost over the MANPAC's life will make the management of SY Ltd more cost-conscious and focused on maintaining profit margins.

(b) *Market-based pricing strategies*

Price skimming
This method of pricing sets high initial prices in an attempt to exploit those sections of the market which are relatively insensitive to price changes.

Penetration pricing
This method sets very low prices in the initial stages of a product's life cycle to gain rapid acceptance of the product and therefore a significant market share. This method of pricing is followed if a company wishes to discourage new entrants to the market. There may also be significant economies of scale to be gained if the low pricing leads to high volume and therefore cost reduction.

Target pricing
This method would mean that SY Ltd would first undertake some market research to determine the target selling price for the MANPAC. As discussed above, it would then use this target selling price to arrive at a target cost.

Recommendation
As the MANPAC is the first of its type to the market, SY Ltd could pursue one of two strategies – market skimming or penetration pricing.

As demand for computer games is generally highly inelastic, SY Ltd would be advised to follow a market skimming strategy and set a high price to take advantage of the new game and the timing of its launch. By doing this, it will exploit customers who are prepared to pay high prices so as to ensure that they have the latest games on the market. It will also be easier for SY Ltd to reduce the price if the product does not reach the level of demand required. It may assist SY Ltd in generating high initial cash flows which would shorten the payback period on the initial investment in the MANPAC which is normally quite long due to high planning and design costs. Also, like many computer games, the MANPAC is likely to have a short life cycle and therefore by setting a high price, SY Ltd will recover the development costs and make a profit more quickly. A skimming policy will also allow SY Ltd to cover any unforeseen cost increases or falls in demand after the novelty appeal has declined.

Furthermore, SY Ltd needs to ensure that it has some significant barriers to entry to deter competitors from entering the market, for example patent protection, otherwise competitors may enter the market with a lower-priced game.

(c)

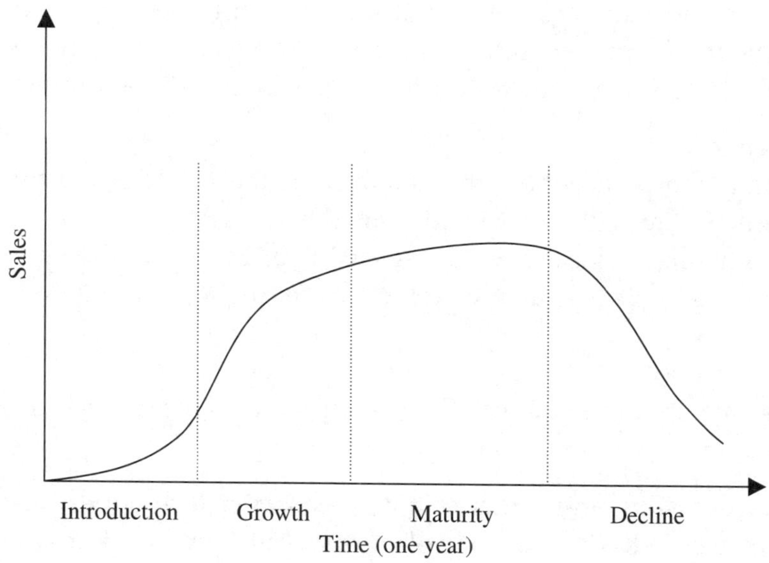

Product life cycle of the MANPAC

The product life cycle of the MANPAC is likely to be short. The life cycle of the MANPAC will significantly influence the pricing strategy. There are four stages in the life cycle:

1 Introduction
The MANPAC is introduced to the market. Due to the nature of the MANPAC and the timing of its launch, it is likely that demand will be reasonably high (as indicated on the diagram). Also, assuming SY Ltd has already established a name in the market, it is likely that the MANPAC will gain market acceptance very quickly. The MANPAC will have already incurred significant costs in its planning, design, development and production stages and it is therefore vital that SY Ltd ensures that the MANPAC is marketed well so that its demand levels are high, otherwise they could stand to incur significant losses. The company therefore needs to ensure that it utilises its existing reputation when marketing the MANPAC.

2 Growth
Assuming the MANPAC is accepted by the market and there has been a reasonable initial uptake (which would be expected at its peak selling season), the product will then enter the growth phase where demand for the MANPAC will increase. At this stage, the company will begin to experience lower costs due to the economies of scale resulting from the higher volume of sales. It is at this point that competitors might enter the market and SY Ltd may need to review its pricing strategy in order to remain competitive with comparable games in the market. It could either pursue a premium pricing strategy, an ongoing or average rate pricing strategy or a discount pricing strategy.

3 Maturity
This is the stage where the MANPAC reaches the mass market and the increase in demand will begin to slow down. As can be seen in the diagram, the sales curve will begin to flatten out. If SY Ltd wishes to maintain demand for the MANPAC, it will need to consider some modification or improvements.

4 Decline
This is the point where the demand for the MANPAC begins to fall. At this point, SY Ltd will need to withdraw the MANPAC from the market and replace it with a new product. Stocks of the MANPAC could then perhaps be bundled with other games in an attempt to recover the costs of unsold units.

9.10

Examiner's note: It is the quality of argument and points made that are important in this answer.

(a) Standard costing and target costing are similar techniques in so far as they are both concerned with the control of cost, but there are a number of differences between the two. The two major differences are:

the approach/attitude used – external/internal approach and the commitment of staff; and the timing of the control, which is illustrated below.

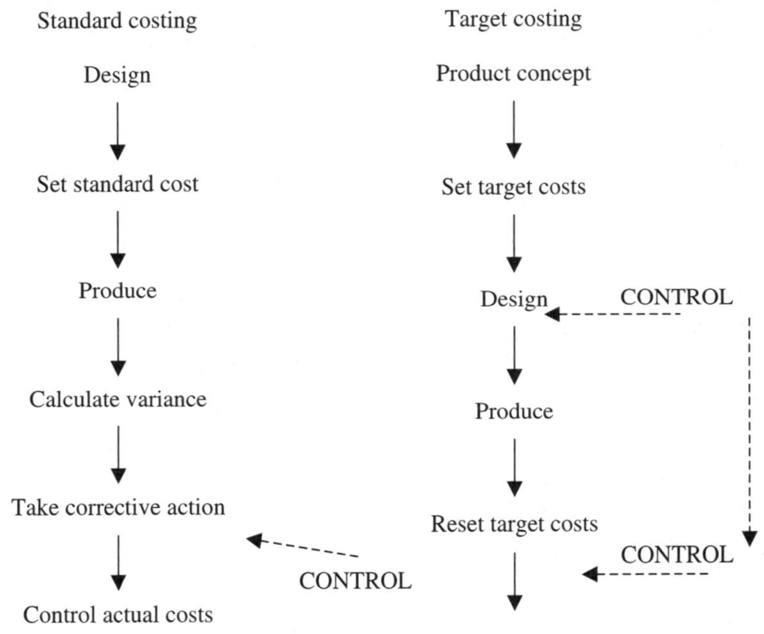

Proactive or not
Standard costing is normally used in a given situation, that is, when products have been in production for some time or when a new product is introduced and a detailed product design has already been produced and production methods determined. Standard times and quantities are determined for each unit and these are turned into costs. Control takes place once in every month when variances (between standard and actual) are calculated. The emphasis is placed on monitoring adverse variances and taking action to reduce these in the future. The selling price of a new product will be determined by estimating its standard

cost and adding the required profit margin to the cost. Thus, standard costing is reactive rather than proactive.

Target costing, on the other hand, is a proactive technique that starts before the design of the product is formalised. The starting point is market research on the price customers would be willing to pay for a product with various specified features. From this price, the required profit margin is deducted to leave a total target cost. This is then split down into a number of different costs for the different product functions. The product is then designed so that it can be manufactured within this cost. If this cannot be done, the product will not be produced. Once in production, the target cost is incorporated in the budgeting process and is reduced steadily over time. Hence, target costing is a cost reduction technique as well.

Agreed by all and rigorously adhered to
It may be untrue to suggest that more people are involved in setting target costs rather than standards, but generally people from a greater number of departments and areas of the business are involved, for example marketing and design. Neither system will work satisfactorily unless those who are responsible for cost have agreed to the target or standard cost. In Japan, where target costing originated, there is more of a consensus approach, which may have influenced the statement in the question. It can be argued that target costs are more rigorously adhered to as it is perceived by all that any increase in cost has a direct effect on profit. In addition, any Japanese manager exceeding the target, once the product is in production, is assigned a supervisory committee for six months to "help" him get the cost to the correct level.

Standard costs may not always be achieved if the situation has changed since the standard was set. For example, if the price of materials has increased, it may not be possible to reduce the actual material cost. This view may be accepted and the standard modified or a planning variance calculated. Furthermore, in some cultures, tight budgets are the norm and adverse variances expected.

Costing system
Whether both are costing systems depends on the definition of a costing system. The CIMA Terminology describes costing as "the process of determining the costs of products, services or activities". So, presumably, any method which determines costs could be called a costing system. This means that both standard costing and target costing could be considered costing systems.

Standard costing has always been considered a costing system because of its tie with budgeting, planning and control. As target costing is used in forecasting, and the Japanese use reducing target costs in their six-month budgets, there would appear to be no difference and both are, therefore, costing systems.

(b) The two systems were developed quite separately in different ages and in different parts of the world for different purposes. The aim of standard costing is to control future costs by looking at past costs and the aim of target costing is to control future costs by considering them in advance and limiting them to an acceptable level. Nevertheless, a company which uses standard costing could adapt the system to embrace the aims of a target costing system. The most important aspect would be to change the mindset of management to make them proactive rather than reactive. This could be quite difficult if target costing is seen simply as an "add-on".

A pharmaceutical company will have heavy research and development costs and a production which may start quite slowly in one market and expand to cover the world until the patent runs out. Because of the patent, there will have been little pressure on the company to control production costs until the patent runs out. (Research and development costs must, of course, be covered, but are usually covered many times on a successful product.) When the patent runs out, other companies can produce the product, but, by this time, doctors may be familiar with the name of the drug and may not switch to prescribing the cheaper drug. However, this scenario is changing and there is pressure on pharmaceutical companies to reduce prices in particular areas of the world where, for example, incomes are low. Therefore, target costing would have advantages because it would force the company to consider how to reduce future costs month by month, based on an experience curve and other factors.

If the pharmaceutical company's target costs are just "targets" rather than the "must achieve" level that the Japanese use, it would be dangerous to base standards on these and then reprimand managers if they did not achieve them. So the mindset behind the system is the important factor, rather than the name of the system, and a standard costing system with learning built in can be used to achieve precisely the same aims as a target costing system. Hence, they are compatible, but they would not be two separate systems. It would be possible to run two systems, but managers are likely to be confused by the difference between the standard cost and the target cost, with its main advantage of "must achieve", and so it is unlikely that many companies would decide to use both together.

Learning Curves 10

The learning effect reflects that as employees repeat a task they get faster at it.

The learning effect has implications for:

- Budgeting – the labour hours required for a given production level will fall over time.
- Capacity – if the total labour hours are fixed then output will increase over time.
- Costing – unit costs will fall with time.
- Pricing – prices below cost at the start of the life cycle may be above cost once learning has an effect.
- Decision-making – the annual cost of production will fall if output levels are fixed.

π To calculate labour time, use the following relationship:

As total production doubles, cumulative average time per unit falls to a fixed percentage of its previous value.

This fixed percentage is called a learning rate.

It is expressed as the following formula:

$$y = ax^b$$

where,
y = cumulative average time per unit
x = cumulative production
a = time for first unit
b = index of learning $= \dfrac{\log(\text{learning rate})}{\log 2}$

When learning stops it is known as the steady state.

? Questions

10.1 GH plc has received an order to make eight units of product K. The time to produce the first unit is estimated to be 100 hours and an 80% learning curve is expected. The rate of pay is £6 for each hour.

The direct materials for each unit is £2,500 and the fixed costs associated with the order are £9,600.

The average cost of each unit (to the nearest £) for this order of product K is

A £4,007
B £4,180
C £6,158
D £10,160
E £12,407

(3 marks)

10.2 BT plc has recently developed a new product. The nature of BT plc's work is repetitive and it is usual for there to be a 75% learning effect when a new product is developed. The time taken for the first unit was 2 hours. Four units have so far been made and sold to an existing customer. These four units included the first unit that took 2 hours to make.

A new customer has asked BT plc to supply an additional four units of the new product. If the labour rate is £12 per hour, how much should BT plc include in the price quotation in respect of labour cost?

A £6
B £27
C £36
D £54
E £81

(4 marks)

10.3 Data relating to the production of the first 16 batches of a new product are as follows:

Cumulative number of batches	*Cumulative total hours*
1	1,562.5
16	12,800

The percentage learning effect is closest to:

A 45%
B 55%
C 65%
D 75%
E 85%

(3 marks)

10.4 Which of the following conditions must exist for there to be a learning curve effect?

(i) The task must be repetitive.
(ii) There must be a significant machine-based element to the work.
(iii) Production must be at an early stage or even be a new product.
(iv) The workforce is motivated to achieve improvements.
(v) There can be extensive breaks in production.

A All of the above
B (i) and (ii) and(iv)
C (i) and (iii) and (iv)
D (i) and (ii) and (iv) and (v)
E (i) and (ii) and (iii) and (iv)

(2 marks)

10.5 The following diagram represents the learning curve effect:

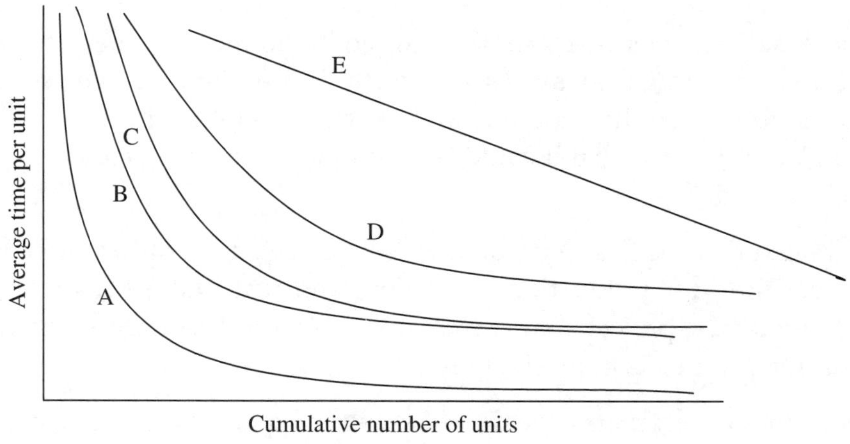

Which of the curves illustrates the highest learning effect?

A Curve A
B Curve B
C Curve C
D Curve D
E Curve E

(2 marks)

10.6 T plc has developed a new product, the TF8. The time taken to produce the first unit was 18 minutes. Assuming that an 80% learning curve applies, the time allowed for the fifth unit (to 2 decimal places) should be

A 5.79 min
B 7.53 min
C 10.72 min
D 11.52 min

Note: For an 80% learning curve $y = ax^{-0.3219}$

(4 marks)

10.7 The following statements concern the learning effect.

When the steady state is reached,

(i) the total time stops rising.
(ii) the cumulative average time stops falling.
(iii) the marginal time stops falling.

Which of these statements is true?

A (i)
B (ii)
C (iii)
D none of them

(2 marks)

10.8 VI plc (IDEC 5/01)

VI plc produces a number of mobile telephone products. It is an established company with a good reputation that has been built on well-engineered, reliable and good-quality products. It is currently developing a product called Computel and has spent £1.5 million on development so far. It now has to decide whether it should proceed further and launch the product in one year's time.

If VI plc decides to continue with the project, it will incur further development costs of £0.75 million straight away. Assets worth £3.5 million will be required immediately prior to the product launch, and working capital of £1.5 million would be required. VI plc expects that it could sell Computel for three years before the product becomes out of date.

It is estimated that the first 500 Computels produced and sold would cost an average of £675 per unit, for production, marketing and distribution costs. The fixed costs associated with the project are expected to amount to £2.4 million (cash outflow) for each year the product is in production.

Because of the cost estimates, the Chief Executive expected the selling price to be in the region of £950. However, the Marketing Director is against this pricing strategy; he says that this price is far too high for this type of product and that he could sell only 6,000 units in each year at this price. He suggests a different strategy: setting a price of £425, at which price he expects sales to be 15,000 units each year.

VI plc has found from past experience that a 70% experience curve applies to production, marketing and distribution costs. The company's cost of capital is 7% a year.

Requirements

(a) The Chief Executive has asked you to help sort out the pricing dilemma. Prepare calculations that demonstrate:

- which of the two suggestions is the better pricing strategy
- the financial viability of the better strategy.

(15 marks)

(b) Discuss other issues that VI plc should consider in relation to the two pricing strategies.

(5 marks)

(c) Discuss the usefulness of the experience curve in gaining market share. Illustrate your answer with specific instances/examples.

(5 marks)
(Total = 25 marks)

10.9 PR plc (IMPM 5/02 (Amended))

PR plc is a marketing consultancy company that offers three different types of service. It is preparing the budget for the year ending 31 December 2002. The details for each type of service are as follows:

	Service A	*Service B*	*Service C*
Estimated demand (number of services)	150	800	200
	£ per service	*£ per service*	*£ per service*
Fee income	2,500	2,000	3,200
Consultant (£300 per day)	900	750	1,500
Specialists' report	400	200	500
Variable overhead	200	160	300

It has been estimated that the consultants will be able to work for a total of 2,400 days during the year. PR plc estimates that the fixed overhead for the year will be £600,000.

Requirements

(a) (i) Prepare calculations that show how many of each type of service should be undertaken in order for PR plc to maximise its profits.

(ii) Prepare a statement that shows the budgeted profit for the year 2002 based on your answer to (i) above.

(8 marks)

The Managing Director has received the service schedule and budget statement that you prepared but would like it to be amended to reflect the following additional information:

- There is a 90% learning curve operating on the consultants' times for service C. The budgeted consultants' time of five days per service C was based on the time taken for the very first service C performed. By the end of December 2001, a total of 100 type C services will have been performed.
- The consultants' salaries will rise by 8% with effect from 1 January 2002.
- Overhead costs will rise by 5% with effect from 1 January 2002.

(b) Calculate the revised optimal service plan and prepare the associated profit statement for the year ending 31 December 2002.

(12 marks)

Note: The formula for a 90% learning curve is $y = ax^{-0.1520}$

(c) Explains the implications of the learning curve effect on service C for PR plc.

(5 marks)
(Total = 25 marks)

Answers

10.1 **A**

If we can find the total cost of making all eight units we can then divide by eight to get the average cost per unit.

Direct materials cost will be = 8 units × £2,500 = £20,000

Fixed costs = £9,600

Labour cost:

Given that there is a learning effect, we must find the total time that is expected to manufacture all eight units.

We can use the law which says that as cumulative output doubles, the *average* time per unit is multiplied by the learning effect percentage.

Going from production of one unit to production of eight units, output doubles three times (1 becomes 2, 2 becomes 4, 4 becomes 8)

First unit produced: average time taken = 100 hours

So to produce eight units:

Average time per unit = 100 hours × 0.8 × 0.8 × 0.8 = 51.2 hours

Given that there are eight units,

Total time = 51.2 hours × 8 units = 409.6 hours

Therefore, labour cost = 409.6 hours × £6 = £2,457.60

So, direct materials cost will be = 8 units × £2,500 = £20,000

Fixed costs = £9,600

Labour cost = £2,457.60

Total cost = £20,000 + £9,600 + £2,457.60 = £32,057.60

Therefore, average cost per unit = £32,056.60/8 units = £4,007.20

10.2 **B**

We can work out the time taken to produce all 8 units that will then have been made using the law which says that as cumulative output doubles, the *average* time per unit is multiplied by the learning effect percentage. We will then need to deduct the time taken to produce the first 4 units in order to arrive at the time expected to be needed for the units to be made for the new customer.

We *cannot* just look at the latter 4 units. We *must* find the time for all 8 units and then deduct the time for the first 4 units.

Time for first 4 units already made and sold:

Going from production of 1 unit to production of 4 units, output doubles *twice* (1 becomes 2, 2 becomes 4)

So,
Average time per unit = 2 hours × 0.75 × 0.75 = 1.125 hours

Therefore, time taken for all 4 units = 4 units × 1.125 hours = 4.5 hours

Now for the time for first 8 units:

Going from production of 1 unit to production of 8 units, output doubles *three* times (1 becomes 2, 2 becomes 4, 4 becomes 8)

So,
Average time per unit = 2 hours × 0.75 × 0.75 × 0.75 = 0.84375 hour

Therefore, time taken for all 8 units = 8 units × 0.84375 hour = 6.75 hours

So, time for *latter* 4 units for new customer = 6.75 hours less 4.5 hours = 2.25 hours

Labour cost = 2.25 hours × £12 = £27

10.3 **E**

To calculate the learning effect percentage we need to use the law which says that as cumulative output doubles, the *average* time per unit is multiplied by the learning effect percentage.

Going from production of 1 unit to production of 16 units, output doubles four times (1 becomes 2, 2 becomes 4, 4 becomes 8, then 8 becomes 16)

First unit produced: average time taken = 1,562.5 hours

16 units produced: average time taken = 12,800 hours/16 units = 800 hours

Let's suppose the learning effect rate is $L\%$

So,
$1{,}562.5 \times L \times L \times L \times L = 800$

That is,
$1{,}562.5 \times L^4 = 800$

$L^4 = 800 \div 1{,}562.5 = 0.512$

So,
$L = \sqrt[4]{0.512}$

$L = 0.846$

That is, the learning effect rate is 84.6%

Say, 85%

10.4 **C**

(i) Is correct. The task involved must be repetitive so that workers can learn to become quicker.
(ii) Is incorrect. There must be a significant manual or labour-based element to the work, NOT a significant machine-based element.
(iii) Is correct. If the product had been made for a long period of time, any learning effect would already have happened and time taken to make each unit would have settled down to a "steady state".
(iv) Is correct. Motivated workers will strive to become better at producing a new or fairly new product, whereas de-motivated workers will not.
(v) Is incorrect. If there are extensive breaks in production, workers will "forget" the skills learned and have to go through a learning effect again once work recommences.

10.5 **A**

The steepest curve which bottoms out the earliest (i.e. reaches "steady state" the earliest) exhibits the highest learning curve percentage.

This is, therefore, Curve A.

10.6 **B**

Unfortunately, we cannot use the learning curve law which says that as cumulative output doubles, the *average* time per unit is multiplied by the learning effect percentage, since to find the time taken for 5 units does not fall into a pattern of doubling up production levels. (Having produced one unit, doubling production levels would double from 1 to 2 units, then 2 to 4 units, then 4 to 8 units.)

Therefore we must use the learning curve equation. This is the reason why the equation has been given to us in the question.

In fact, to find the time taken for the 5th unit, we must find the time to produce all 5 units and then deduct the time taken to produce the first 4 units. We cannot just look at the fifth unit in isolation.

Time for all 5 units:

Using the equation with number of units x being 5

$y = ax^{-0.3219}$

where, "y" is the *average* time per unit produced and "a" is the time taken for the first unit.

So,
$y = ax^{-0.3219} = 18$ multiplied by $5^{-0.3219} = 18$ multiplied by 0.5956

$y = 10.72$ min

So, time taken for all 5 units = 10.72 min × 5 units = 53.60 min

Time for first 4 units:

Using the equation with number of units x being 4

$y = ax^{-0.3219}$

where "y" is the *average* time per unit produced and "a" is the time taken for the first unit.

So,
$y = ax^{-0.3219}$
= 18 multiplied by $4^{-0.3219}$
= 18 multiplied by 0.64

$y = 11.52$ min

So, time taken for first 4 units = 11.52 min × 4 units = 46.08 min

Therefore, time taken for the 5th unit is:

53.6 min − 46.08 min = 7.53 min

10.7 **C**

When the steady state is reached each unit takes the same amount of time as the last one, thus the marginal time is constant. The total time will continue to rise and the average time will continue to fall (albeit at a reduced rate).

10.8

Tutorial note: It is best to work the whole calculation in batches of 500 units, but you would get the same answer if you work in units. In this case you need to work out the time taken for the first unit.

You may get slightly different subtotals to those below due to the rounding conventions used.

To use the learning (experience) effect we will use the following formula, first calculating the index of learning.

(a) $y = ax^b \quad \log 0.7/\log 2 = -0.51457$

15,000 units = 30 batches of 500 units
6,000 units = 12 batches of 500 units

Cost of first batch	(£675 × 500 units)	£337,500
Average cost of 30 batches	(£337,500 × $30^{-0.51457}$)	£58,640
Total cost of 30 batches	(£58,640 × 30)	£1,759,189
Average cost of 12 batches	(£337,500 × $12^{-0.51457}$)	£93,964
Total cost of 12 batches	(£93,964 × 12)	£1,127,568

Similarly for Years 2 and 3:

Units	*Batches*	*Cost per batch* £	*Total cost* £	*Incremental cost* £
15,000	30	58,640	1,759,189	
30,000	60	41,017	2,462,870	703,681
45,000	90	33,318	2,998,620	535,750

	Year 1 £	*Year 2* £	*Year 3* £
Sales revenue			
15,000 × £425	6,375,000	6,375,000	6,375,000
Less: Experience curve costs	1,759,189	703,681	535,750
Differential cash flow	4,615,811	5,671,319	5,839,250

Units	*Batches*	*Cost per batch* £	*Total cost* £	*Incremental cost* £
6,000	12	93,964	1,127,562	
12,000	24	65,774	1,578,588	451,026
18,000	36	53,388	1,921,986	343,398

	Year 1 £	*Year 2* £	*Year 3* £
Sales revenue			
6,000 × £950	5,700,000	5,700,000	5,700,000
Less: Experience curve costs	1,127,562	451,026	343,398
Differential cash flow	4,572,438	5,248,974	5,356,602

Therefore, selling 15,000 units at a price of £425 is the better strategy.

Note: Only Year 1 calculation for 6,000 units is necessary to show this.

Whether this strategy is viable depends on whether it has a positive NPV.

	Year 1	*Year 2*	*Year 3*
	£	£	£
Differential cash flow	4,615,811	5,671,319	5,839,250
Less: Fixed costs	2,400,000	2,400,000	2,400,000
Net cash flow	2,215,811	3,271,319	3,439,250

Year	*Cash flows* £m		*Total flow* £m	*Discount rate*	*NPV* £m
0	(0.75)	Dev	(0.75)	1.000	(0.75)
1	(3.5)	Asset			
	(1.5)	WC	(5.0)	0.935	(4.675)
2	2.216		2.216	0.873	1.935
3	3.271		3.271	0.816	2.669
4	3.439				
	1.5	WC	4.939	0.763	3.768
					2.947

The option of selling 15,000 units a year at £425 is financially viable and gives a NPV over the project's life of £2.9 million.

(b) Other issues to consider include:

If VI plc sets a low price it will gain a greater market share. This may be an advantage in the long term and something that the company could build on with the next generation of products – thus increasing future profits.

On the other hand, VI plc has built its reputation on good quality products and, presumably, it wishes to retain this image. Selling at a low price could harm the company's image, even though the quality of the product is good, because customers may perceive a cheaper product to be inferior.

A larger production volume may require more in the way of production facilities. Could the additional space and equipment be used more profitably for another product?

The product is likely to be under attack from competing products and newer technologies. Will VI plc be able to sustain constant demand (especially at the higher level) for three years?

(c) The experience curve can assist in setting a low price that can be used to enter a market and gain an acceptable market share within a required time period. It can only be used if an experience curve can be determined from previous experience of similar products/markets. Therefore, it requires a certain amount of economic stability and repetition. However, this does not imply large volume of mass production as aircraft manufacturers, for example, have used the technique very successfully.

If a company entering a new market sets a high price, not many units will be sold and the entrant will only achieve a relatively small market share. This could mean that the entrant does not achieve the required critical mass within the required time. If a lower price had been set, volume would be higher, the critical mass might well have been achieved and the market would then be profitable for the company. Setting a low price – one lower than initial cost – is possible if the experience curve factor is known. However, this can be a dangerous strategy if it triggers a price war.

A number of Japanese companies used a low price strategy, based on the experience curve, when entering European markets with electronic/electrical goods for the first time about 30 years ago. Once they became established in the market they could produce a more sophisticated product. This type of product lends itself to this tactic, for example *Amstrad* launched its first computer for £399 plus VAT when other computers were selling for about £1,000. *Texas Instruments* have used this type of tactic. On one occasion, it ended disastrously when competitors lowered their prices aggressively and prevented *Texas Instruments* from selling the volume they had originally planned and hence cost did not reduce as planned.

10.9

(a) (i)

Service type	*A*	*B*	*C*
Contribution/service	£1,000	£890	£900
Consultant days/service	3	2.5	5
Contribution/consultant day	£333.30	£356.00	£180.00
Ranking	2nd	1st	3rd
Demand/usage in services	133*	800	0
Days used	400	2,000	0

* Restricted due to lack of consultant days.

(ii)

Service type	*A*	*B*	*C*	*Total*
Number of each service	133	800	NIL	
	£	£	£	£
Fee charged/service	2,500	2,000	3,200	
Variable cost/service	(1,500)	(1,110)	(2,300)	
Contribution/service	1,000	890	900	
Total contribution	133,000	712,000	NIL	845,000
Fixed costs				(600,000)
Profit				245,000

(b) *Learning curve*:

Project C time per service = 5 days. The time taken for the first service is 5 days so the average time for 100 services and 300 services are:

For 100 Services $y = ax^{-b}$

where,
a is the time for the first service
x is the cumulative number of services
b equals 0.1520
$y = 5 \times 100^{-0.1520} = 2.483$ days

For 300 Services $y = 5 \times 300^{-0.1520} = 2.101$ days

Thus the total time taken:

300 services $\times$ 2.101 = 630.30
100 services $\times$ 2.483 = 248.30
Total time for 200 services in 2002 = 382 days

The learning curve effect changes the ranking of the services:

Service type	*A* £	*B* £	*C* £
Fee charged	2,500	2,000	3,200
Consultant	972	810	619*
Specialist's report	400	200	500
Variable overhead	210	168	315
	1,582	1,178	1,434
Contribution	£918	£822	£1,766
Consultant days/service	3	2.5	1.91*
Contribution/consultant day	£306.00	£328.80	£924.60
Ranking	3rd	2nd	1st
Demand/usage in services	6**	800	200
Days used	18	2,000	382

* Based on average consultant days for the 200 services.

** Restricted due to lack of consultant days.

Service type	*A*	*B*	*C*	*Total*
Number of services	6	800	200	n/a
	£	£	£	£
Fee charged	15,000	1,600,000	640,000	2,255,000
Consultant's time	5,832	648,000	123,768	
Specialist's report	2,400	160,000	100,000	
Variable overhead	1,260	134,400	63,000	
	9,492	942,400	286,768	1,238,660
Contribution	5,508	657,600	353,232	1,016,340
Fixed costs				630,000
Profit				386,340

(c) There are a number of implications of the learning curve, both in general, and with specific relevance to service C.

When comparing the actual performance results from service C against the planned performance, it is realistic to make allowance in the plan for the anticipated effects of the 90% learning curve.

There may also be a learning effect on the usage of the other resources associated with service C. These effects have not been allowed for in the standard costs and thus, unless they are recognised as learning effects, these will give rise to variances that will be reported as operating variances.

The learning curve implications must also be considered from the point of view of the scheduling and planning resource utilisation. As can be seen from the earlier calculations, the effect of the learning curve can significantly affect the optimal utilisation of scarce resources.

Finally, if selling prices are based on costs that do not consider the effects of the learning curve, services can be overpriced, resulting in low demand, which will increase average time per service due to the lower cumulative number of services.

Modern Philosophies

11

A number of changes to management approach have developed in recent years. You must make sure that you understand the ideas that drive them, as well as the consequences for management decisions.

JIT (just in time)

Producing items for immediate despatch to customer rather than for stock.

Often referred to as "demand-pull" production: demand from the customer activates the process.

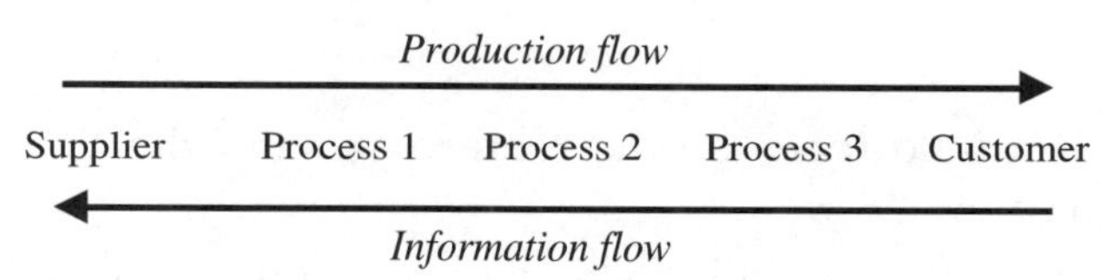

Decisions are based around customer demand, low stocks and quality issues.

TQM (total quality management)

Aim is to continuously improve quality.
Quality is as defined by the customer.
A company should avoid defects rather than correct them.

Costs are categorised into four headings:

Prevention costs
Ensuring failures do not happen, for example, staff training, better quality materials.
Appraisal costs
Checking for failures, for example, quality testing, discarding tested items.
Internal failure costs
Cost of defects discovered in the company, for example, repair costs, scrapping costs.
External failure costs
Cost of defects discovered by the customer, for example, replacement cost, loss of goodwill.

Value analysis

Value is measured in four ways

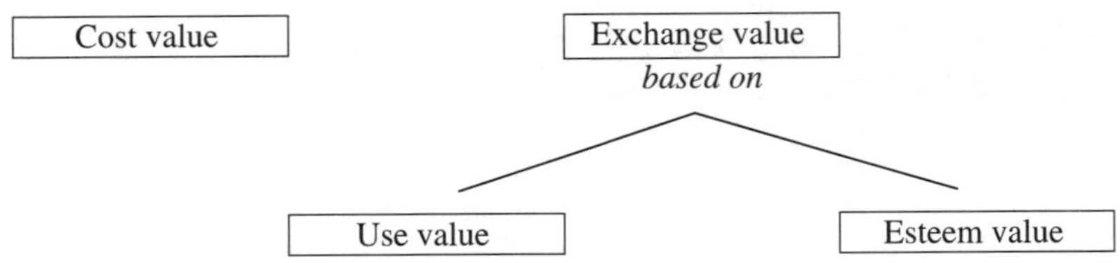

Cost value is the production cost.
Exchange value is the value to the customer (potential selling price).
Use value is the benefit the customer gets from consuming the product.
Esteem value is the prestige (and similar) that the client gets from association with the product.

A company should seek to boost exchange value and/or reduce cost value – it does this by eliminating non-value adding activities.

Questions

11.1 The following statements have all been claimed to relate to the adoption of a TQM approach.

(i) Employees should focus on the requirements of their customers, both internal and external.
(ii) Standard costing is unlikely to be used as a method of control.
(iii) TQM companies often dispense with the quality control department.

Which of these statements are substantially true?

A (i) and (ii) only
B (ii) and (iii) only
C (i) and (iii) only
D all of them

(2 marks)

11.2 Which of the following costs are likely to be reduced on the introduction of a JIT system in a company?

(i) Purchasing costs
(ii) Stockholding costs
(iii) Ordering costs
(iv) Information system costs

A (i) and (ii)
B (ii) and (iii)
C (iii) and (iv)
D (ii) only

(2 marks)

11.3 Which of the following statements relating to JIT and TQM approaches is most closely related to the truth?

A TQM and JIT are not very compatible approaches since their focus is different: one focuses on quality and the other on stock levels.
B TQM and JIT are not usually seen together since TQM is used by service companies and JIT by manufacturing companies.
C TQM and JIT are very compatible approaches as they are both largely focused on customer satisfaction.
D TQM and JIT are not compatible approaches since TQM requires there to be stocks so that quality checking can take place.

(2 marks)

11.4 Which of the following is not a term normally used in value analysis?

A Resale value
B Use value
C Esteem value
D Cost value

(2 marks)

11.5 Which of the following is not suitable for a JIT production system?

A Batch production
B Jobbing production
C Process production
D Service production

(2 marks)

11.6 Companies that embrace TQM often split their costs into four categories: prevention costs, appraisal costs, internal failure costs and external failure costs.

A company wants to categorise the following costs.

(i) Training staff in the importance of quality.
(ii) Replacing, from stock, a defective item returned by a customer.
(iii) Scrapping an item deliberately tested to destruction.
(iv) Losses on the sale of items identified as rejects.

Which categories best reflect the nature of the above costs?

	Prevention costs	*Appraisal costs*	*Internal failure costs*	*External failure costs*
A	(i)	(ii)	(iii)	(iv)
B	(i)	(iii)	(iv)	(ii)
C	(ii)	(iv)	(iii)	(i)
D	(iii)	(i)	(iv)	(ii)

(2 marks)

11.7 C1, C2 and C3 (IDEC 11/02 (Amended))

X Ltd manufactures and distributes three types of car (C1, C2 and C3). Each type of car has its own production line. The company is worried by extremely difficult market conditions and forecasts losses for the forthcoming year.

Management has hired a consultant to advise them on how to reduce costs. The consultant has suggested that the company adopts a JIT manufacturing system.

Requirement

Write a report to the management of X Ltd which states whether costs are likely to reduce and explain the conditions that are necessary for the successful implementation of a JIT manufacturing system.

(10 marks)

11.8 E plc (IMPM 11/03)

E plc provides a computer upgrading, servicing and repair facility to a variety of business and personal computer users.

An issue which concerns the management of E plc is the quality of the service provided for clients. The Operations Manager has suggested that the company should introduce TQM but the management team is unsure how to do this and of the likely costs and benefits that would arise of its introduction.

Requirements

(a) Briefly explain TQM in the context of E plc.

(3 marks)

(b) Discuss the likely costs and benefits that would arise if E plc introduced a TQM policy.

(7 marks)
(Total = 10 marks)

11.9 PG plc (IMPM 11/02)

PG plc manufactures gifts and souvenirs for both the tourist and commercial promotions markets. Many of the items are similar except that they are overprinted with different slogans, logos and colours for the different customers and markets. For many years, it has been PG plc's policy to produce the basic items in bulk and then overprint them as required, but this policy has now been questioned by the company's new Finance Director.

She has also questioned the current policy of purchasing raw materials in bulk from suppliers whenever the periodic stock review system indicates that the re-order level has been reached.

She has said that it is most important in this modern environment to be as efficient as possible, and that bulk purchasing and production strategies are not necessarily the most efficient strategies to be adopted. She has suggested that the company must carefully consider its approaches to production, and the associated costs.

Requirements

(a) Compare and contrast the current strategies of PG plc for raw materials purchasing and production with those that would be associated with a JIT philosophy.

(15 marks)

(b) Explain what is meant by cost reduction.

(3 marks)

(c) Explain how PG plc might introduce a cost reduction programme without affecting its customers' perceptions of product values.

(7 marks)
(Total = 25 marks)

11.10 SG plc (IMPM 11/02)

SG plc is a long-established food manufacturer which produces semi-processed foods for fast-food outlets. While for a number of years it has recognised the need to produce good quality products for its customers, it does not have a formalised quality management programme.

A director of the company has recently returned from a conference, where one of the speakers introduced the concept of TQM and the need to recognise and classify quality costs.

Requirements

(a) Explain what is meant by TQM and use examples to show how it may be introduced into different areas of SG plc's food production business.

(12 marks)

(b) Explain why the adoption of TQM is particularly important within a JIT production environment.

(5 marks)

(c) Explain four quality cost classifications, using examples relevant to the business of SG plc.

(8 marks)
(Total = 25 marks)

✓ Answers

11.1 **D**

(i) Since quality is customer defined, everyone should become customer focused.
(ii) Standard costing implies that there is a standard that is good enough, TQM is based on continuous improvement.
(iii) Quality control departments are believed to reinforce the idea that quality is someone else's problem, instead quality is incorporated into everyone's targets.

11.2 **D**

(i) Purchasing costs will increase due to the extra requirements applied to suppliers.
(ii) Stockholding costs will reduce due to lower stock levels.
(iii) Ordering costs will increase due to the greater specification required and the increased number of small deliveries.
(iv) Information system costs will increase due to the more accurate scheduling tools required.

11.3 **C**

A Unless there is a quality programme of some type, a company cannot afford to have low stocks in case defective items need to be replaced from stock.
B Whilst TQM can be used by service companies, it is also seen in manufacturing and other productive industries along with JIT.
C This is closely related to truth; customer satisfaction as regards quality and delivery times.
D A TQM system is more concerned with ensuring that errors do not occur in the first place. Any checking of items can be undertaken during the production process itself.

11.4 **A**

The resale value is normally referred to as the "exchange value".

11.5 **A**

A Batch production uses stocks to supply customers whilst other products are being produced. Stocks are avoided in a JIT system.
B Jobbing production makes products to customer order, ideal for JIT.
C Process production produces continuous output, as long as the speed of production can be regulated this can be tailored to customer requirements.
D Services are always produced just in time as they cannot be stored.

11.6 **B**

(i) This should help to *prevent* further failures.
(ii) This is the cost of a quality *failure discovered externally* (it has been returned).
(iii) This represents *appraising* the current production.
(iv) This is the cost of a quality *failure discovered internally*.

11.7

REPORT

To: The Management of X Ltd

From: Management Accountant

Date: 20 November 2002

Re: Just In Time

Almost certainly some costs will reduce and some costs will increase.

Storage costs are expected to reduce since there will be less stock.

Purchasing costs will probably increase as orders will be more specific and the company will not be so able to compare suppliers.

Losses should reduce due to the higher quality that is essential in a JIT system.

System and compliance costs will increase due to the more complex system that will be adopted, the equipment needed and staff training.

Conditions
There is a need for smooth uniform production rates, that is, smooth production flow, as fluctuations in production rates will result in delays and excess work in progress.

The pull method of co-ordinating steps in the production process begins at the last stage of the manufacturing process, that is, when additional elements are needed for final assembly, the message goes to the immediately preceding centre to send the amount of elements needed. Therefore, nothing is manufactured until it is triggered from the subsequent process.

There must be multi-skilled workers and flexible facilities in order to produce the different types of cars. Workers should be versatile and capable of moving between production lines in order to keep production flowing. Equipment must be more versatile so that no bottlenecks result.

There must be good teamwork so that efficiency levels are high and any non-value added costs are eliminated. This can sometimes be achieved through the introduction of an incentive scheme.

There must be routine checks and preventative maintenance on equipment to avoid downtime.

There is a need for quick and inexpensive set ups of machinery.

Purchases of materials and production of sub-assemblies should be in small amounts to avoid stock building and the costs associated with this.

High quality material is needed and a reliable working relationship must be established with the supplier to ensure that the materials are available and can be used straight away.

Meeting the above conditions will help to ensure the successful implementation of a JIT manufacturing system for the company.

Signed: Management Accountant.

11.8

(a) Total quality management is a philosophy, based on the ideas of continuous improvement and getting it right first time. E plc would need to initially review the alternative services that it provides to its customers and how it may improve. This review process then needs to be repeated at regular intervals (if not continually) so as to always be improving its services (or the efficiency with which they are provided).

(b) The likely costs to be incurred by E plc will include:

- additional training costs to increase the awareness of employees as to how to use machinery, handle materials and work-in-progress as well as finished items
- supervision/testing expenditure so that E plc can ensure that the items delivered to customers are of good quality
- capital expenditure on testing equipment.

As a consequence, the benefits anticipated by E plc would include:

- lower wastage of damaged components, as the handling of these items and the awareness of their usage is improved
- faster turnaround of customer orders, thus leading to greater customer satisfaction
- fewer customer complaints in respect of being delivered poor quality items or items that are different from those ordered or not serviced correctly.

11.9

(a) Just in time is a relatively recent development in the way in which organisations operate within their "value chains", linking through from material acquisition to servicing the retail customer. The traditional manufacturing system is classified as a "push" system. This is where materials are acquired in bulk, benefiting from quantity discounts, and where production is decoupled from sales, mass production achieving economies of scale, and the marketing function being tasked with selling the goods which have been produced, generally for stock in the first instance.

Should PG plc move to JIT, it would convert to a "pull" system. This would mean that it would only manufacture in response to a customer order, and only acquire materials in response to a requirement from manufacturing. Stocks would be minimised. Some raw material stocks may be held, but no finished items should be in stock. PG plc would therefore need to improve the flexibility of its employees (by making them multi-skilled) and of its equipment (reducing set-up times) so that it could quickly and at minimal cost switch between products in response to customer demand. Material suppliers should ideally deliver in small quantities so that no stock is held. Suppliers should be able to respond immediately to orders, for example, a quantity of labels if a customer order is received for that number of products. To achieve this, competitive quotations would not be requested for each supply, but a small number of approved suppliers would be maintained, with whom there would be a long-term relationship.

While the JIT approach may well improve quality, reduce stock losses (due to obsolescence or deterioration), increase speed of response and improve employee motivation, it is not certain that costs would reduce. A formal cost comparison may well identify cost increases due to the loss, for example, of the economies of bulk purchase. Advocates of JIT would counter that a "tighter" value chain, a more highly trained workforce, quicker identification of production problems, a zero defect philosophy and therefore greater customer satisfaction will lead to more work being done, and therefore to increasing long-term profitability.

The JIT system makes costs more visible than hitherto, and therefore offers greater scope for cost reduction, even though the objective is not to compete on cost as a primary marketing attraction.

(b) Cost reduction is the reduction in output costs without affecting the customer's perception of the value of the output. The attributes of the output are as attractive as before, but the cost of production is lower.

(c) A first step in a cost reduction programme would be to identify the characteristics of the products which are valued by customers. Characteristics or attributes that are not valued (non-value adding) can be considered for elimination, whereas those that add value should be enhanced or retained, and ways sought of reducing their cost without affecting their attractiveness in the perception of the consumer. Indeed, some attributes may be enhanced, even if this means extra cost!

11.10

(a) Total quality management is a management philosophy which emphasises "getting things right first time". It is argued that the costs associated with this policy will be lower than those resulting from the need to rectify defects caused by quality failures.

SG plc, should it introduce TQM, would, for example:

- Improve staff training and retraining, both in the TQM philosophy and in the technical aspects of the job.
- Improve product design so that production is easier and less likely to result in defects.
- Reduce the amount of inspection that is undertaken. As quality increases so should the non-value adding inspection cost decrease.

- Improve the information system so that relevant and timely information is produced and distributed to appropriate personnel.
- With better training, less costs due to spillage or poor storage will be incurred. Better product design in containers may reduce shipping costs and breakages. As quality improves, inspections can be reduced from say one batch per 50 to one batch per 500, with a goal of eventually eliminating them completely. Production employees should be provided with daily throughput figures, set up and changeover time statistics, forward order details and so on, so that they can manage their workloads better.

(b) Within a JIT environment there are no stocks of any quantity, so any quality problem is likely to (and is intended to) immediately affect output levels. Any quality problem is therefore very costly – and a feature of JIT is that it is seen to be costly. To enable the system to work efficiently, therefore, quality is paramount. If this were not the case then the adoption of a JIT system would almost inevitably cause the demise of the organisation as stoppages would multiply, costs would increase significantly, and customer commitments would not be met. JIT therefore is founded on a zero defects goal, which requires TQM.

(c) Four quality cost classifications are:

Prevention costs – Costs associated with preventing the output of products which fail to conform to the specifications. The cost of preventative maintenance on food mixers would be one of such costs.

Appraisal costs – Costs associated with ensuring that production meets standards. The cost of inspecting foodstuffs would be an appraisal cost, whether they are bought-in ingredients or completed foodstuffs.

Internal failure costs – Costs of materials or products that fail to meet specifications. Such costs might be the cost of foodstuffs disposed of due to undercooking, the cost of equipment breakdowns, and associated production stoppages.

External failure costs – Costs arising when poor quality products are delivered to customers. The cost of replacement foodstuffs, of handling customer complaints and possibly of damaged reputation and financial damages if, for example, food poisoning is a result.

May 2005 Questions and Commentary

12

Managerial Level

Management Accounting – Decision Management (Paper P2)

Published separately on the CIMA website (www.cimaglobal.com) from the end of September 2005 is a Post Examination Guide for this paper, which provides much valuable and complementary material including indicative mark information.

© 2005 The Chartered Institute of Management Accountants. All rights reserved. No part of this publication may be reproduced, stored in a retrieval system, or transmitted, in any form or by any means, electronic, mechanical, photocopying, recorded or otherwise, without the written permission of the publisher.

CIMA

Management Accounting Pillar

Managerial Level Paper

P2 – Management Accounting - Decision Management

25 May 2005 – Wednesday Morning Session

Instructions to candidates

You are allowed three hours to answer this question paper
You are allowed 20 minutes reading time *before the examination begins* during which you should read the question paper, and if you wish, make annotations on the question paper. However, you will *not* be allowed, *under any circumstances*, to open the answer book and start writing or use your calculator during this reading time.
You are strongly advised to carefully read the question requirement before attempting the question concerned. The requirements for the questions in Sections B and C are contained in a dotted box.
Answer the ONE compulsory question in Section A. This is comprised of eight sub-questions and is on pages 186 to 188.
Answer ALL THREE compulsory questions in Section B on pages 189 to 191.
Answer TWO of the three questions in Section C on pages 192 to 195.
Maths Tables and Formulae are provided on pages 196 to 201.
Write your full examination number, paper number and the examination subject title in the spaces provided on the front of the examination answer book. Also write your contact ID and name in the space provided in the right-hand margin and seal to close.
Tick the appropriate boxes on the front of the answer book to indicate which questions you have answered.

SECTION A – 20 MARKS

[the indicative time for answering this section is 36 minutes]

ANSWER *ALL* EIGHT SUB-QUESTIONS

Instructions for answering Section A:

The answers to the eight sub-questions in Section A should ALL be written in your answer book.

Your answers should be clearly numbered with the sub-question number and then ruled off, so that the markers know which sub-question you are answering.

For sub-questions **1.6**, **1.7** and **1.8** you should show your workings, as marks are available for the method you use to answer these sub-questions.

? Question One

1.1 The following details relate to ready meals that are prepared by a food processing company:

Ready meal	*K*	*L*	*M*
	$/meal	*$/meal*	*$/meal*
Selling price	5.00	3.00	4.40
Ingredients	2.00	1.00	1.30
Variable conversion costs	1.60	0.80	1.85
Fixed conversion costs*	0.50	0.30	0.60
Profit	0.90	0.90	0.65
Oven time (minutes per ready meal)	10	4	8

Each of the meals is prepared using a series of processes, one of which involves cooking the ingredients in a large oven. The availability of cooking time in the oven is limited and, because each of the meals requires cooking at a different oven temperature, it is not possible to cook more than one of the meals in the oven at the same time.

*The fixed conversion costs are general fixed costs that are not specific to any type of ready meal.

The most and least profitable use of the oven is

	Most profitable	*Least profitable*
A	Meal K	Meal L
B	Meal L	Meal M
C	Meal L	Meal K
D	Meal M	Meal L

(2 marks)

1.2 A company provides three different levels of customer service support for one of its software products.

The following data relate to these three levels of support:

Support level	*Superior $ per contract*	*Standard $ per contract*	*Basic $ per contract*
Annual fee	1,000	750	400
Annual variable costs	450	250	180
Annual fixed costs (see note below)	200	100	50
Profit	350	400	170

Note: The total annual fixed costs are budgeted to be $1,000,000. None of these costs are specific to any type of customer service support.

Assuming that the number of customer service support contracts sold are in the proportion:

Superior 20% Standard 30% Basic 50%

The annual revenue needed to be generated to break even is closest to

A $1,690,000
B $1,695,000
C $1,710,000
D $2,270,000

(2 marks)

1.3 A company is preparing a quotation for a one-month consultancy project and seeks your help in determining the relevant cost of one of the members of its project team. Currently the company employs the consultant on an annual salary of £36,000. In addition, the company provides the consultant with a company car which incurs running costs of £6,000 each year. The car will be continuously provided to the consultant whether this project is undertaken by the company or not.

This consultant is fully employed on current projects and, if she were to be transferred to this new project, then an existing junior consultant would be used to cover her current work. The junior consultant would be paid a bonus of £5,000 for undertaking this additional responsibility.

Another alternative that the company is considering is hiring an external consultant who has the necessary technical knowledge to work on the new consultancy project on a one-month contract at a cost of £4,500.

The relevant cost to be used in preparing the quotation is

A £3,000
B £3,500
C £4,500
D £5,000

(2 marks)

1.4 A company has determined that the net present value of an investment project is $12,304 when using a 10% discount rate and $(3,216) when using a discount rate of 15%.

Calculate the Internal Rate of Return of the project to the nearest 1%.

(2 marks)

1.5 A company has a nominal (money) cost of capital of 18% per annum. If inflation is 6% each year, calculate the company's real cost of capital to the nearest 0.01%.

(2 marks)

1.6 A company is considering the price that it should charge for a repeat order. Fifteen units of the product have already been made and supplied to the customer and the company has experienced an 80% learning curve so far. The first unit required 54 hours of labour to complete the manufacture, assembly and testing processes.

Assuming that the 80% learning curve continues, calculate the expected time to be taken for the 16th unit.

Note: The learning index for an 80% learning curve is −0.3219.

(3 marks)

1.7 A company has estimated the selling prices and variable costs of one of its products as follows:

Selling price per unit		*Variable cost per unit*	
$	*Probability*	$	*Probability*
40	0.30	20	0.55
50	0.45	30	0.25
60	0.25	40	0.20

Given that the company will be able to supply 1,000 units of its product each week irrespective of the selling price, and that selling price and variable cost per unit are independent of each other, calculate the probability that the weekly contribution will exceed $20,000.

(3 marks)

1.8 A company is considering the pricing of one of its products. It has already carried out some market research with the following results:

The quantity demanded at a price of $100 will be 1,000 units.

The quantity demanded will increase/decrease by 100 units for every $50 decrease/increase in the selling price.

The marginal cost of each unit is $35.

Note that if Selling Price (P) = a − bx, then Marginal Revenue = a − 2bx.

Calculate the selling price that maximises company profit.

(4 marks)

(Total marks for Section A = 20)

SECTION B – 30 MARKS

[the indicative time for answering this section is 54 minutes]

ANSWER *ALL* THREE QUESTIONS

? Question Two

The X group is a well-established manufacturing group that operates a number of companies using similar production and inventory holding policies. All of the companies are in the same country though there are considerable distances between them.

The group has traditionally operated a constant production system, whereby the same volume of output is produced each week, even though the demand for the group's products is subject to seasonal fluctuations. As a result there is always finished goods inventory in the group's warehouses waiting for customer orders. This inventory will include a safety inventory equal to two weeks' production.

Raw material inventories are ordered from suppliers using the Economic Order Quantity (EOQ) model in conjunction with a computerised inventory control system which identifies the need to place an order when the re-order level is reached. The purchasing department is centralised for the group. On receiving a notification from the computerised inventory control system that an order is to be placed, a series of quotation enquiries are issued to prospective suppliers so that the best price and delivery terms are obtained for each order. This practice has resulted in there being a large number of suppliers to the X group. Each supplier delivers directly to the company that requires the material.

The Managing Director of the X group has recently returned from a conference on World Class Manufacturing and was particularly interested in the possible use of Just In Time (JIT) within the X group.

Requirement

Write a report, addressed to the Managing Director of the X group, that explains how the adoption of JIT might affect its profitability.

(10 marks)

? Question Three

A company is considering the replacement of its delivery vehicle. It has chosen the vehicle that it will acquire but it now needs to decide whether the vehicle should be purchased or leased.

The cost of the vehicle is £15,000. If the company purchases the vehicle it will be entitled to claim tax depreciation at the rate of 25% per year on a reducing balance basis. The vehicle is expected to have a trade-in value of £5,000 at the end of three years.

If the company leases the vehicle, it will make an initial payment of £1,250 plus annual payments of £4,992 at the end of each of three years. The full value of each lease payment will be an allowable cost in the computation of the company's taxable profits of the year in which the payments are made.

The company pays corporation tax at the rate of 30% of its profits.

50% of the company's corporation tax is payable in the year in which profits are made and 50% in the following year. Assume that the company has sufficient profits to obtain tax relief on its acquisition of the vehicle in accordance with the information provided above.

The company's after-tax cost of capital is 15% per year.

Note: Tax depreciation is not a cash cost but is allowed as a deduction in the calculation of taxable profits.

Requirement

Calculate whether the company should purchase or lease the vehicle and clearly state your recommendation to the company.

(10 marks)

? Question Four

Z manufactures three joint products (M, N and P) from the same common process. The following process account relates to the common process last month and is typical of the monthly results of operating this process:

Common Process Account

	Litres	*$*		*Litres*	*$*
Opening work in process	1,000	5,320	Normal loss	10,000	20,000
Materials	100,000	250,000	Output M	25,000	141,875
Conversion costs:			Output N	15,000	85,125
Variable		100,000	Output P	45,000	255,375
Fixed		180,000	Closing work in process	800	3,533
			Abnormal loss	5,200	29,412
	101,000	535,320		101,000	535,320

Each one of the products can be sold immediately after the common process, but each one of them can be further processed individually before being sold. The following further processing costs and selling prices per litre are expected:

Product	*Selling price after common process $/litre*	*Selling price after further processing $/litre*	*Further variable processing cost $/litre*
M	6.25	8.40	1.75
N	5.20	6.45	0.95
P	6.80	7.45	0.85

Requirements

(a) State the method used to apportion the common costs between the products M, N and P and comment on its acceptability. Explain why it is necessary to apportion the common costs between each of the products.

(5 marks)

(b) Evaluate the viability of the common process, and determine the optimal processing plan for each of the three products showing appropriate calculations.

(5 marks)
(Total marks = 10)

(Total marks for Section B = 30)

SECTION C – 50 MARKS

[the indicative time for answering this section is 90 minutes]

ANSWER *TWO* QUESTIONS OUT OF THREE

? Question Five

A printing company is considering investing in new equipment which has a capital cost of £3 million. The machine qualifies for tax depreciation at the rate of 25% per year on a reducing balance basis and has an expected life of five years. The residual value of the machine is expected to be £300,000 at the end of five years.

An existing machine would be sold immediately for £400,000 if the new machine were to be bought. This existing machine has a tax written down value of £250,000.

The existing machine generates annual revenues of £4 million and earns a contribution of 40% of sales. The new machine would reduce unit variable costs to 80% of their former value and increase output capacity by 20%. There is sufficient sales demand at the existing prices to make full use of this additional capacity.

The printing company pays corporation tax on its profits at the rate of 30%, with half of the tax being payable in the year that the profit is earned and half in the following year.

The company's after-tax cost of capital is 14% per year.

Requirements

(a) Evaluate the proposed purchase of the new printing machine from a financial perspective using appropriate calculations, and advise the company as to whether the investment is worthwhile.

(15 marks)

(b) Explain sensitivity analysis and prepare calculations to show the sensitivity of the decision to independent changes in each of the following:

(i) annual contribution,
(ii) rate of corporation tax on profits.

(10 marks)
(Total marks = 25)

? Question Six

(a) The CS group is planning its annual marketing conference for its sales executives and has approached the VBJ Holiday company (VBJ) to obtain a quotation.

VBJ has been trying to win the business of the CS group for some time and is keen to provide a quotation which the CS group will find acceptable in the hope that this will lead to future contracts.

The manager of VBJ has produced the following cost estimate for the conference:

	$
Coach running costs	2,000
Driver costs	3,000
Hotel costs	5,000
General overheads	2,000
Sub-total	12,000
Profit (30%)	3,600
Total	15,600

You have considered this cost estimate but you believe that it would be more appropriate to base the quotation on relevant costs. You have therefore obtained the following further information:

Coach running costs represent the fuel costs of $1,500 plus an apportionment of the annual fixed costs of operating the coach. No specific fixed costs would be incurred if the coach is used on this contract. If the contract did not go ahead, the coach would not be in use for eight out of the ten days of the conference. For the other two days a contract has already been accepted which contains a significant financial penalty clause. This contract earns a contribution of $250 per day. A replacement coach could be hired for $180 per day.

Driver costs represent the salary and related employment costs of one driver for 10 days. If the driver is used on this contract the company will need to replace the driver so that VBJ can complete its existing work. The replacement driver would be hired from a recruitment agency that charges $400 per day for a suitably qualified driver.

Hotel costs are the expected costs of hiring the hotel for the conference.

General overheads are based upon the overhead absorption rate of VBJ and are set annually when the company prepares its budgets. The only general overhead cost that can be specifically identified with the conference is the time that has been spent in considering the costs of the conference and preparing the quotation. This amounted to $250.

Requirement

Prepare a statement showing the total relevant cost of the contract. Explain clearly the reasons for each of the values in your quotation and for excluding any of the costs (if appropriate).

(10 marks)

(b) Now that the quotation has been prepared, it is realised that there is some uncertainty concerning the hotel cost and the fuel cost. Further investigation has shown that these costs may be higher or lower than the original estimates. Estimated costs with their associated probabilities are as follows:

Estimated hotel cost ($)	*Probability* %	*Estimated fuel cost* ($)	*Probability* %
4,000	20	1,200	10
5,000	50	1,500	50
6,000	30	2,000	40

The following two-way data table shows the effect on the total relevant cost of these alternative values. All figures are in $:

			Hotel	
		$4,000	$5,000	$6,000
	$1,200	−1,300	−300	+700
Fuel	$1,500	−1,000	0	+1,000
	$2,000	−500	+500	+1,500

Requirements

(i) Explain the meaning of the above two-way data table.
(ii) Produce and interpret a table that shows how the two-way data table may be used in conjunction with the probabilities to improve the information available to the manager of VBJ.

(15 marks)
(Total marks = 25)

? Question Seven

(a) The Q organisation is a large, worldwide respected manufacturer of consumer electrical and electronic goods. Q constantly develops new products that are in high demand as they represent the latest technology and are "must haves" for those consumers that want to own the latest consumer gadgets. Recently Q has developed a new handheld digital DVD recorder and seeks your advice as to the price it should charge for such a technologically advanced product.

Requirement

Explain the relevance of the product life cycle to the consideration of alternative pricing policies that might be adopted by Q.

(10 marks)

(b) Market research has discovered that the price–demand relationship for the item during the initial launch phase will be as follows:

Price (£)	*Demand (units)*
100	10,000
80	20,000
69	30,000
62	40,000

Production of the DVD recorder would occur in batches of 10,000 units, and the production director believes that 50% of the variable manufacturing cost would be affected by a learning and experience curve. This would apply to each batch produced and continue at a constant rate of learning up to a production volume of 40,000 units when the learning would be complete. Thereafter, the unit variable manufacturing cost of the product would be equal to the unit cost of the fourth batch. The production director estimates that the unit variable manufacturing cost of the first batch would be £60 (£30 of which is subject to the effect of the learning and experience curve, and £30 of which is unaffected), whereas the average unit variable manufacturing cost of all four batches would be £52.71.

There are no non-manufacturing variable costs associated with the DVD recorder.

Requirements

(i) Calculate the rate of learning that is expected by the production director.

(4 marks)

(ii) Calculate the optimum price at which Q should sell the DVD recorder in order to maximise its profits during the initial launch phase of the product.

(8 marks)

(iii) Q expects that after the initial launch phase, the market price will be £57 per unit. Estimated product specific fixed costs during this phase of the product's life are expected to be £15,000 per month. During this phase of the product life cycle, Q wishes to achieve a target monthly profit of £30,000 from the product.

Calculate the number of units that need to be sold each month during this phase in order that Q achieves this target monthly profit.

(3 marks)

(Total marks = 25)

(Total marks for Section C = 50)

Indicative Maths Tables and Formulae

Area Under the Normal Curve

This table gives the area under the normal curve between the mean and a point Z standard deviations above the mean. The corresponding area for deviations below the mean can be found by symmetry.

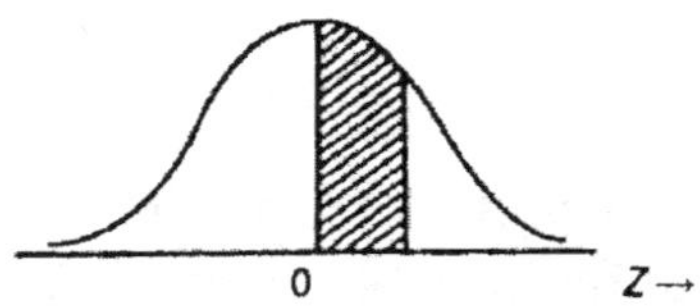

$Z = \frac{(x - \mu)}{\sigma}$	*0.00*	*0.01*	*0.02*	*0.03*	*0.04*	*0.05*	*0.06*	*0.07*	*0.08*	*0.09*
0.0	0.0000	0.0040	0.0080	0.0120	0.0159	0.0199	0.0239	0.0279	0.0319	0.0359
0.1	0.0398	0.0438	0.0478	0.0517	0.0557	0.0596	0.0636	0.0675	0.0714	0.0753
0.2	0.0793	0.0832	0.0871	0.0910	0.0948	0.0987	0.1026	0.1064	0.1103	0.1141
0.3	0.1179	0.1217	0.1255	0.1293	0.1331	0.1368	0.1406	0.1443	0.1480	0.1517
0.4	0.1554	0.1591	0.1628	0.1664	0.1700	0.1736	0.1772	0.1808	0.1844	0.1879
0.5	0.1915	0.1950	0.1985	0.2019	0.2054	0.2088	0.2123	0.2157	0.2190	0.2224
0.6	0.2257	0.2291	0.2324	0.2357	0.2389	0.2422	0.2454	0.2486	0.2518	0.2549
0.7	0.2580	0.2611	0.2642	0.2673	0.2704	0.2734	0.2764	0.2794	0.2823	0.2852
0.8	0.2881	0.2910	0.2939	0.2967	0.2995	0.3023	0.3051	0.3078	0.3106	0.3133
0.9	0.3159	0.3186	0.3212	0.3238	0.3264	0.3289	0.3315	0.3340	0.3365	0.3389
1.0	0.3413	0.3438	0.3461	0.3485	0.3508	0.3531	0.3554	0.3577	0.3599	0.3621
1.1	0.3643	0.3665	0.3686	0.3708	0.3729	0.3749	0.3770	0.3790	0.3810	0.3830
1.2	0.3849	0.3869	0.3888	0.3907	0.3925	0.3944	0.3962	0.3980	0.3997	0.4015
1.3	0.4032	0.4049	0.4066	0.4082	0.4099	0.4115	0.4131	0.4147	0.4162	0.4177
1.4	0.4192	0.4207	0.4222	0.4236	0.4251	0.4265	0.4279	0.4292	0.4306	0.4319
1.5	0.4332	0.4345	0.4357	0.4370	0.4382	0.4394	0.4406	0.4418	0.4430	0.4441
1.6	0.4452	0.4463	0.4474	0.4485	0.4495	0.4505	0.4515	0.4525	0.4535	0.4545
1.7	0.4554	0.4564	0.4573	0.4582	0.4591	0.4599	0.4608	0.4616	0.4625	0.4633
1.8	0.4641	0.4649	0.4656	0.4664	0.4671	0.4678	0.4686	0.4693	0.4699	0.4706
1.9	0.4713	0.4719	0.4726	0.4732	0.4738	0.4744	0.4750	0.4756	0.4762	0.4767
2.0	0.4772	0.4778	0.4783	0.4788	0.4793	0.4798	0.4803	0.4808	0.4812	0.4817
2.1	0.4821	0.4826	0.4830	0.4834	0.4838	0.4842	0.4846	0.4850	0.4854	0.4857
2.2	0.4861	0.4865	0.4868	0.4871	0.4875	0.4878	0.4881	0.4884	0.4887	0.4890
2.3	0.4893	0.4896	0.4898	0.4901	0.4904	0.4906	0.4909	0.4911	0.4913	0.4916
2.4	0.4918	0.4920	0.4922	0.4925	0.4927	0.4929	0.4931	0.4932	0.4934	0.4936
2.5	0.4938	0.4940	0.4941	0.4943	0.4945	0.4946	0.4948	0.4949	0.4951	0.4952
2.6	0.4953	0.4955	0.4956	0.4957	0.4959	0.4960	0.4961	0.4962	0.4963	0.4964
2.7	0.4965	0.4966	0.4967	0.4968	0.4969	0.4970	0.4971	0.4972	0.4973	0.4974
2.8	0.4974	0.4975	0.4976	0.4977	0.4977	0.4978	0.4979	0.4980	0.4980	0.4981
2.9	0.4981	0.4982	0.4983	0.4983	0.4984	0.4984	0.4985	0.4985	0.4986	0.4986
3.0	0.49865	0.4987	0.4987	0.4988	0.4988	0.4989	0.4989	0.4989	0.4990	0.4990
3.1	0.49903	0.4991	0.4991	0.4991	0.4992	0.4992	0.4992	0.4992	0.4993	0.4993
3.2	0.49931	0.4993	0.4994	0.4994	0.4994	0.4994	0.4994	0.4995	0.4995	0.4995
3.3	0.49952	0.4995	0.4995	0.4996	0.4996	0.4996	0.4996	0.4996	0.4996	0.4997
3.4	0.49966	0.4997	0.4997	0.4997	0.4997	0.4997	0.4997	0.4997	0.4997	0.4998
3.5	0.49977									

Present Value Table

Present value of £1 i.e. $(1 + r)^{-n}$ where r = interest rate; n = number of periods until payment or receipt.

Periods	Interest rates (r)																			
(n)	1%	2%	3%	4%	5%	6%	7%	8%	9%	10%	11%	12%	13%	14%	15%	16%	17%	18%	19%	20%
1	0.990	0.980	0.971	0.962	0.952	0.943	0.935	0.926	0.917	0.909	0.901	0.893	0.885	0.877	0.870	0.862	0.855	0.847	0.840	0.833
2	0.980	0.961	0.943	0.925	0.907	0.890	0.873	0.857	0.842	0.826	0.812	0.797	0.783	0.769	0.756	0.743	0.731	0.718	0.706	0.694
3	0.971	0.942	0.915	0.889	0.864	0.840	0.816	0.794	0.772	0.751	0.731	0.712	0.693	0.675	0.658	0.641	0.624	0.609	0.593	0.579
4	0.961	0.924	0.888	0.855	0.823	0.792	0.763	0.735	0.708	0.683	0.659	0.636	0.613	0.592	0.572	0.552	0.534	0.516	0.499	0.482
5	0.951	0.906	0.863	0.822	0.784	0.747	0.713	0.681	0.650	0.621	0.593	0.567	0.543	0.519	0.497	0.476	0.456	0.437	0.419	0.402
6	0.942	0.888	0.837	0.790	0.746	0.705	0.666	0.630	0.596	0.564	0.535	0.507	0.480	0.456	0.432	0.410	0.390	0.370	0.352	0.335
7	0.933	0.871	0.813	0.760	0.711	0.665	0.623	0.583	0.547	0.513	0.482	0.452	0.425	0.400	0.376	0.354	0.333	0.314	0.296	0.279
8	0.923	0.853	0.789	0.731	0.677	0.627	0.582	0.540	0.502	0.467	0.434	0.404	0.376	0.351	0.327	0.305	0.285	0.266	0.249	0.233
9	0.914	0.837	0.766	0.703	0.645	0.592	0.544	0.500	0.460	0.424	0.391	0.361	0.333	0.308	0.284	0.263	0.243	0.225	0.209	0.194
10	0.905	0.820	0.744	0.676	0.614	0.558	0.508	0.463	0.422	0.386	0.352	0.322	0.295	0.270	0.247	0.227	0.208	0.191	0.176	0.162
11	0.896	0.804	0.722	0.650	0.585	0.527	0.475	0.429	0.388	0.350	0.317	0.287	0.261	0.237	0.215	0.195	0.178	0.162	0.148	0.135
12	0.887	0.788	0.701	0.625	0.557	0.497	0.444	0.397	0.356	0.319	0.286	0.257	0.231	0.208	0.187	0.168	0.152	0.137	0.124	0.112
13	0.879	0.773	0.681	0.601	0.530	0.469	0.415	0.368	0.326	0.290	0.258	0.229	0.204	0.182	0.163	0.145	0.130	0.116	0.104	0.093
14	0.870	0.758	0.661	0.577	0.505	0.442	0.388	0.340	0.299	0.263	0.232	0.205	0.181	0.160	0.141	0.125	0.111	0.099	0.088	0.078
15	0.861	0.743	0.642	0.555	0.481	0.417	0.362	0.315	0.275	0.239	0.209	0.183	0.160	0.140	0.123	0.108	0.095	0.084	0.074	0.065
16	0.853	0.728	0.623	0.534	0.458	0.394	0.339	0.292	0.252	0.218	0.188	0.163	0.141	0.123	0.107	0.093	0.081	0.071	0.062	0.054
17	0.844	0.714	0.605	0.513	0.436	0.371	0.317	0.270	0.231	0.198	0.170	0.146	0.125	0.108	0.093	0.080	0.069	0.060	0.052	0.045
18	0.836	0.700	0.587	0.494	0.416	0.350	0.296	0.250	0.212	0.180	0.153	0.130	0.111	0.095	0.081	0.069	0.059	0.051	0.044	0.038
19	0.828	0.686	0.570	0.475	0.396	0.331	0.277	0.232	0.194	0.164	0.138	0.116	0.098	0.083	0.070	0.060	0.051	0.043	0.037	0.031
20	0.820	0.673	0.554	0.456	0.377	0.312	0.258	0.215	0.178	0.149	0.124	0.104	0.087	0.073	0.061	0.051	0.043	0.037	0.031	0.026

Cumulative Present Value of £1

This table shows the Present Value of £1 per annum. Receivable or Payable at the end of each year for n years $\frac{1 - (1 + r)^{-n}}{r}$.

Periods (n)	Interest rates (r) 1%	2%	3%	4%	5%	6%	7%	8%	9%	10%	11%	12%	13%	14%	15%	16%	17%	18%	19%	20%
1	0.990	0.980	0.971	0.962	0.952	0.943	0.935	0.926	0.917	0.909	0.901	0.893	0.885	0.877	0.870	0.862	0.855	0.847	0.840	0.833
2	1.970	1.942	1.913	1.386	1.859	1.833	1.808	1.783	1.759	1.736	1.713	1.690	1.668	1.647	1.626	1.605	1.585	1.566	1.547	1.528
3	2.941	2.884	2.829	2.775	2.723	2.673	2.624	2.577	2.531	2.487	2.444	2.402	2.361	2.322	2.283	2.246	2.210	2.174	2.140	2.106
4	3.902	3.808	3.717	3.630	3.546	3.463	3.387	3.312	3.240	3.170	3.102	3.037	2.974	2.914	2.855	2.798	2.743	2.690	2.639	2.589
5	4.853	4.713	4.580	4.452	4.329	4.212	4.100	3.993	3.890	3.791	3.696	3.605	3.517	3.433	3.352	3.274	3.199	3.127	3.058	2.991
6	5.795	5.601	5.417	5.242	5.076	4.917	4.767	4.623	4.486	4.355	4.231	4.111	3.998	3.689	3.784	3.685	3.589	3.498	3.410	3.326
7	6.728	6.472	6.230	6.002	5.786	5.582	5.389	5.206	5.033	4.868	4.712	4.564	4.423	4.288	4.160	4.039	3.922	3.812	3.706	3.605
8	7.652	7.325	7.020	6.733	6.463	6.210	5.971	5.747	5.535	5.335	5.146	4.968	4.799	4.639	4.487	4.344	4.207	4.078	3.954	3.837
9	8.565	8.162	7.786	7.435	7.108	6.802	6.515	6.247	5.995	5.759	5.537	5.328	5.132	4.946	4.772	4.607	4.451	4.303	4.163	4.031
10	9.471	8.983	8.530	8.111	7.722	7.360	7.024	6.710	6.418	6.145	5.889	5.650	5.426	5.216	5.019	4.833	4.659	4.494	4.339	4.192
11	10.368	9.787	9.253	8.760	8.306	7.887	7.499	7.139	6.805	6.495	6.207	5.938	5.687	5.453	5.234	5.029	4.836	4.656	4.486	4.327
12	11.255	10.575	9.954	9.385	8.863	8.384	7.943	7.536	7.161	6.814	6.492	6.194	5.918	5.660	5.421	5.197	4.988	4.793	4.611	4.439
13	12.134	11.348	10.635	9.986	9.394	8.853	8.358	7.904	7.487	7.103	6.750	6.424	6.122	5.842	5.583	5.342	5.118	4.910	4.715	4.533
14	13.004	12.106	11.296	10.563	9.899	9.295	8.745	8.244	7.786	7.367	6.982	6.628	6.302	6.002	5.724	5.468	5.229	5.008	4.802	4.611
15	13.865	12.849	11.938	11.118	10.380	9.712	9.108	8.559	8.061	7.606	7.191	6.811	6.462	6.142	5.847	5.575	5.324	5.092	4.876	4.675
16	14.718	13.578	12.561	11.652	10.838	10.106	9.447	8.851	8.313	7.824	7.379	6.974	6.604	6.265	5.954	5.668	5.405	5.162	4.938	4.730
17	15.562	14.292	13.166	12.166	11.274	10.477	9.763	9.122	8.544	8.022	7.549	7.120	8.729	6.373	6.047	5.749	5.475	5.222	4.990	4.775
18	16.398	14.992	13.754	12.659	11.690	10.828	10.059	9.372	8.756	8.201	7.702	7.250	6.840	6.467	6.128	5.818	5.534	5.273	5.033	4.812
19	17.226	15.679	14.324	13.134	12.085	11.158	10.336	9.604	8.950	8.365	7.839	7.366	6.938	6.550	6.198	5.877	5.584	5.316	5.070	4.843
20	18.046	16.351	14.878	13.590	12.462	11.470	10.594	9.818	9.129	8.514	7.963	7.469	7.025	6.623	6.259	5.929	5.628	5.353	5.101	4.870

Formulae

Probability

$A \cup B$ = **A or B**. $A \cap B$ = **A and B** (overlap).
$P(B|A)$ = probability of B, **given** A.

Rules of addition

If A and B are mutually exclusive: $P(A \cup B) = P(A) + P(B)$
If A and B are **not** mutually exclusive: $P(A \cup B) = P(A) + P(B) - P(A \cap B)$

Rules of multiplication

If A and B are *independent*: $P(A \cap B) = P(A) * P(B)$
If A and B are **not** *independent*: $P(A \cap B) = P(A) * P(B|A)$
$E(X) = \sum(\text{probability} * \text{payoff})$

Quadratic equations

If $aX^2 + bX + c = 0$ is the general quadratic equation, the two solutions (roots) are given by:

$$X = \frac{-b \pm \sqrt{b^2 - 4ac}}{2a}$$

Descriptive statistics

Arithmetic mean

$$\bar{x} = \frac{\sum x}{n} \quad \bar{x} = \frac{\sum fx}{\sum f} \quad \text{(frequency distribution)}$$

Standard deviation

$$SD = \sqrt{\frac{\sum(x - \bar{x})}{n}} \quad SD = \sqrt{\frac{\sum fx^2}{\sum f} - \bar{x}^2} \quad \text{(frequency distribution)}$$

Index numbers

Price relative = $100 * P_1/P_0$ Quantity relative = $100 * Q_1/Q_0$

Price: $$\frac{\sum w * \left(\frac{P_1}{P_0}\right)}{\sum w} \times 100$$

Quantity: $$\frac{\sum w * \left(\frac{Q_1}{Q_0}\right)}{\sum w} \times 100$$

Time series

Additive model
Series = Trend + Seasonal + Random
Multiplicative model
Series = Trend * Seasonal * Random

Linear regression and correlation

The linear regression equation of y on x is given by:

$$Y = a + bX \quad \text{or} \quad Y - Y = b(\overline{X} - \overline{X})$$

where

$$b = \frac{\text{Covariance}(XY)}{\text{Variance}(X)} = \frac{n\sum XY - (\sum x)(\sum y)}{n\sum x^2 - (\sum x)^2}$$

and

$$a = \overline{Y} - b\overline{X}$$

or solve

$$\sum Y = na + b\sum x$$
$$\sum XY = a\sum x + b\sum x^2$$

Coefficient of correlation

$$r = \frac{\text{Covariance}(XY)}{\sqrt{Var(X).Var(Y)}} = \frac{n\sum XY - (\sum X)(\sum Y)}{\sqrt{\{n\sum x^2 - (\sum x)^2\}\{n\sum y^2 - (\sum y)^2\}}}$$

$$R(\text{rank}) = 1 - \frac{6\sum d^2}{n(n^2 - 1)}$$

Financial mathematics

Compound interest (values and sums)

Future Value of S, of a sum of X, invested for n periods, compounded at $r\%$ interest

$S = X[1 + r]n$

Annuity

Present value of an annuity of £1 per annum receivable or payable for *n* years, commencing in one year, discounted at *r* % per annum:

$$PV = \frac{1}{r}\left[1 - \frac{1}{[1 + r]^n}\right]$$

Perpetuity

Present value of £1 per annum, payable or receivable in perpetuity, commencing in one year, discounted at *r*% per annum:

$$PV = \frac{1}{r}$$

Review of May 2005 paper

Section A

Question 1: 20 marks

Question 1 comprised 8 compulsory objective test sub-questions for 2, 3 and 4 marks each.

The topics to which these questions related were
Key factor/limiting factor analysis
Breakeven analysis
Relevant costing
Internal rate of return
Cost of capital
Learning curves
Probability theory
Selling price to maximise profit

Section B: 3 compulsory 10 mark questions

Question 2: 10 marks

Question 2 required students to produce a report to the managing director of a manufacturing group.

The question related to stock control and stock ordering in a business that manufactures the same volume of production each week and experiences seasonal demand for the product so ending up with fluctuating levels of finished goods inventory.

The managing director has just become aware of the Just In Time (JIT) element of World Class Manufacturing.

The report required students to discuss the effect of introducing JIT on the profit of the group.

This necessitated a discussion of both the current and the proposed new (JIT) approach towards production and stockholding.

It would have been easy to lose marks here by discussing the new approach only rather than discussing both the existing and the proposed new approach.

Question 3: 10 marks

This question related to the lease or buy decision for a business acquiring a new vehicle.

The vehicle is expected to have a three-year life. The cost of capital was given along with the tax rate and tax regime.

Students were required to produce a table of relevant costs including tax-related cash flows using their relevant costing knowledge. These cash flows then had to be discounted to arrive at a net present value for each of the lease and buy decisions.

Question 4: 10 marks

This question had two requirements for 5 marks each.

Part (a) tested knowledge of joint cost apportionment for a business manufacturing 3 products in a common or joint manufacturing process.

Part (b) related to the decision to sell products as soon as they result from the common manufacturing process as against undertaking further processing and selling the product as a further processed version.

Students should have used their relevant costing knowledge to compare the additional processing costs with the additional revenue that could be generated if further processing is undertaken.

Section C: Two 25 mark questions to be attempted from a choice of three questions

Question 5: 25 marks

This question had two requirements – Part (a) for 15 marks and Part (b) for 10 marks.

This gives rise to a very important examination technique issue.

Time should be allocated to the separate parts of the requirement according to the marks available!

Part (a) required the use of the net present value investment appraisal technique to determine whether or not a printing company should make an investment in new equipment. The cost of capital was given along with the tax rate and tax regime.

Students were required to produce a table of relevant costs including tax-related cash flows using their relevant costing knowledge. These cash flows then had to be discounted to arrive at the net present value.

Part (b) also related to investment appraisal. It required students to explain what is meant by sensitivity analysis and calculate how sensitive would be the investment decision from Part (a) to a change in the tax rate or a change in the annual contribution cash flows.

Question 6: 25 marks

This question had two requirements – Part (a) for 10 marks and Part (b) for 15 marks.

This gives rise to a very important examination technique issue.

Time should be allocated to the separate parts of the requirement according to the marks available!

Part (a) required students to produce a statement of relevant costs in order to tender for a piece of work with a potential customer.

This would require careful application not only of relevant costing knowledge but also of examination technique. The requirement asked for explanation of relevant and non-relevant items. Marks would have been lost if a table of relevant costs had been produced without these supporting explanations.

Part (b) tested expected value calculations using a two-way data. Students had to interpret the table in terms of how it had been prepared and what the information within it says as well as showing how the information could improve the information provided in Part (a) of the question.

Part (b) was the most challenging part of the question.

Question 7: 25 marks

This question had two requirements – Part (a) for 10 marks and Part (b) had three sub-requirements totalling 15 marks.

This gives rise to a very important examination technique issue.

Time should be allocated to the separate parts of the requirement according to the marks available!

Part (a) required discussion of the use of the product life cycle model when deciding on the selling price to be charged for a new product. In this instance, the new product is a high-tech product: a handheld digital DVD recorder. It would have been important to make comments which were relevant to this type of high-tech product rather than just discussing pricing policy in general. Comments were required in relation to the passage of the product through the various phases of the product life cycle from introduction through to decline.

Part (b) tested knowledge of the use of learning curve knowledge for 4 marks, optimal price to charge to maximise profits for 8 marks and the number of units that must be sold in order to achieve a profit target for 3 marks.

November 2005 Questions and Answers

13

Managerial Level

Management Accounting – Decision Management (Paper P2)

The answers published here have been written by the Examiner and should provide a helpful guide for both tutors and students.

Published separately on the CIMA website (www.cimaglobal.com) from the end of February 2006 is a Post Examination Guide for this paper, which provides much valuable and complementary material including indicative mark information.

© 2005 The Chartered Institute of Management Accountants. All rights reserved. No part of this publication may be reproduced, stored in a retrieval system, or transmitted, in any form or by any means, electronic, mechanical, photocopying, recorded or otherwise, without the written permission of the publisher.

© The Chartered Institute of Management Accountants 2005

CIMA

Management Accounting Pillar

Managerial Level Paper

P2 – Management Accounting - Decision Management

23 November 2005 – Wednesday Morning Session

Instructions to candidates

You are allowed three hours to answer this question paper
You are allowed 20 minutes reading time **before the examination begins** during which you should read the question paper, and if you wish, make annotations on the question paper. However, you will **not** be allowed, **under any circumstances**, to open the answer book and start writing or use your calculator during this reading time.
You are strongly advised to carefully read ALL the question requirements before attempting the question concerned (that is, all parts and/or sub-questions). The requirements for the questions in Sections B and C are contained in a dotted box.
Answer the ONE compulsory question in Section A. This is comprised of eight sub-questions and is on pages 207 to 208.
Answer ALL THREE compulsory questions in Section B on pages 209 to 211.
Answer TWO of the three questions in Section C on pages 212 to 216.
Maths Tables and Formulae are provided on pages 217 to 219.
Write your full examination number, paper number and the examination subject title in the spaces provided on the front of the examination answer book. Also write your contact ID and name in the space provided in the right hand margin and seal to close.
Tick the appropriate boxes on the front of the answer book to indicate which questions you have answered.

SECTION A – 20 MARKS

[the indicative time for answering this section is 36 minutes]

ANSWER *ALL* EIGHT SUB-QUESTIONS

Instructions for answering Section A:

The answers to the eight sub-questions in Section A should ALL be written in your answer book.

Your answers should be clearly numbered with the sub-question number and then ruled off, so that the markers know which sub-question you are answering. For multiple choice questions, you need only write the sub-question number and the letter of the answer option you have chosen. You do not need to start a new page for each sub-question.

For sub-questions **1.6**, **1.7**, and **1.8** you should show your workings as marks are available for the method you use to answer these sub-questions.

? Question One

1.1 A five-year project has a net present value of $160,000 when it is discounted at 12%. The project includes an annual cash outflow of $50,000 for each of the five years. No tax is payable on projects of this type.

The percentage increase in the value of this annual cash outflow that would make the project no longer financially viable is closest to

A 64%
B 89%
C 113%
D 156%

(2 marks)

The following data are to be used when answering questions 1.2 and 1.3

A company expects to sell 1,000 units per month of a new product but there is uncertainty as to both the unit selling price and the unit variable cost of the product. The following estimates of selling price, variable costs and their related probabilities have been made:

Selling Price		*Unit Variable Cost*	
£ per unit	*Probability*	*£ per unit*	*Probability*
20	25%	8	20%
25	40%	10	50%
30	35%	12	30%

There are specific fixed costs of £5,000 per month expected for the new product.

1.2 The expected value of monthly contribution is

A £5,890
B £10,300
C £10,890
D £15,300

(2 marks)

1.3 The probability of monthly contribution from this new product exceeding £13,500 is

A 24.5%
B 30.5%
C 63.0%
D 92.5%

(2 marks)

1.4 PT has discovered that when it employs a new test engineer there is a learning curve with a 75% rate of learning that exists for the first 12 customer assignments. A new test engineer completed her first customer assignment in 6 hours.

Calculate the time that she should take for her 7th assignment to the nearest 0.01 hours.

Note: The index for a 75% learning curve is −0.415.

(2 marks)

The following data are to be used when answering questions 1.5 and 1.6

JKL plc has $1 million available for investment. It has identified three possible investments, J, K and L, which each have a life of three years. The three-year period coincides with JKL plc's investment plans. JKL plc uses a 15% cost of capital when appraising investments of this type. Details of these investments are set out below:

	J	*K*	*L*
	$'000	$'000	$'000
Initial investment	400	500	300
Net positive cashflows			
Year 1	40	70	50
Year 2	80	90	50
Year 3	510	630	380
Net present value	31	43	31

1.5 Assuming that each of the investments is divisible, they are not mutually exclusive and cannot be invested in more than once, state the optimum investment plan for JKL plc.

(2 marks)

1.6 Calculate the Internal Rate of Return of an investment in project K to the nearest 0.01%.

(3 marks)

1.7 FH is an electronics company that has developed a new product for the video conferencing market. The product has successfully completed its testing phase and FH has now produced the first four production units. The first unit took 3 hours of labour time and the total time for the first four units was 8.3667 hours.

Calculate the learning curve improvement rate (rate of learning) to the nearest 0.1%.

(3 marks)

1.8 A baker is trying to decide the number of batches of a particular type of bread that he should bake each day. Daily demand ranges from 10 batches to 12 batches. Each batch of bread that is baked and sold yields a positive contribution of £50, but each batch of bread baked that is not sold yields a negative contribution of £20.

Assuming the baker adopts the *minimax regret* decision rule, calculate the number of batches of bread that he should bake each day. You must justify your answer.

(4 marks)

(Section A = 20 marks)

SECTION B – 30 MARKS

[the indicative time for answering this section is 54 minutes]

ANSWER *ALL* THREE QUESTIONS

Question Two

The owner of a taxi company is considering the replacement of his vehicles. He is planning to retire in 6 years' time and is therefore only concerned with that period of time, but cannot decide whether it is better to replace the vehicles every two years or every three years.

The following data have been estimated (all values at today's price levels):

Purchase cost and trade in values

Taxi cost	£15,000
Trade-in value of taxi	
after 2 years	£7,000
after 3 years	£4,000

Annual costs and revenues

Vehicle running cost	£20,000 per year
Fares charged to customers	£40,000 per year

Vehicle servicing and repair costs

Vehicle servicing and repair costs depend on the age of the vehicle. In the following table, Year 1 represents the cost in the first year of the vehicle's ownership; Year 2 represents the cost in the second year of ownership and so on:

Year 1	£500
Year 2	£2,500
Year 3	£4,000

Inflation

New vehicle costs and trade-in values are expected to increase by 5% per year.
Vehicle running costs and fares are expected to increase by 7% per year.
Vehicle servicing and repair costs are expected to increase by 10% per year.

Requirement

Advise the company on the optimum replacement cycle for its vehicles and state the net present value of the opportunity cost of making the wrong decision. Use a discount rate of 12% per year. All workings and assumptions should be shown. Ignore taxation.

(10 marks)

Question Three

ML is an engineering company that specialises in providing engineering facilities to businesses that cannot justify operating their own facilities in-house. ML employs a number of engineers who are skilled in different engineering techniques that enable ML to provide a full range of engineering facilities to its customers. Most of the work undertaken by ML is unique to each of its customers, often requiring the manufacture of spare parts for its customers' equipment, or the building of new equipment from customer drawings. As a result most of ML's work is short-term, with some jobs being completed within hours while others may take a few days.

To date ML has adopted a cost plus approach to setting its prices. This is based upon an absorption costing system that uses machine hours as the basis of absorbing overhead costs into individual job costs. The Managing Director is concerned that over recent months ML has been unsuccessful when quoting for work with the consequence that there has been an increase in the level of unused capacity. It has been suggested that ML should adopt an alternative approach to its pricing based on marginal costing since "any price that exceeds variable costs is better than no work".

Requirement

With reference to the above scenario

(i) briefly explain absorption and marginal cost approaches to pricing;
(ii) discuss the validity of the comment "any price that exceeds variable costs is better than no work".

(10 marks)

Question Four

You are the assistant management accountant within PK plc. PK plc manufactures high-quality self-assembly furniture from raw materials utilising highly skilled labour within a computer-controlled manufacturing facility. The company produces a range of furniture, and, because of the lead time to receive delivery of its raw materials, has a finished goods inventory policy of holding an average of two weeks estimated sales in inventory. Customer demand is seasonal and, as a consequence, this finished goods inventory level fluctuates throughout the year. The company also holds inventories of raw materials based upon estimates of its production requirements. An absorption costing system is used to attribute all manufacturing costs to output.

Increasingly PK plc is facing competition, particularly from overseas manufacturers and its sales team have to make decisions about the extent to which it can offer price discounts in order to win customer orders.

Requirement

Prepare a report addressed to the Management Team of PK plc that explains the changing nature of cost structures in the modern manufacturing environment and the implications for PK plc's

(i) inventory valuation
(ii) short-term decision making

(10 marks)

Note: There are 2 marks available for format and presentational style.

(Section B = 30 marks)

SECTION C – 50 MARKS

[the indicative time for answering this section is 90 minutes]

ANSWER *TWO* QUESTIONS OUT OF THREE

? Question Five

The MP Organisation is an independent film production company. It has a number of potential films that it is considering producing, one of which is the subject of a management meeting next week. The film which has been code named CA45 is a thriller based on a novel by a well-respected author.

The script has already been written at a cost of $10,000 and preliminary discussions have been held with the lead actors. The MP Organisation has incurred travel and other incidental costs of $4,000 to date. The following additional costs have been estimated in order to produce the film:

	$'000
Production director's fee	100
Set design	10
Costumes and wardrobe	20
Actors' fees	50
Musician/Songwriter for soundtrack	5
Camera and equipment hire	20
Actors' travel and accommodation costs	10
Other production costs	5

Production of the film is estimated to take 16 weeks, and all of the above costs would be incurred during this period, though there is some uncertainty about the accuracy of these cost estimates. These cost values are those most likely to be incurred. With the exception of the payment to the production director which is a fixed fee, the other costs could be up to 10% higher or lower than the values estimated.

In addition there will be advertising, promotion and marketing costs of $15,000 immediately, $10,000 in each of Years 1 and 2, and then $5,000 during each of the next three years. These figures are not subject to any uncertainty.

The film is expected to have a life of five years. During the first three years the film will be sold to cinemas through distributors and MP will receive 25% of the gross revenues. The film will be sold as a DVD for the remaining two years and MP will receive 100% of these revenues. The expected gross revenues are as follows:

Year	*Source*	*Gross revenue*	*MP's share*
1	Cinema	$400,000	25%
2	Cinema	$600,000	25%
3	Cinema	$450,000	25%
4	DVD	$50,000	100%
5	DVD	$30,000	100%

However it is thought that the gross revenues could vary by as much as 20% higher or lower than those stated, depending on the popularity of the film. The initial level of popularity will continue for all five years.

The MP Organisation evaluates new films using a cost of capital of 15% per year.

Requirements

(a) Prepare calculations for each combination of the most likely, optimistic and pessimistic cost **and** revenue values to evaluate whether or not the MP Organisation should continue with the production of the film. Discuss your analysis and make a recommendation to MP.

(15 marks)

(b) Prepare notes for the management meeting that explain how probabilities can be used,

(i) to calculate the expected NPV; and

(ii) in a simulation model to evaluate the risk of a long-term decision.

(10 marks)

(Total for Question Five = 25 marks)

? Question Six

QP plc is a food processing company that produces pre-prepared meals for sale to consumers through a number of different supermarkets. The company specialises in three particular pre-prepared meals and has invested significantly in modern manufacturing processes to ensure a high quality product. The company is very aware of the importance of training and retaining high quality staff in all areas of the company and, in order to ensure their production employees' commitment to the company, the employees are guaranteed a weekly salary that is equivalent to their normal working hours paid at their normal hourly rate of £7 per hour.

The meals are produced in batches of 100 units. Costs and selling prices per batch are as follows:

Meal	*TR £/batch*	*PN £/batch*	*BE £/batch*
Selling Price	340	450	270
Ingredient K (£5/kg)	150	120	90
Ingredient L (£10/kg)	70	90	40
Ingredient M (£15/kg)	30	75	45
Labour (£7/hour)	21	28	42
Factory costs absorbed	20	80	40

QP plc has adopted throughput accounting for its short-term decisions.

Requirement

(a) State the principles of throughput accounting and the effects of using it for short-term decision making.

(6 marks)

(b) QP plc is preparing its production plans for the next three months and has estimated the maximum demand from its customers to be as follows:

TR	500 batches
PN	400 batches
BE	350 batches

These demand maximums are amended figures because a customer has just delayed its request for a large order and QP has unusually got some spare capacity over the next three months. However, these demand maximums do include a contract for the delivery of 50 batches of each to an important customer. If this minimum contract is not satisfied then QP plc will have to pay a substantial financial penalty for non-delivery.

The Production Director is concerned at hearing news that two of the ingredients used are expected to be in short supply for the next three months. QP plc does not hold inventory of these ingredients and although there are no supply problems for ingredient K, the supplies of ingredients L and M are expected to be limited to:

Ingredient L	7,000 kilos
Ingredient M	3,000 kilos

The Production Director has researched the problem and found that ingredient V can be used as a direct substitute for ingredient M. It also costs the same as ingredient M. There is an unlimited supply of ingredient V.

Requirement

Prepare calculations to determine the production mix that will maximise the profit of QP plc during the next three months.

(10 marks)

(c) The World Health Organisation has now announced that ingredient V contains dangerously high levels of a chemical that can cause life-threatening illnesses. As a consequence it can no longer be used in the production of food.

As a result, the production director has determined the optimal solution to the company's production mix problem using linear programming. This is set out below:

Objective function value	110,714
TR value	500
PN value	357
BE value	71
TR slack value	0
PN slack value	43
BE slack value	279
L value	3
M value	28

Requirement

Explain the meaning of each of the values contained in the above solution.

(9 marks)

(Total for Question Six = 25 marks)

Question Seven

ZP plc is a marketing consultancy that provides marketing advice and support to small and medium-sized enterprises. ZP plc employs 4 full-time marketing consultants who each expect to deliver 1,500 chargeable hours per year and each receive a salary of £60,000 per year. In addition the company employs 6 marketing support/administration staff whose combined total salary cost is £120,000 per year.

ZP plc has estimated its other costs for the coming year as follows:

	£'000
Office premises: rent, rates, heating	50
Advertising	5
Travel to clients	15
Accommodation whilst visiting clients	11
Telephone, fax, communications	10

ZP plc has been attributing costs to each client (and to the projects undertaken for them) by recording the chargeable hours spent on each client and using a single cost rate of £75 per chargeable hour. The same basis has been used to estimate the costs of a project when preparing a quotation for new work.

ZP plc has reviewed its existing client database and determined the following three average profiles of typical clients:

Client profile	*D*	*E*	*F*
Chargeable hours per client	100	700	300
Distance (Miles) to client	50	70	100
Number of visits per client	3	8	3
Number of clients in each profile	10	5	5

The senior consultant has been reviewing the company's costing and pricing procedures. He suggests that the use of a single cost rate should be abandoned and, where possible, activities should be costed individually. With this in mind, he has obtained the following further information:

- It is ZP plc's policy that where a visit is made to a client and the distance to the client is more than 50 miles, the consultant will travel the day before the visit and stay in local accommodation so that the maximum time is available for meeting the client the following day.

- The cost of travel to the client is dependent on the number of miles travelled to visit the client.
- Other costs are facility costs – at present the senior consultant cannot identify an alternative basis to that currently being used to attribute costs to each client.

Requirements

(a) Prepare calculations to show the cost attributed to each client group using an activity based system of attributing costs.

(7 marks)

(b) Discuss the differences between the costs attributed using activity based costing and those attributed by the current system and advise whether the senior consultant's suggestion should be adopted.

(9 marks)

(c) In a manufacturing environment, activity based costing often classifies activities into those that are: unit; batch; product sustaining and facility sustaining. Discuss, giving examples, how similar classifications may be applied to the use of the technique in consultancy organisations such as ZP plc.

(9 marks)

(Total for Question Seven = 25 marks)

(Section C = 50 marks)

PRESENT VALUE TABLE

Present value of $1, that is $(1 + r)^{-n}$ where r = interest rate; n = number of periods until payment or receipt.

Periods (n)	Interest rates (r)									
	1%	2%	3%	4%	5%	6%	7%	8%	9%	10%
1	0.990	0.980	0.971	0.962	0.952	0.943	0.935	0.926	0.917	0.909
2	0.980	0.961	0.943	0.925	0.907	0.890	0.873	0.857	0.842	0.826
3	0.971	0.942	0.915	0.889	0.864	0.840	0.816	0.794	0.772	0.751
4	0.961	0.924	0.888	0.855	0.823	0.792	0.763	0.735	0.708	0.683
5	0.951	0.906	0.863	0.822	0.784	0.747	0.713	0.681	0.650	0.621
6	0.942	0.888	0.837	0.790	0.746	0.705	0.666	0.630	0.596	0.564
7	0.933	0.871	0.813	0.760	0.711	0.665	0.623	0.583	0.547	0.513
8	0.923	0.853	0.789	0.731	0.677	0.627	0.582	0.540	0.502	0.467
9	0.914	0.837	0.766	0.703	0.645	0.592	0.544	0.500	0.460	0.424
10	0.905	0.820	0.744	0.676	0.614	0.558	0.508	0.463	0.422	0.386
11	0.896	0.804	0.722	0.650	0.585	0.527	0.475	0.429	0.388	0.350
12	0.887	0.788	0.701	0.625	0.557	0.497	0.444	0.397	0.356	0.319
13	0.879	0.773	0.681	0.601	0.530	0.469	0.415	0.368	0.326	0.290
14	0.870	0.758	0.661	0.577	0.505	0.442	0.388	0.340	0.299	0.263
15	0.861	0.743	0.642	0.555	0.481	0.417	0.362	0.315	0.275	0.239
16	0.853	0.728	0.623	0.534	0.458	0.394	0.339	0.292	0.252	0.218
17	0.844	0.714	0.605	0.513	0.436	0.371	0.317	0.270	0.231	0.198
18	0.836	0.700	0.587	0.494	0.416	0.350	0.296	0.250	0.212	0.180
19	0.828	0.686	0.570	0.475	0.396	0.331	0.277	0.232	0.194	0.164
20	0.820	0.673	0.554	0.456	0.377	0.312	0.258	0.215	0.178	0.149

Periods (n)	Interest rates (r)									
	11%	12%	13%	14%	15%	16%	17%	18%	19%	20%
1	0.901	0.893	0.885	0.877	0.870	0.862	0.855	0.847	0.840	0.833
2	0.812	0.797	0.783	0.769	0.756	0.743	0.731	0.718	0.706	0.694
3	0.731	0.712	0.693	0.675	0.658	0.641	0.624	0.609	0.593	0.579
4	0.659	0.636	0.613	0.592	0.572	0.552	0.534	0.516	0.499	0.482
5	0.593	0.567	0.543	0.519	0.497	0.476	0.456	0.437	0.419	0.402
6	0.535	0.507	0.480	0.456	0.432	0.410	0.390	0.370	0.352	0.335
7	0.482	0.452	0.425	0.400	0.376	0.354	0.333	0.314	0.296	0.279
8	0.434	0.404	0.376	0.351	0.327	0.305	0.285	0.266	0.249	0.233
9	0.391	0.361	0.333	0.308	0.284	0.263	0.243	0.225	0.209	0.194
10	0.352	0.322	0.295	0.270	0.247	0.227	0.208	0.191	0.176	0.162
11	0.317	0.287	0.261	0.237	0.215	0.195	0.178	0.162	0.148	0.135
12	0.286	0.257	0.231	0.208	0.187	0.168	0.152	0.137	0.124	0.112
13	0.258	0.229	0.204	0.182	0.163	0.145	0.130	0.116	0.104	0.093
14	0.232	0.205	0.181	0.160	0.141	0.125	0.111	0.099	0.088	0.078
15	0.209	0.183	0.160	0.140	0.123	0.108	0.095	0.084	0.079	0.065
16	0.188	0.163	0.141	0.123	0.107	0.093	0.081	0.071	0.062	0.054
17	0.170	0.146	0.125	0.108	0.093	0.080	0.069	0.060	0.052	0.045
18	0.153	0.130	0.111	0.095	0.081	0.069	0.059	0.051	0.044	0.038
19	0.138	0.116	0.098	0.083	0.070	0.060	0.051	0.043	0.037	0.031
20	0.124	0.104	0.087	0.073	0.061	0.051	0.043	0.037	0.031	0.026

Cumulative present value of $1 per annum, Receivable or Payable at the end of each year for n years $\frac{1-(1+r)^{-n}}{r}$

Periods (n)	Interest rates (r)									
	1%	2%	3%	4%	5%	6%	7%	8%	9%	10%
1	0.990	0.980	0.971	0.962	0.952	0.943	0.935	0.926	0.917	0.909
2	1.970	1.942	1.913	1.886	1.859	1.833	1.808	1.783	1.759	1.736
3	2.941	2.884	2.829	2.775	2.723	2.673	2.624	2.577	2.531	2.487
4	3.902	3.808	3.717	3.630	3.546	3.465	3.387	3.312	3.240	3.170
5	4.853	4.713	4.580	4.452	4.329	4.212	4.100	3.993	3.890	3.791
6	5.795	5.601	5.417	5.242	5.076	4.917	4.767	4.623	4.486	4.355
7	6.728	6.472	6.230	6.002	5.786	5.582	5.389	5.206	5.033	4.868
8	7.652	7.325	7.020	6.733	6.463	6.210	5.971	5.747	5.535	5.335
9	8.566	8.162	7.786	7.435	7.108	6.802	6.515	6.247	5.995	5.759
10	9.471	8.983	8.530	8.111	7.722	7.360	7.024	6.710	6.418	6.145
11	10.368	9.787	9.253	8.760	8.306	7.887	7.499	7.139	6.805	6.495
12	11.255	10.575	9.954	9.385	8.863	8.384	7.943	7.536	7.161	6.814
13	12.134	11.348	10.635	9.986	9.394	8.853	8.358	7.904	7.487	7.103
14	13.004	12.106	11.296	10.563	9.899	9.295	8.745	8.244	7.786	7.367
15	13.865	12.849	11.938	11.118	10.380	9.712	9.108	8.559	8.061	7.606
16	14.718	13.578	12.561	11.652	10.838	10.106	9.447	8.851	8.313	7.824
17	15.562	14.292	13.166	12.166	11.274	10.477	9.763	9.122	8.544	8.022
18	16.398	14.992	13.754	12.659	11.690	10.828	10.059	9.372	8.756	8.201
19	17.226	15.679	14.324	13.134	12.085	11.158	10.336	9.604	8.950	8.365
20	18.046	16.351	14.878	13.590	12.462	11.470	10.594	9.818	9.129	8.514

Periods (n)	Interest rates (r)									
	11%	12%	13%	14%	15%	16%	17%	18%	19%	20%
1	0.901	0.893	0.885	0.877	0.870	0.862	0.855	0.847	0.840	0.833
2	1.713	1.690	1.668	1.647	1.626	1.605	1.585	1.566	1.547	1.528
3	2.444	2.402	2.361	2.322	2.283	2.246	2.210	2.174	2.140	2.106
4	3.102	3.037	2.974	2.914	2.855	2.798	2.743	2.690	2.639	2.589
5	3.696	3.605	3.517	3.433	3.352	3.274	3.199	3.127	3.058	2.991
6	4.231	4.111	3.998	3.889	3.784	3.685	3.589	3.498	3.410	3.326
7	4.712	4.564	4.423	4.288	4.160	4.039	3.922	3.812	3.706	3.605
8	5.146	4.968	4.799	4.639	4.487	4.344	4.207	4.078	3.954	3.837
9	5.537	5.328	5.132	4.946	4.772	4.607	4.451	4.303	4.163	4.031
10	5.889	5.650	5.426	5.216	5.019	4.833	4.659	4.494	4.339	4.192
11	6.207	5.938	5.687	5.453	5.234	5.029	4.836	4.656	4.486	4.327
12	6.492	6.194	5.918	5.660	5.421	5.197	4.988	7.793	4.611	4.439
13	6.750	6.424	6.122	5.842	5.583	5.342	5.118	4.910	4.715	4.533
14	6.982	6.628	6.302	6.002	5.724	5.468	5.229	5.008	4.802	4.611
15	7.191	6.811	6.462	6.142	5.847	5.575	5.324	5.092	4.876	4.675
16	7.379	6.974	6.604	6.265	5.954	5.668	5.405	5.162	4.938	4.730
17	7.549	7.120	6.729	6.373	6.047	5.749	5.475	5.222	4.990	4.775
18	7.702	7.250	6.840	6.467	6.128	5.818	5.534	5.273	5.033	4.812
19	7.839	7.366	6.938	6.550	6.198	5.877	5.584	5.316	5.070	4.843
20	7.963	7.469	7.025	6.623	6.259	5.929	5.628	5.353	5.101	4.870

FORMULAE

Time series

Additive model:

Series = Trend + Seasonal + Random

Multiplicative model:

Series = Trend * Seasonal * Random

Regression analysis

The linear regression equation of Y on X is given by:

$$Y = a + bX \quad \text{or} \quad Y - \overline{Y} = b(X - \overline{X}),$$

where

$$b = \frac{\text{Covariance } (XY)}{\text{Variance } (X)} = \frac{n\Sigma XY - (\Sigma X)(\Sigma Y)}{n\Sigma X^2 - (\Sigma X)^2}$$

and

$$a = \overline{Y} - b\overline{X}$$

or solve

$$\Sigma Y = na + b\Sigma X$$

$$\Sigma XY = a\Sigma X + b\Sigma X^2$$

Exponential

$$Y = ab^x$$

Geometric

$$Y = aX^b$$

Learning curve

$$Y_x = aX^b$$

where

Y_x = the cumulative average time per unit to produce X units;
a = the time required to produce the first unit of output;
X = the cumulative number of units;
b = the index of learning.

The exponent b is defined as the log of the learning curve improvement rate divided by log 2.

The Examiner for Management Accounting – Decision Management offers to future candidates and to tutors using this booklet for study purposes, the following background and guidance on the questions included in this examination paper.

Section A – Compulsory

Question One comprises eight sub-questions in objective testing format. Some of the questions provide a choice of answers of which only one is correct whilst others require solution by the candidate. This question covers a number of syllabus areas and learning outcomes and is designed to complement the syllabus coverage of the remaining questions on the paper.

Section B – Compulsory

Question Two requires candidates to determine the optimum replacement cycle for the vehicles of a taxi company and advise the company accordingly. The question addresses the learning *outcome "Evaluate project proposals using the techniques of investment appraisal"*.

Question Three requires candidates to interpret a short scenario and to then briefly explain absorption and marginal cost approaches to pricing and discuss a comment made by one of the managers concerning the acceptance of prices which are lower than full cost. This question addresses the learning outcome *"Explain the particular issues that arise in pricing decisions and the conflict between marginal cost principles and the need for full recovery of all costs incurred"*.

Question Four requires candidates to interpret a short scenario and then prepare a report that explains the changing nature of cost structures in the modern manufacturing environment and its implications for stock valuation and short-term decision making. This question addresses the learning outcome *"Explain the possible conflicts between cost accounting for profit reporting and stock valuation and the convenient availability of information for decision making"*.

Section C – Answer two of three questions

Question Five requires candidates to prepare calculations to enable them to evaluate whether or not the organisation in the scenario should continue with the production of a film in Part (a) and then to discuss the use of probabilities in long-term decision making in Part (b). This question addresses the learning outcomes *"Evaluate project proposals using the techniques of investment appraisal"* and *"Evaluate the impact of uncertainty and risk on decision models that may be based on CVP analysis, relevant cash flows, learning curves, discounting techniques, etc"*.

Question Six requires candidates to state the principles of throughput accounting in part (a), determine an optimum production mix when there is a single scarce resource in part (b) and explain the meaning of a linear programming solution in Part (c). This question addresses the learning outcomes *"Discuss the meaning of optimal solutions and show how linear programming methods can be employed for profit maximising, revenue maximising and satisfying objectives"* and *"Evaluate the impacts of just in time production, the theory of constraints and total quality management on efficiency, inventory and cost"*.

Question 7 requires candidates to apply the principles of activity based costing to a marketing consultancy in Part (a), to discuss the differences between an activity based approach and a tradition overhead absorption approach in Part (b) and to explain how activity based costing cost classifications could be used in consultancy organisations in Part (c). This question addresses the learning outcomes "*Apply the techniques of activity-based management in identifying cost drivers/activities and explain how process re-engineering can be used to eliminate non-value adding activities and reduce activity costs*" and "*Apply activity based costing ideas to analyse direct customer profitability and extend this analysis to distribution channel profitability*".

Examiner's Answers

SECTION A

Question One

1.1 B

Years 1–5 \$50,000 × 3.605 = \$180,250
\$160,000/\$180,250 = 0.8876

1.2 D

	£
Selling price expected value = (£20 × 25%) + (£25 × 40%) + (£30 × 35%)	= 25.50
Variable cost expected value = (£8 × 20%) + (£10 × 50%) + (£12 × 30%)	= 10.20
Expected unit contribution	15.30
1,000 units × £15.30 = £15,300	

1.3 C

The total contribution must exceed £13,500, so to achieve this from a volume of 1,000 units, the unit contribution must exceed £13.50. The following combinations of selling price and variable cost and their respective combined probabilities meet this target:

Selling Price £	*Variable cost* £	*Probability*
25	8	0.4 × 0.2 = 0.08
25	10	0.4 × 0.5 = 0.20
30	8	{
30	10	{0.35 × 1.0 = 0.35
30	12	{
Combined probability total		0.63

1.4 The average time for 7 assignments = $6 \times 7^{-0.415}$ = 2.6757 hours

Total time for 7 assignments = 7 × 2.6757 hours	18.730 hours
The average time for 6 assignments = $6 \times 6^{-0.415}$ = 2.8525 hours	
Total time for 6 assignments = 6 × 2.8525 hours	17.115 hours
Time for the 7th assignment	1.615 hours
i.e. 1.62 hours	

1.5 Profitability Index values are:

J	31/400 = 0.0775	3rd
K	43/500 = 0.0860	2nd
L	31/300 = 0.1033	1st

Therefore the investment plan should be to invest:

L in full
K in full
J × 50%

1.6 The return is greater than 15% so try 20%:

Year	*Cashflow* $'000	*Discount Factor*	*Present Value* $'000
0	(500)	1.000	(500.00)
1	70	0.833	58.31
2	90	0.694	62.46
3	630	0.579	364.77
		NPV	(14.46)

Since the NPV is negative when the cashflows are discounted at 20%, the IRR of the project lies between 15% and 20%.

The IRR = 15% + [(43/57.46) × 5] = 18.74%

1.7 The average time per unit for 4 units = 8.3667/4 = 2.0917 hours

2.0917/3 = 0.6972
$\sqrt{0.6972} = 0.835$

The rate of learning is 83.5%

1.8 Contribution table (all contribution figures in £):

	Sale/Demand		
Make	*10*	*11*	*12*
10	500	500	500
11	480	550	550
12	460	530	600

Regret table (all contribution figures in £):

	Sale/Demand			*Maximum Regret*
Make	*10*	*11*	*12*	
10	0	50	100	100
11	20	0	50	50
12	40	20	0	40

The answer is to make 12.

SECTION B

Question Two

2-year plan

Year			*Cashflow* £	*Discount Factor*	*Present Value* £
2	Replacement	8,000 × 1.05^2	8,820	.797	7,030
3	Servicing	500 × 1.10^3	666	.712	474
4	Servicing	2,500 × 1.10^4	3,660		
	Replacement	8,000 × 1.05^4	9,724		
			13,384	.636	8,512
5	Servicing	500 × 1.10^5	805	.567	456
6	Servicing	2,500 × 1.10^6	4,429		
	Trade-In Value	7,000 × 1.05^6	(9,381)		
			(4,952)	.507	(2,511)
					13,961

3-year plan

Year			*Cashflow* £	*Discount Factor*	*Present Value* £
3	Servicing	4,000 × 1.10^3	5,324		
	Replacement	11,000 × 1.05^3	12,734		
			18,058	.712	12,857
4	Servicing	500 × 1.10^4	732	.636	466
5	Servicing	2,500 × 1.10^5	4,026	.567	2,283
6	Servicing	4,000 × 1.10^6	7,086		
	Trade-In Value	4,000 × 1.05^6	(5,360)		
			1,726	.507	875
					16,481

The above values exclude the non-relevant costs.

The 2-year replacement cycle is the lower cost option by £2,510 in present value terms.

Question Three

(i) There are a number of approaches to pricing that may be used by organisations depending on the nature of their business, their products and services and the extent to which these are personalised to the requirements of their customers. ML is an engineering company that provides a unique service to each of their customers using a range of engineering skills. As a consequence there is no "real" market for their services so a cost-based approach to pricing must be used. There are a number of cost based approaches to pricing that may be adopted by ML ranging from a variable cost-approach (Marginal costing) to a total cost approach (Absorption costing). The main difference between these approaches is their differing treatment of fixed production overhead costs.

Absorption costing attributes fixed production overhead costs to individual jobs or units using an absorption rate which in ML is based on machine hours, whereas marginal costing makes no attempt to attribute fixed production overhead costs to individual jobs. This results in a lower unit cost under marginal costing compared to absorption costing.

As a consequence the percentage mark-up added to these absorption/-marginal costs to determine the selling price will be different so as to result in the same level of profits overall. However, the use of absorption costing approaches may lead the manager to believe that the fixed production overhead cost absorbed per unit is incurred at a unit level (which is wrong). In turn this may mean that the manager will not be prepared to offer a price below this absorption cost because to do so "incurs a loss." However, the marginal costing approach may lead the manager to ignore the fixed production overhead costs with the consequence that the overall performance of ML may be loss making.

(ii) In the short term the comment is valid since the fixed costs will continue to be incurred whether work is being undertaken or not. Any price is excess of variable costs provides a contribution towards the fixed costs of ML. Therefore it would be true to say that "any price that exceeds variable costs is better than no work" in the short term. However, care needs to be taken when accepting work at lower than normal profit margins because it is very difficult to increase prices in the future when the same customer requires further spare parts for its machine.

Furthermore, in the long term, a company needs to be profitable to survive, so that there is a need to charge selling prices that fully recover all of the costs incurred. The acceptance of lower prices in order to utilise spare capacity is acceptable in the short term but cannot continue into the long term because the fixed costs are still being incurred and need to be at least covered by the overall contribution earned.

Question Four

REPORT

To: Management Team

From: Assistant Management Accountant

Subject: Cost Structures

Date: November 2005

Introduction

The company is facing increasing competition particularly from overseas suppliers. It is thus becoming more and more important that we understand the cost structures of the company so that our managers can make informed decisions about the price discounts that may be offered in order to win customer orders. The purpose of this report is to explain the implications of the changing nature of cost structures in our company.

Traditional classifications for management decisions

Traditionally, costs were classified between those that are affected by a change in the level of activity (known as variable costs) and those that are not affected by a change in the level of activity (known as fixed costs). For this purpose the level of activity was an output measure, often the number of units of a product or the number of hours of output. In PK plc, because we produce a range of self assembly furniture, a number of hours measure would need to be used in order to allow us to accumulate the total output of a particular accounting period by adding the equivalent standard hours of each unit produced.

The modern manufacturing environment

PK plc operates a computer-controlled manufacturing facility using highly skilled labour. Therefore many of its production costs will be incurred as a consequence of investing in the production system and employing skilled staff on a salaried basis. As a consequence the majority of its costs would be classified as fixed if the traditional cost classification were to be applied. The development of modern manufacturing systems has resulted in greater investigation into the causes of costs rather than the simple assumption that costs can be classified according to their behaviour in relation to changes in output. As a result, activity is considered from a number of different perspectives, including the measurement of the activities carried out in order to produce the output and the costs incurred in relation to each of those input activities. This is known as activity based costing, and when this system is fully applied costs that were previously believed to be fixed are in fact found to be variable in relation to a particular input activity.

Stock valuation

The need for profit reporting and stock valuation is usually the result of external reporting requirements imposed by legislation and governed by accounting standards. These stock valuation rules require that the stock be valued at the lower of cost or net realisable value (the latter being the application of the prudence concept). In this context cost is explained to be "the total cost incurred in bringing the item to its present location and condition, including an appropriate proportion of production overhead cost." In other words, stock should be valued at total production cost, including both fixed and variable production costs. Thus for the purposes of stock valuation it is not necessary to classify costs according to whether or not they are affected by changes in activity.

Short-term decision making

The majority (if not all) short-term decisions involve changes in activities; either a change in the level of output or a change in the activities used to create the output. Thus it is appropriate when making such decisions to be aware of the expected changes in costs as a result of the proposed changes in activity. An analysis of the causes of costs allows managers to predict the cost changes that are expected as a result of the changes to the activity and thus make the appropriate decision.

Conclusion

Thus there is a conflict between the accounting classifications and techniques that are most useful for short-term decision making and those that are required for external profit reporting and stock valuation.

SECTION C

Question Five

(a)

Expected relevant production costs $220,000

Present value of expected relevant production costs = $220,000 × 0.870 = $191,400

But there could be a ± 10% variation in some of the costs so the present value of these costs could be as low as $180,960 or as high as $201,840.

Present value of other costs are expected to be as follows:

Year	*Cost* $	*Discount Factor*	*Present Value* $
0	15,000	1.000	15,000
1–2	10,000	1.626	16,260
3–5	5,000	1.726	8,630
			39,890

Present value of revenues are expected to be as follows:

Year	*Revenue* $	*Discount Factor*	*Present Value* $
1	100,000	.870	87,000
2	150,000	.756	113,400
3	112,500	.658	74,025
4	50,000	.572	28,600
5	30,000	.497	14,910
			317,935

But there could be a ± 20% variation so the present value of these revenues could be as low as $254,348 or as high as $381,522.

Thus the following nine combinations could occur:

*Production Costs** $	*Other Costs** $	*Revenues** $	*NPV* $
180,960	39,890	254,348	33,498
180,960	39,890	317,935	97,085
180,960	39,890	381,522	160,672
191,400	39,890	254,348	23,058
191,400	39,890	317,935	86,645
191,400	39,890	381,522	150,232
201,840	39,890	254,348	12,618
201,840	39,890	317,935	76,205
201,840	39,890	381,522	139,792

* values shown are present values

It can be seen that the film has a positive NPV at all anticipated levels of costs and revenues. Therefore film production should continue.

(b) Although any number of possible values may be used for each variable, the use of probabilities when evaluating the risk of long-term decisions is usually based on three possible values being determined for each input variable. It is then possible to evaluate each of the most likely, optimistic and pessimistic outcomes that could occur (as in (a) above), and make a decision based upon the range of results.

The next step is to assign probabilities to each of the possible input values (production costs and revenues) and determine the combined probability of each combination of these input values occurring. These combined probabilities can then be used with the output values (NPV values) to calculate the expected NPV and the probability of the NPV exceeding a target value set by management.

Alternatively, the input value probabilities can be used to assign random number ranges to each input value. Random number generators may then be used to determine many combinations of input values in a simulation modelling technique and for each combination the model determines the output value (NPV). The output values can then be analysed to determine the range of values that could occur and make the decision depending on the manager's attitude to risk.

Question Six

(a) Throughput accounting falls within a wider management philosophy known as the theory of constraints. It recognises that where production is carried out through a series of processes on machines then there may be varying capacities in each of these resources. If production demand is high then it may be the case that total demand cannot be met and the organisation needs to identify the bottleneck resource that is causing the constraint.

Having done this, the short-term objective is to maximise the return yielded by this scarce resource and we seek to utilise it on those products that yield the highest contribution per unit of scarce resource.

Here contribution is defined as sales revenue less directly attributable variable costs. In the modern manufacturing environment it is commonly perceived that the only truly variable cost in the short term is materials since other costs that have been traditionally regarded as variable such as direct labour and some expenses are the subject of minimum payment arrangements and are therefore fixed costs. As a consequence the calculation of contribution in this modern business environment is sales revenue less direct material cost.

(b)

	TR *£/batch*	*PN* *£/batch*	*BE* *£/batch*	*Total*
Selling Price	340	450	270	
K	150	120	90	
L	70	90	40	
M/V	30	75	45	
Contribution	90	165	95	
Kgs of L	7	9	4	
Contribution per kg of L	12.86	18.33	23.75	
Ranking	3rd	2nd	1st	
Minimum output (batches)	50	50	50	
Uses (kg of L)	350	450	200	1,000
Balance (kg of L)	1,650	3,150	1,200	6,000
Discretionary manufacture (batches)	235	350	300	
Total output (batches)	285	400	350	

(c) Objective function value of £110,714 is the contribution from the optimal solution which is to produce 500 batches of TR, 357 batches of PN and 71 batches of BE.

The product slack values of 0, 43 and 279 represent the unsatisfied demand (in batches) of products TR, PN, and BE, respectively.

The slack values for ingredients L and M of £3 and £28, respectively represent the shadow prices of the scarce resources. There is no shadow price for ingredient K because the supply is unlimited.

Question Seven

(a)

Client profile	*D*	*E*	*F*
Number of visits	30	40	15
Return mileage	100	140	200
Total mileage	3,000	5,600	3,000

Costs	£	£	£
Travel to clients	3,880	7,240	3,880
Accommodation	Nil	8,000	3,000
Other	70,833	247,917	106,250
Total costs	74,713	263,157	113,130

Travel costs

$$\frac{\text{Total cost}}{\text{Total mileage}}\ \frac{£15{,}000}{11{,}600} = £1.29/\text{mile}$$

Accommodation costs

$$\frac{\text{Total cost}}{\text{Number of overnight stays}}\ \frac{£11{,}000}{55} = £200/\text{stay}$$

Other costs

$$\frac{\text{Total cost}}{\text{Chargeable hours}}\ \frac{£425{,}000}{6{,}000} = £70.833/\text{hour}$$

(b)

	D	*E*	*F*
Chargeable hours	1,000	3,500	1,500
Total cost attributed using current system	£75,000	£262,500	£112,500
Activity based cost attributed	£74,713	£263,157	£113,130

(£1,000 not attributed due to roundings)

Although there are some differences between the costs attributed to each type of client they are not significant and it is questionable whether the added complexity of the ABC approach can be justified in these circumstances. However, the senior consultant's suggestion is theoretically correct, and if the profile of prospective clients were to be significantly different from those of the existing client profiles then the use of ABC would be justified.

One of the main reasons for the similarity in the cost values is that only 6% of the existing costs are believed to be caused by activities other than chargeable hours. In fact the senior consultant recognises that the majority of the costs that are incurred are facility type costs that will continue to exist (in the short term at least) as a consequence of a past decision to engage the consultants and their support staff. These costs would continue to be incurred even if there were no client projects to be undertaken. The validity of attempting to attribute these costs to such clients is therefore questionable.

(c) The four classifications are based upon the different factors that may cause a cost to vary. Unit level costs are driven by the quantity of products made. These costs may typically include raw material.

Batch level costs are those that are incurred every time a batch is processed. However large a batch is (whether it is, for example, 1 unit or 1,000 units), there may be a cost such as tool setting which falls under this category.

Product sustaining costs are those that exist as long as the product or product range continues to be manufactured. Such costs may include the salary of the "Product Manager" who is responsible for the overall marketing of the product.

Facility sustaining costs are seen as the costs that are truly fixed and relate to the overall organisation. These costs may include the rent on a factory that manufactures the full range of the company's products or head office costs that do not relate to any specific product.

ZP is a service organisation, but there may still be some relevance in the above classifications.

The unit level costs relate to the chargeable hour. Although the consultants are salaried, they are expected to deliver 1,500 hours of chargeable effort per year at a cost of £40 per hour.

The batch concept also exists in that there will be a number of contracts involved in this type of business. Each contract may involve any number of chargeable hours. The client director may have to spend the same amount of time negotiating each contract whether it is large or small. Similarly some administrative functions may be batch/contract related; for example it takes just as long for credit control to chase payment on a £750 contract as it does to chase a £7,500 contract.

The product sustaining level may be related to each client. If each client has a number of contracts then there may be a "Client director" and other administrative costs that are incurred on a client basis.

The facility sustaining costs are also in evidence; these include the infrastructure costs of telephone, fax and communications.

In conclusion, the four classifications do appear to be of potential use to a service organisation such as ZP.

)rder Form

r CIMA Official Study Materials for 2006 Exams

ELSEVIER

CIMA PUBLISHING

Title	Author	ISBN	ISBN 13	Price	Total
		CIMA Official Study Systems			
Management Accounting Fundamentals	Walker	0750667087	9780750667081	£33.00	
Financial Accounting Fundamentals	Lunt	0750667044	9780750667043	£33.00	
Business Mathematics	Peers	0750667052	9780750667050	£33.00	
Economics for Business	Adams	0750667060	9780750667067	£33.00	
Business Law	Sagar	0750667079	9780750667074	£33.00	
Performance Evaluation	Scarlett	0750667117	9780750667111	£33.00	
Decision Management	Wilks	0750667125	9780750667128	£33.00	
Risk and Control Strategy	Collier	0750667168	9780750667166	£33.00	
Organisational Management and Information Systems	Perry	0750667095	9780750667098	£33.00	
Integrated Management	Harris	0750667109	9780750667104	£33.00	
Business Strategy	Botten	0750667184	9780750667180	£33.00	
Financial Accounting and Tax Principles	Rolfe	0750667133	9780750667135	£33.00	
Financial Analysis	Gowthorpe	0750667141	9780750667142	£33.00	
Financial Strategy	Ogilvie	075066715X	9780750667159	£33.00	
TOP CIMA	Barnwell	0750667176	9780750667173	£33.00	
		CIMA Official Exam Practice Kits			
Management Accounting Fundamentals	Allan	0750665807	9780750665803	£14.99	
Financial Accounting Fundamentals	Allan	0750665831	9780750665834	£14.99	
Business Mathematics	Allan	0750665866	9780750665865	£14.99	
Economics for Business	Allan	075066584X	9780750665841	£14.99	
Business Law	Benton	0750665858	9780750665858	£14.99	
Performance Evaluation	Barnett	0750669322	9780750669320	£14.99	
Decision Management	Barnett	0750669292	9780750669290	£14.99	
Risk and Control Strategy	Robertson	0750669373	9780750669375	£14.99	
Organisational Management & Information Systems	Robertson	0750669306	9780750669306	£14.99	
Integrated Management	dalton	0750669314	9780750669313	£14.99	
Business Strategy	Allan	0750669365	9780750669368	£14.99	
Financial Accounting and Tax Principles	Patel	0750669330	9780750669337	£14.99	
Financial Analysis	Rodgers	0750669349	9780750669344	£14.99	
Financial Strategy	Allan	0750669357	9780750669351	£14.99	
TOPCIMA	Little	0750666277	9780750666275	£14.99	
		CIMA Revision Cards			
Management Accounting Fundamentals	Walker	0750664770	9780750664776	£6.99	
Financial Accounting Fundamentals	Holland	0750664762	9780750664769	£6.99	
Business Mathematics	Peers	0750664800	9780750664806	£6.99	
Economics for Business	Adams	0750664789	9780750664783	£6.99	
Business Law	Sagar	0750664797	9780750664790	£6.99	
Performance Evaluation	Scarlett	0750664819	9780750664813	£6.99	
Decision Management	Avis	0750664827	9780750664820	£6.99	
Risk and Control Strategy	Harris	0750664835	9780750664837	£6.99	
Organisational Management and Information Systems	Perry	0750664843	9780750664844	£6.99	
Integrated Management	Harris	0750664851	9780750664851	£6.99	
Business Strategy	Botten	075066486X	9780750664868	£6.99	
Financial Accounting and Tax Principles	Rolfe	0750664878	9780750664875	£6.99	
Financial Analysis	Gowthorpe	0750664886	9780750664882	£6.99	
Financial Strategy	Ogilvie	0750664894	9780750664899	£6.99	
				P+P (£)	2.95
				Total (£)	

Post this form to:

CIMA Publishing Customer Services
Elsevier
FREEPOST (OF 1639)
Linacre House, Jordan Hill
OXFORD, OX2 8DP, UK

Or FAX +44 (0)1865 474 010
Or PHONE +44 (0)1865 474 014

Email: cimaorders@elsevier.com

www.cimapublishing.com

Name: ____________________

Organisation: ____________________

Invoice Address: ____________________

____

____

Postcode: ____________________

Phone number: ____________________

Email: ____________________

Delivery Address if different:

FAO: ____________________

Address: ____________________

____

____

Postcode: ____________________

Please note that all deliveries must be signed for

1. Cheques payable to Elsevier.
2. Please charge my:

Visa ☐ ☐ MasterCard
Amex ☐ ☐ Switch Issue No.______

Card No: ____________________

Expiry Date: ____________________

Cardholder Name: ____________________

Signature: ____________________

Date: ____________________

Elsevier retains certain personal information about you in hard copy form and on computer. It will be used to inform you about goods and services from Elsevier and its associated companies in which you may be interested. _ please tick this box if you do not want to receive this information.

ELSEVIER

CIMA PUBLISHING

CIMA Official *Study Systems*

These comprehensive ring-binders are the only texts written and endorsed by the CIMA Faculty. As writers of the new 2006 syllabus and exams, nobody is better qualified to explain how to pass.

- Step-by-step subject coverage directly linked to CIMA's learning outcomes
- Extensive question practice throughout
- Complete revision section
- Pilot papers on the new syllabus, complete with examiner's solutions
- Two mock exams for Certificate subjects

CIMA Official *Revision Cards*

- Pocket-sized books for learning all the key points – especially for students on the move
- Relevant, succinct and compact reminders of all the bullet points and diagrams needed for the new CIMA 2006 exams
- Break down the syllabus into memorable bite-size chunks

CIMA Official *Exam Practice Kits*

Supplement the Study Systems with a bank of additional questions focusing purely on applying what has been learnt to passing the exam. Ideal for independent study or tutored revision courses. Prepare with confidence for exam day, and pass the new syllabus first time.

- Practice applying and displaying knowledge so CIMA examiners can award you marks
- Avoid common pitfalls with fully worked model answers which include analysis of typical incorrect answers
- Type and weighting of questions match the format of the exam by paper, helping you prepare by giving you the closest available preview of the exam
- Certificate subjects include 200 exam standard multiple choice questions. All have detailed explanations or calculations to show how to arrive at the correct answer
- Written by an outstanding team of freelance tutors with established reputations for success. The only materials endorsed by CIMA.

CIMA *Introduction to Business Taxation*

We continue to publish the authors of the syllabus with this first CIMA CPD product. Chris Jones is Tax Training Director at Lexis Nexis UK, with 10 years experience in training on tax issues. He prepared both the syllabus and this Official study manual.

Fully equips those studying for the new CIMA Certificate in Business Taxation. There is only one paper to be examined and one book for the course – this one.

Each chapter has full explanation of the rules and calculations as required by the Finance Act 2005. Short summaries then provide a "pocket digest" and together form a comprehensive overview of the syllabus. Each chapter contains examples questions to assess knowledge ahead of the CBA.

CIMA Publishing is an imprint of Elsevier
Registered Office
The Boulevard, Langford Lane, Kidlington, Oxford OX5 1GB, UK
Registered in England: 3099304, VAT 494 627212